66 DAYS
ADRIFT

William Butler

66 DAYS ADRIFT

A True Story of Disaster and Survival on the Open Sea

International Marine / McGraw-Hill

Camden, Maine • New York • Chicago • San Francisco • Lisbon • London • Madrid • Mexico City
Milan • New Delhi • San Juan • Seoul • Singapore • Sydney • Toronto

The McGraw·Hill Companies

1 2 3 4 5 6 7 8 9 10 DOC DOC 0 9 8 7 6 5

This edition published 2005 by International Marine, a division of The McGraw-Hill Companies. Previously published in a different format as *Our Last Chance* by Exmart Press.

Library of Congress Cataloging-in-Publication Data
Butler, Bill, 1929–
[Our last chance]
66 days adrift : a true story of disaster and survival on the open sea / William A. Butler.
   p.   cm.
Originally published: Our last chance. Miami, FL : Exmart Press, c1991.
ISBN 0-07-143874-2 (pbk. : alk. paper)
1. Siboney (Ship) 2. Shipwrecks—Pacific Ocean. 3. Survival after airplane accidents, shipwrecks, etc. 4. Butler, Bill, 1929– 5. Butler, Simonne, 1937– I. Title: Sixty-six days adrift. II. Title.
G530.S574B88 2005
910´.9164´9—dc22   2004027314

Questions regarding the content of this book should be addressed to
International Marine
P.O. Box 220
Camden, ME 04843
www.internationalmarine.com

Questions regarding the ordering of this book should be addressed to
The McGraw-Hill Companies
Customer Service Department
P.O. Box 547
Blacklick, OH 43004
Retail customers: 1-800-262-4729
Bookstores: 1-800-722-4726

Map on pages vi–vii by International Mapping Associates.

Author's Note

I have always maintained a detailed log when at sea. When the moment came to abandon Siboney, *I made sure the ship's log went with me as I stepped aboard the raft. While adrift, I entered wind and wave conditions, attacks by predators, domino game scores, and all significant activity several times a day. I kept the log up to date until day fifty-two, when sharks and dolphins, in a wild display of energy, tore the floor of our raft. Seawater soaked the logbook and made further direct entries impossible, though I did continue to make penciled notes on a small paper pad. Once I was safely ashore in a Costa Rican hospital, long-nailed nurses helped me separate and dry each page. To my surprise, the log remained fully legible. The log became a valuable tool when I wrote this book by providing me with a true and chronological sequence of events.*

PACIFIC
OCEAN

Hawaii
(U.S.)

Violent
storms

Birds
left

Siboney sank
June 15, 1989

	Voyage of *Siboney*
– – –	Voyage of *Last Chance*

PROLOGUE

THIS STORY BEGINS in 1941, in Cuba, when I was twelve. My mother, exhausted by my mischievous energy, surrendered me to the care of a sailboat captain. "Take him as crew," my mother insisted. Soon, the sea held me in a solid grip that lasts to this very day.

Two years later, when my father took notice of my interest in sailing and how it kept me out of his hair, he bought me a twelve-foot flat-bottom Snorky Class skiff named *Pallas*. Several years later, he gave me a fifteen-foot Snipe, *Bluebird*, #5181. My young brother got the skiff.

I met world-renowned Argentinean solo circumnavigator Vito Dumas as he passed through Havana in 1946 aboard *Lehg II*. I'd just won a race sailing solo in *Pallas*, and Dumas, as guest of honor, was handing out the trophies at the Havana Yacht Club. When he shook my hand and compared my solo sail with his, he drove into my heart the dream of circling the globe in a sailboat. Forty years would pass before I set off to turn this dream into reality.

Together with my buddy Bob Harras as crew, I began serious open-ocean cruising with a two-hundred-and-twenty-mile, two-week sail aboard *Bluebird*. We tacked upwind from Havana to Matanzas for the 1948 Snipe Nationals, then on to Varadero Beach to visit friends, and back to Havana. For provisions we had a five-gallon jug of water, a large can of crackers, four cans of sardines, a bar of guava paste, and ten dollars. Needless to say, we didn't pass up a free meal nor did we put on any weight.

My engineering degree from Purdue led me to a job with General Electric in Cuba. When Castro closed GE in 1960, I was posted to Manila. On my first visit to the Manila Yacht Club, *Mysterious*, a thirty-nine-foot cutter, caught my eye. It was love at first sight. But she wasn't for sale. Besides, I couldn't afford her. I bought a Star boat instead, which I turned into a cruiser for trips out of Manila Bay.

Two years later, I bought *Monsoon*, thirty-two feet on the deck, but with a five-foot bowsprit and four-foot bumpkin she had the sail plan of a forty-one-footer. She'd spent the war years sunk up the Pearl River from Hong Kong. I cruised the waters off Batangas and Bataan in *Monsoon*, raced her in Manila Bay, and enjoyed fine family outings.

Still, each time I sailed out of the yacht basin, my eyes were glued on the beautiful lines of the thirty-nine-foot cutter. In 1966, *Mysterious* became mine. One of more than thirty boats of the Mystery Class designed by Robert Clark, she was built at the Sussex Yacht Works in Shoreham during 1937. Warehoused during the war, she sailed British waters until 1956 when a new owner shipped her to Manila.

I changed her name to *Siboney*, from a Cuban love song, and with friends raced or cruised her every weekend. During a school break in November 1967, I sailed with my wife, Elsie, and three pre-teen children past Corregidor and out of Manila Bay to a beautiful sandy beach thirty miles to the south. On our third day out, a violent typhoon changed course and headed our way. On first notice, we lifted anchor and raced for the quasi-protection of Manila Bay. By two A.M. all sails had been lowered, the boom tied to the deck. Winds out of the northeast soon exceeded sixty knots. We flew right along under bare poles, unable though to head for the Manila Yacht Club as the winds were right on the nose.

With my wife and children below, I sat on the cockpit floor securely roped in. The barometer plummeted as winds increased to a steady seventy-five knots out of the northeast. At two in the morning, two waves in succession, both more than twenty feet high, broke on us. *Siboney* slid mast down in the rushing sea, shook herself loose, and kept going.

When dawn broke, it was obvious the typhoon was headed straight for us. I ordered my wife and kids to inflate their life jackets and put on shoes as I had decided to head for shore, three miles off, and beach the boat. When released, the mainsail quickly filled much like a parachute to speed us on our way. I aimed the bow directly at a large building onshore that I had been watching. We surfed down the breaking waves, the shoreline racing toward us. The keel touched bottom several times until, at a speed of more than ten knots, *Siboney* climbed up on the sandy beach like a wild crocodile and ground to a stop.

I threw open the hatch and over the howling wind screamed to my wife to gather up the children and get out. A dozen waiting hands scooped all four up and led them away. I couldn't move. A glance at the wind-speed indicator showed steady winds of more than ninety knots. The events of the past twelve hours had me paralyzed, in shock. Against all odds, I had managed to save the lives of my wife and my three young children. A true miracle. I shook and cried in amazement and ecstasy, oblivious to the pleas of men onshore who themselves risked their lives as they struggled to stand while dodging sheets of galvanized roofing. Yielding to their incessant calls, I glanced at the wind-speed indicator on my way to shore. It pegged at ninety-five knots.

Weeks later, with a borrowed twenty-ton floating crane, we lifted *Siboney* from the beach and dropped her off at the Manila Yacht Club, where with the help of master carpenter Pacífico Cadión and many others, we totally rebuilt her—frames, hull, deck, and cabin. Seventeen carpenters built a new *Siboney* in less than three months.

With wood shavings still covering the deck, I cast off with five friends in April 1968 and headed for Hong Kong to join the China Sea Race to Manila. We didn't win but had a great voyage.

When GE posted me to Caracas, *Siboney* followed atop a bulk sugar carrier to Panama. With two sons and longtime friend Siro Cugini, I sailed her to La Guaira in nineteen blustery days. *Siboney* cruised to every Caribbean island over the following seven years with my three sons as a built-in crew.

• ◆ •

Simonne is French, and as a young girl she escaped the worst of the war years on a farm in the hills northwest of Nice. In the 1950s her family moved to Menton, a small town on the Mediterranean between Monte Carlo and the Italian border. There, with her sister and brother, she came to know and love the sea. After completing secondary school, she traveled to England, Germany, and Spain, where she studied, worked, and added three more languages to her native French and her mother's Italian.

Simonne and I met during the 1973 Caracas carnival season at the bar by the Tamanaco Hotel pool. A restless forty-year-old with five young children, I was there with a few GE coworkers. She had just sent her kids home after a day at the pool. She had bright blue eyes, sensuous lips, and an irresistible French accent, and yes, she would accept a drink. Her marriage, like mine, had lost its luster. She knocked me out cold. That poolside spark flared quickly into the full blaze of love. In the following years, we contrived to see each other weekly. Her sparkling personality and her old-country sensuous warmth were like a high-powered magnet from which there was no escape. When GE transferred me to Miami in 1978, I sailed *Siboney* across the Caribbean with three friends and Simonne. When we bid each other a tearful adieu at the airport in Miami, we both agreed that this was to be the final farewell. To continue our love affair would make no sense. We would cut it short now before anyone got hurt.

Months later she called me. She had divorced her husband and had moved to Miami with her two sons. I hesitated to rekindle the affair, then succumbed totally. A year later, I separated from the mother of my five children, resigned a great post with GE, and moved in with Simonne to begin a new life together.

Besides being captivated by Simonne, I had also been bitten by the entrepreneurial bug. I formed not one but four Florida corporations, one an export business in partnership with Simonne that we called SIBU Export. We worked side by side selling and shipping heavy electrical equipment to Venezuela during the day and running a paint-stripping business, aptly named Sim's Dip and Strip, by night.

Talk about a rough day. We'd leave home at seven A.M. to beat the traffic, drive to our export business, where we'd go nonstop until four in the afternoon, then head north ten miles to Opa-locka, where we'd strip down and really go to work. I moved large doors and other furniture, some with ten layers of old paint, into large hot vats filled with lye, let them soak for a half hour, then lifted them over to where Simonne could blast off all the old paint with a high-pressure hose. We'd get home at eleven P.M. or later, eat something, sleep for a few hours, and then at six A.M. start the new day. We used weekends to catch up on house chores. It was a tough life, but we both loved it, and our love grew deeper. In 1983 we married.

When exchange controls in 1988 within Venezuela froze new orders, we closed down our sales operation, got rid of the paint-stripping fiasco, and prepared to travel, aboard *Siboney*. Though Simonne understood what my dream of circumnavigating meant to me, she was equally reluctant to leave her children. She insisted we wait a year or two, but I argued that this was the moment to go. Finally, reluctantly, she agreed and began to cast off all ties to shore. One son went to college, and the other moved into an apartment I bought. She emptied her home and put it up for sale.

My lifetime dream was about to become reality. I owned the right boat, and in a short time I would set sail on a four-year circumnavigation. Soon, very soon, my dream of dreams would be fulfilled.

After crossing the Caribbean, we planned to transit the Panama Canal. From there, Hilo, Hawaii, lay forty-five hundred miles ahead. There we would stop briefly to buy fresh food before continuing to Honolulu, the first major stop in our four-year, globe-circling sail. From Honolulu, we'd sail to Hiroshima, Japan, with twenty-five other boats in a cruising rally that was to start June 18. Not only would it be safer to sail in company with other boats, but our arrival in Japan also would be more fun. We would carry Japanese books and tapes aboard to help Sim, the ship's linguist, pick up basic Japanese during our long sail.

Sailing the inland waters of Japan in the late summer months of 1989 was to be the true highlight of our trip. October would see *Siboney* cruising through the Ryukyus, past Taiwan, and on to the Philippines. I dreamed of following *Siboney*'s wake in waters I had often sailed when living in Manila. We would enter Manila Bay between Corregidor and Bataan and then sail on to the Manila Yacht Club, where I had been commodore from 1967 to 1969. With all flags flying, I longed to salute old friends.

In February 1990 or earlier, we planned to sail south to Brunei, over to Singapore, to Sri Lanka, and the Maldives, unable to linger as we had to stay ahead of the monsoons. From Djibouti, we hoped to push up the Red Sea before headwinds set in. A marina in Turkey would be our home for the winter of 1990.

We planned to cruise the Greek islands, Yugoslavia, and parts of Italy in 1991 to end up in a wintering spot near Menton in the south of France. There, we'd lie in a marina less than a mile from Sim's childhood home, which she had left at age twenty to discover the world.

In early June 1992, we would anchor in Cádiz, Spain, to join the America's 500 regatta. The start would take place in Palos, from where Columbus set sail in 1492, and would finish in Miami, with stops in the Canary Islands and San Salvador in the Bahamas. This five-hundredth anniversary rally, to follow Columbus's "small-boat cruise" of 1492, would be the perfect finale for my induction into that so-exclusive group of circumnavigators.

Siboney became a beauty as we approached our scheduled departure date of early April 1989. New roller-furling gear was installed on both headsails. The main had boom furling. A Fleming wind-powered self-steering gear would do most of the hard work by keeping *Siboney* on course, day and night. I bought a twelve-hundred-dollar Survivor 35 manual desalinator. With this gadget, which had just hit the market, we should never run out of clean drinking water—that is, if it worked as advertised.

A major innovation for me would be to have an inflatable life raft aboard. Wherever we had sailed to date, to Hong Kong in 1968 and to New York City in 1986, plus twelve thousand miles in between, I had planned to rely on our dinghy in an emergency. With a four-year circumnavigation ahead of us, I decided to invest in a life raft. Simonne and I shopped a half-dozen boat shows and looked into just about every raft on the market. In my own mind I settled on a Switlik life raft since it met my budget and was neither too heavy nor too bulky.

I went without Simonne to the Switlik dealer in Miami, took another look at his price list, and selected the four-man coastal raft because it was compact and light at forty pounds. When the salesman asked if I wanted the inflatable floor, I asked how much and how heavy. It would cost four hundred dollars and weigh another twenty pounds. No way, I had told him. I wasn't planning to use the raft, so why spend more money and add weight?

I sailed away on April 21, three weeks behind schedule and without Simonne, accompanied instead by Gustavo Ponzoa, a good friend from my youthful sailing days in Cuba. Simonne remained behind to wrap up a myriad of loose ends, and would meet us in Nassau. When I called her from the fuel dock in Nassau, she said she still couldn't make it. We filled up and headed for George Town, Exuma, where days later Sim joined the boat. Gus flew back to Miami.

In a tight beat against a howling southeasterly, Simonne and I approached Great Inagua late in the afternoon of May 5. Spray flew high over the cabin. *Siboney* leaped over the waves as I raced her toward shore in the waning light. Night was nearly upon us when a young man waved *Siboney* into the island's minute basin, then helped secure our lines.

Next day we asked everyone we met about the whereabouts of Woosh. Woosh had helped save *Siboney* when, on a stop in Great Inagua on our way to Miami from Venezuela in 1979, we had run aground. Woosh and three friends had brought their fishing boat out, tossed us a line, and pulled us off the beach. An old-timer told us Woosh drowned after falling overboard at night while on a fishing trip off the coast. Sim and I had so looked forward to seeing him again to thank him one more time for his help. Simonne prayed long into the evening for Woosh.

Later, while I slept, Simonne lay awake reading. At eleven, on a trip to the head, she stepped down from her bunk to find ten inches of water over the cabin sole. She shook me awake and switched on the bilge pump. The bilge emptied in minutes. The boat was so heavy with stores that the bilge outlet was underwater. Seawater had siphoned back into the boat through a valve that normally didn't need to be closed unless underway. Had Sim been asleep, the water would have reached us at bunk level and soaked many of my electronic spares. We worked most of the night tidying the mess.

This had to be a warning from Woosh, Sim said in the morning. In a fitful dream in the dregs of the night, she had heard him call out:

"Be careful. Be careful, my friends. There are dangers on this trip. Take good care of yourselves." Poor Woosh. Such a great guy. His time had come much too soon.

Calls to the owner of the island's fuel truck always ended with a promise that he would arrive in less than an hour. At three in the afternoon, we gave up and sailed for Panama with our fuel tanks short twenty gallons.

The Windward Passage was totally windless. Seas calmed as we approached Haiti. We motored to distance ourselves from land, yet wishing to conserve fuel for use later in the trip, we did a lot of drifting. During the ensuing days, the current pushed us south and west, much too close to Jamaica and the perilous reefs that surround it. A favorable wind shift got *Siboney* back on track.

At eleven in the morning on May 11, a tall white lighthouse stood off our port bow. Morant Cays, an inviting set of tiny islands fifty miles east of Jamaica, tempted us to pay a call, a means to break up the trip, but better judgment drew me away. Better to let unknown places be. We worried about piracy in this part of the Caribbean, so when one of several fishing boats working nets to seaward turned our way, I brought our 9 mm handgun on deck, just in case. Two fishermen motored up, waved, and asked for cigarettes. We had none and tossed them a couple of cold drinks instead. They tossed three snappers on the deck and, with a wave, sped away.

The rest of the Caribbean was equally windless. How we wished we'd been patient and loaded the extra fuel in Great Inagua. On May 17, a month out of Miami, we approached the entrance to the Panama Canal. With Sim at the helm we followed a string of green high-intensity lights into Cristóbal, where I dropped the anchor in an area set aside for small boats. Seconds later, we were both enjoying a dead man's sleep.

Six days later, fully provisioned and with the required complement of line handlers and the pilot aboard, we were herded into Gatun Locks along with six other sailboats. Before noon on May 24, *Siboney* reentered the Pacific Ocean.

We topped off our fuel and water tanks at the Balboa Yacht Club, loaded the coolers with ice, and added picturesque club T-shirts to our collection. Late in the afternoon of May 24, 1989, with a single farewell wave from the fuel attendant, we set out on the longest leg of our voyage around the world.

A bright rainbow to the south drew us away from the Balboa Yacht Club. My heart raced with excitement as I aimed the bow of our sturdy boat away from land without so much as a backward glance. I was eager to swing into the open ocean, where peace reigns, where man tests his skills against the forces that govern the earth. I was now on my way to fulfill my lifelong dream.

I gripped Simonne's hand as we motored away. Again and again, I noticed her look out past the stern, her eyes reaching out to land, which she well knew would soon not be there. Later she told me that she had prayed for a miracle, even secretly hoping she would break a bone so as not to make this leg of the trip. She sailed only because she loved me.

Simonne disliked long ocean passages. Her longest so far aboard *Siboney* had been seven days. On this leg, she had argued for a course that would take us coast-hopping along Central America, up as far as Puerto Vallarta in Mexico. She could handle the three- or four-week sail from there to Hawaii. Unfortunately, the end of May was too late in the year for a direct shot toward Hawaii via the great circle route that skirts the coast of Central America. The hurricane season in the eastern North Pacific had started in April. We couldn't risk it. We had to play it safe and take the southern route to Hawaii. This called for a two-hundred mile leg south out of Panama, away from Hawaii, until we reached the westerly flowing winds and current. At 4 degrees North latitude, we would head west and sail twenty-four hundred miles before turning north toward Hilo on the island of Hawaii.

Winds were light and variable, and the skies were overcast. Anxious to reach our turning point at Isla de Malpelo, we burned half of our fuel exiting the Bay of Panama.

Malpelo. What a strange, ominous name for an island. In Spanish slang, *malpelo* means "lousy luck." A dark, cloudy, foggy night found us closing in on this spooky island. At midnight, the radar range to Malpelo was twelve miles due west. The breeze was gentle and steady out of the southwest. Sim napped below and I catnapped on deck. At one in the morning, when Sim joined me on deck, the range was seven miles, still west.

The black night and heavy mist dropped visibility to less than a half mile. Simonne sidled up next to me. I felt her shudder and pulled her in more tightly as we strained to see a sign of Malpelo in the inky blackness. The name connotes so much evil that we grew uneasy every time I made a new plot of our position. Light rain began to fall.

At two in the morning, the radar showed Malpelo at five miles. At three A.M., the radar range was seven miles. We were going backward. At three thirty, Malpelo suddenly disappeared from the radar screen. While I tinkered with the radar knobs, I began to wonder: Who discovered it? What happened there over the years? Why is it considered bad luck? What disaster overtook mariners on Malpelo? Some unseen force was drawing us ever closer. When I mentioned some of my concerns to Simonne, she shook visibly and said she didn't like where we were at all. She pushed closer to me as if looking for protection from this invisible evil.

Sim of a sudden turned toward me and whispered, "Bill, let's get out of here. I'm scared."

I needed no further coaxing. I tacked the boat right off to the south and put us on a course parallel to the spooky rock. At dawn, when we had again tacked, the island loomed large on the horizon to the north. It stayed with us throughout the day. When the wind died, we ran the engine, using precious fuel to distance us from its clutches by nightfall.

On the following night, two fishing trawlers passed close by headed out to sea. Soon after, the weather turned nasty and stayed that way for the next two weeks. The wind velocity changed every five hours. No sooner did I have the sails set to handle a blow than the wind died. Or when calm, with full sails flying, the wind in just minutes would begin to whistle. Unless I kept the sails properly set, the boat wouldn't move at her best speed. We would reach Honolulu days later than planned.

After midnight on June 11, about five hundred miles north of the Galápagos Islands, the wind shifted from southeast to south. Dawn revealed an overcast sky with low, dirty, fast-moving clouds scudding toward the north. Sunrise was red and ominous. The wind steadily increased and, within an hour, reached twenty-five knots. Soon we had gusts of thirty. I rushed to deeply reef all sails as Sim secured all hatches and the skylight. Seas continued to build as thirty-five-foot swells from the south roared and broke on *Siboney*. Each wave sent sheets of wind-driven spray over the boat. The self-steering gear struggled to maintain course.

We hurtled over waves and rode atop swells larger than railroad cars. Mountains of frothy seawater buried boat and crew. Whenever the self-steering gear lost control of the twelve-ton boat, I would grab the helm and coax her back on course.

Then a second storm broke.

Late on the second day of the southerly, I noticed Simonne had become quieter than normal. She didn't read or listen to her Walkman radio. When I stroked her head, she exploded and lashed out at me for bringing her on this trip she didn't want to go on, for taking her away from her children and the life she loved, for putting her in danger. I was a monster and a terrorist, she screamed. I tried to calm her, but my every try wound her up all the more.

Her fury lasted hours. I tried to soothe her without success. Frustrated, I dug into the cooler for one of my last cold Heinekens and escaped to the equally stormy deck.

Eventually, she calmed, then slept. Later, as we talked, I confessed that I too had a feeling of foreboding. She said she knew. She had watched me sneak quietly on deck during the storm. She saw me flash the lantern on the rigging as I checked and rechecked new creaking sounds. We hugged each other, made love, and slept.

Flying spray lashed *Siboney* endlessly. White water cascaded over the cabin and down the deck to gush over the lee side. Hour after hour, the wind howled and the ocean screamed at us as if questioning our right to exist. The self-steering gear battled the monster seas, which insisted on pushing *Siboney*'s bow to the north. Unable to control the boat, I gave up. I let her run where she wanted. Unbridled, she took off like a runaway mare. In the next two days, we logged three hundred miles on a course closer to 300 degrees than the 270 we needed.

While the storm blew, we spent most of the time in our bunks sandwiched between pillows. When we awoke around midmorning on June 13, the wind and seas had calmed. The sun again warmed the deck. We opened the boat and hung our bedding out to dry. A seawater bath and brunch in the cockpit revived us.

A dozen satellite fixes over the past two days confirmed that the storm had pushed us ninety miles north, off our intended track and right into the strong North Pacific Equatorial Countercurrent. This easterly current flows at about one knot, thus reducing our miles made good by close to twenty-five miles a day. The start for the race to Hiroshima, Japan, was but a few days away. When we had committed to enter this regatta three months before, I had told the race committee we'd be late for the start, but I still needed to find a way to make the boat move faster.

I pored over the marine current diagrams in the pilot chart for the North Pacific Ocean in search of a way out of our plight. The westerly current was about a hundred miles to the south. If we tightened up, we could get there in a couple of days unless, of course, another storm blew in. Another was due soon, for they hit in weekly cycles. Or we could head north with the next big blow, across the doldrums in search of the easterlies and the westerly current. That three-hundred-mile trek might take a week even if we burned up most of our fuel.

What to do? It was June 14, nearly midnight. I went up on deck to take a look around, hoping the fresh air would clear my mind. It was then that a large school of what I thought at first were dolphins caught me by surprise.

ABOARD *SIBONEY*
2400 WEDNESDAY • JUNE 14, 1989

ENTLE SPLASHES and faint blowing sounds surround me. I lean over the lifelines for a better look. Streamlined shapes plow the water alongside. *Siboney* is surrounded by dozens of them! They pace the boat, surface to blow out old air and suck in new, and then, with a deliberate, well-timed twist of their tail, dive and vanish into the inky sea. Wherever I look, quarter-moon-shaped dorsal fins cut the surface. In the darkness, they appear to be dolphins. I love dolphins, their antics and their company. I hope they'll stay for a while.

The southeasterly has blown steadily throughout the long Pacific night, generating a deep swell, which our thirty-nine-foot cutter, *Siboney*, slices through on her westward course. An oppressive overcast smothers all starlight. Our masthead light produces the sole glow in the immense blackness of the vast ocean we now traverse.

The Pacific Ocean, twelve hundred miles west of Panama, is more intimidating than usual tonight, as neither moon nor starlight penetrates the dense, low-lying clouds that stretch to the horizon. With every roll, *Siboney* speaks softly with her many voices: the creak of the dinghy pulling against its lashings, the rattle of the leeward backstay banging against a stanchion, the knock-knock inside one of the storage lockers. Like a faithful workhorse, *Siboney* plows on, jousting intrepidly with both wind and waves. Her heavy oak frames yield ever so slightly to the pressure of the sea, working with the elements at hand. The wind-driven autopilot holds an almost perfect course of 270 degrees West.

The warm breeze fills our three sails to push our speed over the water to four and a half knots, the best we've been able to maintain, deeply loaded as we are with fuel, water, and stores for the sixty-day passage from Panama to Hawaii. The almost one-knot easterly current, right on our nose, continues to slow our progress. Hawaii still lies more than three thousand miles to the northwest. Not only are we hopelessly late for the start of the race to Hiroshima, but it's now obvious that just catching the stragglers will be an impossible feat for *Siboney*.

Dropping down into the cabin, where Simonne sleeps soundly, I work the satellite navigator in search of a position update. Our last fix—obtained at six P.M. yesterday, June 14—put us at 5 degrees 30 minutes North latitude and 98 degrees 1 minute West longitude. My anxious finger punches the keypad on the satellite navigator. There is nothing new. I question the little black box for future satellite passes, and within seconds it displays its answer: the next acceptable satellites will be overhead at three thirty this morning, still three hours away. I go back on deck to join my favorite animals.

When Simonne stirs, I whistle lightly. Within moments, she sits alongside me on deck and peers over the side. "They're wonderful!" she says. "You know, Bill, we haven't seen dolphins in nearly three weeks, not since we left the Panama Canal."

"Well, I'll tell you what, we're seeing them now! Look at them, Sim. There must be hundreds."

Simonne leans across the lifelines to get a closer look at our visitors. Not satisfied, she reaches for the electrical panel and flips on the switch to the tower spotlight. Instantly, the boat is bathed in a spectral whitish green aura, the black masses now brilliantly alive. She studies the shapes closely, then slips her arm through mine and whispers, "They're not dolphins, Bill. They're whales. Pilot whales. I'm sure of it! In French we call them *cachalots*."

They move like an armada on a purposeful mission. With each plunge of *Siboney*'s bow, larger whales appear. There is a notable tightening of the herd. Up to now I have had only good, positive thoughts and an all-encompassing bonding with these mammals. But is their mood changing? A flash of tension passes through our clutched hands. Are we infringing on their space?

Sim shivers and without a word returns below. An hour passes, then another, each half hour dutifully announced by the ship's clock. Soon, I hope, the pod will move on, and we'll be alone once again in the vast emptiness of this unfriendly ocean. How I wish we were sailing the Caribbean, where the water is deep blue, stars twinkle, and flying fish play.

I return below. The display on the satellite navigator tells me it's four in the morning, June 15, Miami time. I'll change the ship's clock to Hawaii time in a couple of weeks. I touch the update button on the position pad and instantly get our new location fix:

0342 THURSDAY JUNE 15 1989 5 DEGREES
30 MINUTES NORTH 99 DEGREES 3 MINUTES
WEST.

I do some quick math and find that our speed since the last fix at six yesterday evening has been just three knots. That damn current still has us in its hold. We're losing at least twenty miles of headway each day to the current. I must make a move soon. But to where? How? To work our way south a hundred miles in search of the westerly current will take days and draw us away from our destination, Hawaii. My best bet might be to wait for the next storm out of the south and ride it into the doldrums. It will be a wild ride, thirty-five-knot winds and thirty-foot waves. Wild, but that's what I'll do. I have no other choice.

Back on deck, I find the whales are now bigger, some half as long as *Siboney*. When they exhale, the noise they make is louder, and the spray flies higher. They truly act annoyed now. They rush at one another in an apparent struggle of titans for position. A sandpaper-like scratching sound echoes along the starboard side, a long, rough caress that rights the boat and lets it go again.

"Bill, did you feel that?" Sim's dimmed voice calls from below.

"Yes," comes my terse reply. I have much to add, but I am speechless. What I want to say is that the whales now are bigger, they surface more often, and when they blow, it's more like the belch of a steam locomotive going uphill. Water caught in their blow rises like a geyser at Yellowstone. They are clearly angry at one another. Or are they irritated by our intrusion?

I can't put a finger on it, but something is wrong. The mood of the whales has definitely changed. Ever-larger whales close in on both sides of our boat. As they pace *Siboney*, they rush and push one another for a position close to the hull. Now, when they blow, air and water fly over the boom. I feel imprisoned, surrounded, encircled, held hostage by a pack of mad whales—whales turned terrorists. My admiration has changed to cold fear. I disengage the self-steering gear, then grab the tiller to head the boat into the wind as another whale scrapes the bottom of *Siboney* from stern to stem.

A whale bumps us to starboard. In rapid succession, two hard blows to port echo like the boom of a kettledrum. The boat heels far over to starboard, holds, and straightens up. More black shapes close in. These whales are no longer a mindless force, but a tenacious one, seemingly with a single-minded mission: our destruction. I hold the tiller way over to bring the boat up into the wind when a titanic jolt knocks me into the lifelines. *Siboney* reels way over to port. Sim is heaved from her bunk and cracks her head against the galley wall. The shout most dreaded by any sailor rings in my ears: "Bill! We're taking on water! Oh God, it's coming in fast!"

I head below as Simonne leaps out of the cabin and into the cockpit. An ominous noise much like a waterfall meets me. Water gushes through the floorboards. The ocean pours in with riptide determination. I start the bilge pump, then search for the damage. The sound of water pouring in comes from behind the cooler and the galley range, deep below the waterline. It couldn't be in a worse place. The icebox insulation has six inches of foam covered with fiberglass. The panel behind the stove consists of a heavy sheet of stainless steel for fireproofing. Water is coming in so fast I'll never have time to rip everything out, then locate and repair the damage.

Frantic, I start the engine, close the engine's saltwater intake, and remove the top of the filter. This turns the motor into a giant bilge pump, drawing its cooling water out of the bilge. Will it be enough to keep the boat from sinking? Is the leak behind the engine? I pull off the engine box and toss it on a bunk. My lantern reveals no rush of water from the stern. It's all happening too fast. Disbelief, confusion, and fear paralyze me, but as the water rises over my feet, one thought becomes clear: we must save the boat.

That's all that counts. We'll have to bail. I call to Simonne to toss me the bucket.

Water rises up my legs. I plunge the bucket wildly into the water and rush it into Sim's waiting hands. A second later, she thrusts the bucket back at me. My eyes are glued to the water inching up my legs. The engine roars. We fight to save the boat.

Water rises faster than our bailing and the pumps can manage. Obsessed with the need to keep the boat afloat, I hardly hear Sim's scream over the roar of the engine.

"Bill, we're sinking. Stop bailing. The boat is going down! We need to inflate the raft. Hand me the knife." I can see the knife in the sink but remain immobile, bucket in hand, stunned by the stark reality of the situation. The engine noise is deafening. Sim screams once again, this time louder:

"BILL, *SIBONEY* IS SINKING! PASS UP THE KNIFE!"

Water has reached the engine. Water-soaked drive belts shriek and spin salt spray throughout the cabin. Blinded, I start to turn off the engine and hesitate. I need this backup pump, but I also need to see what's going on. I reach over and stop the diesel. An eerie silence follows, broken only by the splash of knee-high water rushing from one side of the cabin to the other.

Without a word, I push the knife into Simonne's waiting hands and continue to heave water out of the cabin. Sim screams and I rush on deck. Knife in hand, she is unable to cut through the half-inch ropes that hold our fiberglass tender to its cradle, under which we have stowed our life raft. I cut through two lines, then give a back-breaking tug on the blue bag under the dinghy. It suddenly breaks loose, almost sending me over the side. That's when I notice the deck is less than a foot above the ocean. Whales still swim alongside, seemingly oblivious to our torment. An enormous bull whale splashes next to the boat. Inches closer, and it would have struck us again.

I drag the heavy bag down the deck and roll it into the cockpit. I leave it to Sim to ready, then head below to place a Mayday call before the water reaches the radio and the batteries.

I turn on the single-sideband radio transmitter, tune it to the U.S. Coast Guard emergency frequency, and yell desperately into the microphone:

MAYDAY MAYDAY MAYDAY. THIS IS SAILING
VESSEL SIBONEY WHISKEY X-RAY UNIFORM
5908. MAYDAY MAYDAY STATION KILO CHARLIE
FOUR JULIET CHARLEY VICTOR. WE ARE SINK-
ING. POSITION 99 DEGREES 10 MINUTES WEST
LONGITUDE 5 DEGREES 30 MINUTES NORTH
LATITUDE. HIT BY WHALES. WE ARE GOING
TO THE RAFT. MAYDAY MAYDAY MAYDAY.

Hundreds of thoughts race through my mind as I repeat the call
on two other frequencies. A plane that crashed in the Everglades
many years ago comes to mind, the captain calling "Mayday! Mayday!" as it plunged toward the ground. I am one with all the pilots,
captains, and sailors who have ever sent SOS messages. The distress
they felt in their time of need is now mine.

Sim breaks my musing with a scream: "BILL, THIS BAG HAS A
SAIL IN IT." I look up to be met by her look of helplessness and
total despair. I point to the other side of the dinghy. "There, Sim,
on the other side. I can see it from here. Keep your cool. You're
doing fine. Call me when you have it."

Sim edges back out on the deck. Whales blow and splash inches
away. An animal could easily slide up onto the deck. A powerful sea
breaks over the bow and washes down the deck. Sim struggles with
the ropes that hold the second bag, harder to cut when they are loose.
After much sawing, she pulls the bag loose. It is much heavier than
the bag with the sail, and she strains to drag it along the deck to the
cockpit. She opens the bag and sighs with relief when the raft pops
out. She yells down, "I'VE GOT IT! IT'S HERE! COME UP NOW!"

I shove my way through the flooded cabin to the companion-
way, water inching closer to my waist. My fingers tremble as I rush
to untie the layers of protection surrounding the life raft's valise. At
last, the raft pops out—new, compact, and so very small.

I start to pull the handle to inflate the raft but stop. First, we
must clear the deck so we can launch it. I loosen one of the ties that
holds down our bimini, the cover that kept us dry during rainsqualls. Sim unties the other side. The wind quickly catches the

bright-blue bimini top and carries it over our heads and out of the way. I then move to the starboard deck and lean heavily on the stanchions that hold the lifelines. There is no way we can lift the raft over this three-foot barrier. With some unknown force, I rip three of the stanchions out of their brackets and drop them, with the lifelines attached, over the side. So far, so good.

Seas roll down the deck. I take one more look around and say to Sim, "Stand back. I'm going to inflate the raft." The raft has a handle with large letters that read: "Pull here to inflate." I pull about twenty-five feet of line out until one last hard tug catches us by surprise. Totally unprepared for the explosion of high-pressure air that rushes into the raft, we lose precious minutes, stunned. Air hisses into the neatly folded plastic, each crease popping out in succession. Within seconds, a sturdy yellow raft fills the cockpit. A sudden puff of wind lifts it off the deck and threatens to blow it away. Sim holds onto it as I tie the inflation lanyard to the winch. "Let's load it," I order Simonne. With no further word, I return below.

She loads everything on deck into the raft: bucket, cushions, flashlight, compass, gloves, T-shirts, shorts. From a cockpit locker, she pulls out all the bottles of water and soft drinks she can find and drops them into the raft.

Below, I fight my way back to the radio to search the twenty-meter amateur band for radio traffic. It is deathly quiet. Either the band is dead or everyone's asleep. In Australia and the Far East, it's four in the afternoon, a bad hour for reception. Back in the States, it's four in the morning, and even the hardiest ham radio operators are in bed. I tune to 13113.2 kilohertz, the Coast Guard weather broadcast frequency, and transmit a signal that I hope will get through to some ship awaiting the latest weather forecast. As a last shot, I tune back into the Pacific Maritime Net, send my last Mayday, then lock the radio into transmit mode in the hope that someone with a radio direction finder will pick up the dying signal.

Now to load the raft with stores. We keep our food under the port bunk, which is now piled high with the computer, the weather fax, the camcorder, and heaps of bedding and clothing. I throw everything onto the starboard bunk, tear off the cushions, and plunge my head into the diesel-laden water to grope for the cans stored below. I drop each can into a plastic bag and, when it's full, pass it up to Sim, then reach for another bag. Suddenly, I remember there is something important I must do.

In water way above my waist, I struggle with the heavy motor cover and cushions that block my way toward the bow compartment. In total darkness, I force my way in. An impossible mountain of cushions bars me. I squeeze past them and blindly grope in the dark. I locate the water desalinator and two life jackets, then fight my way out, swimming more than treading. Sim takes all three out of my hands. She slips into her jacket and places my jacket and the water-maker atop the boat cushions she has loaded into the raft.

I return to the main cabin, water up to my armpits, in search of food, exhaling in desperation, blowing like one of the whales. Whales. I've forgotten about them. Are they still with us? Will they attack the raft once we launch it? I recover from a secluded locker a large ziplock bag with our passports, credit cards, money, and traveler's checks and order Sim to put them into a pocket of her life jacket. I then toss up a large plastic bag with unused bedding. With water covering the lower lockers, I blindly empty cans from them into small plastic bags and hand each up to Sim.

A bottle of cognac, half full, floats next to a can of crackers. I pass both up. The raft overflows with stores. I think I have it all. With water up to my chin, I must get out. I hesitate and look around. I just cannot accept that my beloved boat is sinking. And to think of where we have been together: Hong Kong, Manila, New York City, Maine, Bermuda, Venezuela, and to every island in the Caribbean. More than thirty-two thousand miles together. And now we must part . . . forever.

Simonne's call jars me. "Bill, that's it. There's no more room. Let's get the raft in the water." I am not through. I fumble in the tool compartment, find a screwdriver, and pry off the ship's clock and the barometer from their traditional places above the navigation station, toss them into a plastic bag, and hand them up. Sim waves and points to the ship's logbook and her yellow Walkman radio. I grab both.

I can't pull myself away from the boat I've grown to love. I've spent hours at anchor and at sea breathing in the coziness and warmth of the beautifully varnished cabin. The boat lurches as I grab an overhead bracket, step over the now strangely quiet engine, and emerge on deck.

The floodlight shines brightly on the mainsail as it flails like a bird about to take flight. C'mon, *Siboney*, get up! Let's go! You and I were ready to conquer the world. Don't leave me now. You are part of my life. You and I have done much in these twenty-two years. Don't rob me of my dream. We have so much yet to do. But the pull of the sea is relentless. Sim's pleas bring me back to the moment.

"Bill, quickly! The boat's going to sink. We must get off! Now!"

We must go. What am I forgetting?

"Butler, what's wrong with you? COME ON, LET'S GO!" she screams.

"I'm not ready." I know how my boat settles. My sons sank her twice in Biscayne Bay, and I refloated her both times. She's not yet ready to sink. She has been my faithful partner, and I will stay with her until she leaves me.

"Lord, have mercy on us. This guy is crazy!" screams Sim. "Who do you think you are? Captain Ahab?"

I look at Simonne. "I repeat: I'm not ready. Besides, I need to get fishhooks out of the cockpit lockers."

"Bill, put the raft in the water. The boat could go down and pull us with it. I want to get off. Now."

Siboney, full of water, rocks gently as if held in a giant cradle. Sim's desperate pleading gets through to me. I turn to her and say, "OK, let's launch the raft. Grab the other end."

We inch the heavily loaded raft toward the gunwale and slide it into the water. I take the twenty-foot inflation lanyard and cleat it. When Sim jumps on top of our load of supplies, I push the raft off. It floats away with its bow line tied to *Siboney*.

I spot the fishing rod and set it aside. I probe in the aft locker for a bag of hooks. Six packages sorted by size should be there, each in its own ziplock bag. I search blindly in the rising water but find only four coconuts, which I place on the deck. I feel around for a face mask. No masks. No hooks, either.

I call out, "Sim, where are the face masks?" She yells back that they are in the bow, now unreachable.

"Bill, for God's sake. Get off!" She hasn't stopped calling me since she jumped into the raft.

The deck wallows under me. Waves roll over my feet. Should I take the fiberglass dinghy or not? It's been on my mind since we started to sink. It would give us a backup for the raft. On the other hand, in rough weather, the dinghy would surely fill with water and sink. What would happen then? It could puncture the raft. Or perhaps tear it. Many reasons for and many against. I decide to leave it.

The bow is heavy with water. Waves roll down the full length of the deck and spill over the stern. I will stay with you, *Siboney*, to the last. Soon you will be alone, resting eternally on the muddy seabed, two thousand fathoms of black ocean pressing down on you, trapped forever in a solitary frigid tomb, never again to sail into a strange port or to bound carelessly over the oceans of the world. We rode out a typhoon together, with winds of more than eighty knots. Your masthead touched the waves twice, but you emerged stronger and sailed farther than ever before. Much water has passed under your keel, but on this last two-mile leg, you will need to sail alone.

Simonne is barely visible just beyond the circle of light. Her desperate scream reaches me: "BILL, IF YOU DON'T GET INTO THE RAFT RIGHT NOW, I WILL CUT THE LINE! YOU'RE CRAZY! THE BOAT IS GOING DOWN! GET OFF NOW!"

The boat lurches drunkenly. Waves roll down the deck, flow into the cabin, and fill the last remaining spaces. Nothing can save her now. It is time for me to abandon my ship.

A great sea lifts *Siboney*, then breaks as it reaches the stern, propelling a ton of white water into the open lazarette to hasten *Siboney's* now inevitable plunge to the bottom. The glare from the spotlight accentuates the grim finality of our situation. Seawater pours into the cabin where Simonne and I have passed the last two months in cozy comfort. The brightly lit mainsail waves a painful good-bye. I turn toward Sim, in whose expression fear, exasperation, and disbelief are mingled. A wave breaks against the cabin and covers my ankles. It is time to abandon my love of loves.

I pull the raft toward my stricken boat. Bright yellow and rugged-looking, it rides high, though heavily loaded. Simonne, hair wind-blown and lips pursed, hangs over the near end of the raft, ready to fend off from the self-steering gear and the stern pulpit now beginning to go under. The roar of a breaking wave startles me. It washes over the cockpit coaming and collides with the raft, propelling it into *Siboney*. The surge overpowers Simonne, and the raft brushes the stern. A loud blast of air rushes from the raft. The end closest to the boat deflates and sinks under Sim's weight. The raft begins to go under, full of the stores we've saved. I start to pull it aboard in hopes I have time to loosen and load the dinghy, but with a pop, the raft fills out and continues to float as before. Its internal sleeves filled, acting as a backup air chamber. Sim, her left hand outstretched, terror in her eyes, looks to me for an answer. I nod. We're OK for now.

I stare at the three-inch gash in the raft. What if water floods in? Will the raft sink? Though it has lost half its air, the raft floats high. Will it hold the two of us? I hesitate to jump in, afraid my added weight may cause the raft to fill with water. I move toward the dinghy, but another wave breaks over the cabin. White foamy water cascades down the deck and pummels the raft. I can stay aboard no longer. *Siboney* is going down.

MARLTON, NEW JERSEY
0430 THURSDAY • JUNE 15, 1989

Jim Butler lies sprawled across his king-size waterbed. He dreams. His father is at the helm of Siboney *sailing along in a gentle breeze far off in the Pacific Ocean. Jim is on board. The night is dark and ominous. A strange object approaches* Siboney. *The object strikes the boat a solid blow.* Siboney *shudders and heels way over. Water floods the cabin. Then suddenly, the sea is empty. There is no trace of* Siboney *or her crew. They have disappeared. What happened to Dad?*

ABOARD THE RAFT
LAST CHANCE
0450 THURSDAY • JUNE 15, 1989

I PULL THE RAFT CLOSER to hand Sim the fishing rod, then untie the line from the winch. Sim steadies me while I slide in next to her. The four coconuts float by, out of reach. We drift away from *Siboney*. I am unable to speak, stunned and overwhelmed with unknowns. Amazingly, *Siboney*'s masthead light continues to burn even though the batteries are submerged. The distance between us widens quickly.

Sim and I remain motionless as the sea swallows *Siboney* and so many of our possessions. She squeezes my hand. We kiss. I search for words to reassure her, but come up empty. Moments later, the tower is underwater. Lights flicker, and then the boat disappears. Left in total darkness and utterly alone, we embrace, and with anguish deeper than we have ever experienced, we cry uncontrollably, howling louder than lonely hyenas.

I tighten my hold on Sim and search the horizon. Search for what? We haven't seen a living thing above water except for birds during the past three weeks. Never have I seen a night this dark and dismal. Adrift in the Pacific Ocean in an overloaded and torn raft, we are castaways in the full sense of the word. When I glance at Simonne, her face somber and stiff, I remember all too quickly that she is in peril solely because of me. Her death will rest at my doorstep forever.

Dark clouds press down and compress our universe into a tiny ball of terror and anguish. Unquenchable tears and loud cries fill the night. I fight to remain strong but fail miserably. I howl loudest and longest. I know better than Sim the magnitude of our plight.

Sim moves her wristwatch near a small greenish emergency light attached to the raft. It's 0520. At 0420, we sailed along without a care, pleased to have the whales as company. Whales! Whatever happened to the whales? I scan the water around us and find the sea empty. Most probably they continue to whack *Siboney* as she heads for the bottom.

In sixty minutes, our lives and destiny have been irrevocably altered. And in less than an hour of use, our raft appears much less sturdy than when first inflated. Then it felt solid; now it is soft and low in the water. We must fill it with air before it sinks. But where is the pump? I don't even know what it looks like. Sim rummages among our stores and locates the emergency kit. In it she finds a flashlight, two patches, a packet of seasickness pills, two plastic knobs, and a small, bellows-type pump.

She turns the flashlight to the instructions printed on the side of the raft near the valve. Large black letters read, "Screw the pump on clockwise until it is tight, and then open the valve two turns." I hold the flashlight while Sim screws the pump into the valve. She turns the knob on the valve clockwise and starts to pump. The air chamber fills and soon becomes much firmer. She turns the valve to close it and removes the pump.

I don't dare tell Sim we're in a coastal raft designed to be used for a week or ten days. I bought this model to save money, space, and weight. Why in the devil didn't I buy a top-of-the-line offshore raft? Will this one last until we're spotted? I look into Sim's disbelieving eyes, and when they catch mine, both of us wail like lonesome coyotes. What will happen to us now? Will our family ever see us again? When will help come? Our lives now dangle from the thinnest of threads hundreds of miles from land in a minuscule plastic vessel.

No question, the emergency sleeves inherent in the design of this raft have saved our lives. When the canister of compressed gas first expanded the raft, both halves of the air chambers inflated equally. Air pressure pressed the internal sleeves into tight balls in the middle of each side of the raft. When the raft tore, air from the full half chamber filled the sleeves, which then expanded into the empty half chamber. The raft floated as before. Where would we be now if the raft had filled with water? Dead or dying.

Tens of thousands of square miles of empty ocean surround us. If we only had a moon or a few stars, daylight, anything at all to reach out to, I would feel less alone. The gloomy blackness of night drags on. Our anxiety deepens. We're coming up on 0600 Miami time. Out here, where we drift, the day runs about two hours later; first light is before eight and the sun rises no earlier than 0830, perhaps closer to nine. This night, a night that has brought us closer to death than either of us could have imagined, still has a long way to run.

To the east, the coast of Central America is more than eleven hundred nautical miles away. Acapulco is seven hundred miles to the north. The wind could push us north, but the current will take us east. The Galápagos Islands are six hundred miles to the southeast, directly upwind. To the west lie four thousand miles of empty ocean. Westerly flowing currents lie a hundred miles to the south and one hundred fifty miles or less to the north. If we're pushed into either, we will drift into emptiness. Distance and time are our enemies.

I need not close my eyes to see *Siboney* in her final moments, deck awash, sails full. Then the ruptured raft. Could I have launched the dinghy in time? Should I have brought it? What will happen if the other end of the raft tears and the raft goes down? A vision of the raft sinking with all our stores sends new shivers through me.

Yet we are alive! Someone will surely find us soon. We have some food, and the desalinator will provide us with all the fresh water we need. When I bought it and the raft, I also purchased an emergency position-indicator radio beacon (EPIRB), a handheld device that transmits signals on two frequencies monitored by aircraft and satellites. Upon receiving a signal from an EPIRB, the receiving station can track the approximate location of the signal. For the system to work, our EPIRB must be within line of sight from an airplane or satellite.

Are we near a commercial airline route? Chile–San Francisco or New Zealand–Los Angeles? What other routes could there be? None come close to where we now float. Should I activate the EPIRB now or wait until we're closer to shore? If I wait, it may be too late to do any good. We could be dead. We need help now.

If the EPIRB or Mayday signals fail us, our family will certainly take the necessary steps for our rescue. Today is June 15. We talked to

Simonne's eldest son, Cris, and to my daughter Susan on June 11. Susan reported that my son Joe's baby, a girl, had been born a day earlier. Joe awaits our congratulatory phone call. Cris expects an answer on whether to rent the house or not. I almost called the children last night, but now I'm glad I didn't. In a week, on June 22, it will have been more than ten days since they've heard from us. After we left Panama, we called home every three or four days. Our silence will have to be a strong signal that something has happened. When the boys compare notes, the air search will certainly be on.

Is there any chance a freighter will sight us? Not really. Ships from Panama to Hawaii and the Far East all run farther north, and shipping from South America to the West Coast runs to the east of us. It's obvious. We are out of all regular shipping routes.

On the positive side, however, we're in a strong easterly current that will push us toward shore. Aboard *Siboney*, the current was our enemy, slowing us down. Now it's our hope and, very possibly, our salvation. The North Pacific Equatorial Countercurrent flows as steadily as the Gulf Stream. If we're lucky, we'll stay in it all the way to the coast. If not, we'll drift into the trackless wastes of the Pacific Ocean . . . or into an endless eddy, to drift in circles forever, our bleached bones picked clean by the birds or the fish.

We remain motionless atop all the stores gathered in those last few grueling minutes before *Siboney* sank. Petrified that the raft will capsize, I dare not move. We hang onto straps sewn into the top of the air cylinder to keep our balance. The two of us perching on the mountain of stores make the raft terribly top-heavy. But though its freeboard is no more than eight or ten inches, we float easily over the passing swells. Not a single wave has washed aboard. Above, the dark, unfriendly sky presses close. A sense of utter loneliness sets in, stronger than I have ever felt before. For Sim's sake, I must keep a strong, positive attitude. Poor Sim, she's so quiet. I can only imagine what desperate thoughts run through her mind.

Neither of us can doze, much less sleep. My eyes refuse to close. Sim lies in my arms with her eyes shut, lips compressed. The green glow from the tiny saltwater-activated emergency light helps fight our overwhelming feeling of loneliness. I look at the pain highlighted on Sim's face and think of how much more pain she will have to bear before we are delivered. How do we get out of this one? I've sailed the oceans for more than forty years. I must find a way.

A pale glow in the eastern sky makes the horizon more distinct. Then touches of pink tint the eastern and western horizons. At sea, on *Siboney*, I always stood the early watch to experience first light, that splendid moment when night suddenly yields to the force of a new day and the horizon emerges from hours of darkness. It is at this moment, when both stars and the horizon are visible, that ocean navigators the world over work their sextants and shoot stars to determine their position. Minutes later, even the brightest star is no longer visible. First light finds us trapped between the long sweep of the swells and a multilayered sky.

As morning dawns, black clouds turn gray, then slowly evolve into isolated shapes that glide in from the southern horizon, pass closely overhead, and quickly disappear far off to the north. The horizon lies before us, naked except for the incessant waves that form a jagged, tooth-shaped silhouette where ocean joins sky.

We bob easily atop the ceaseless swells as the seas continue to calm. The sun, hidden behind thick clouds, is surely up. I change position slightly and stretch slowly. Simonne looks up and hugs me. Tears run down her cheeks while prayers form on her lips. We hold each other tightly as time stands still.

The skies lighten. We have enough light to look after the tear in the raft. The emergency kit contains two mechanical patches. Each patch consists of three pieces: an aluminum oval disk with a rubber gasket slips inside the tear; a long threaded screw runs up from the middle of this disk; and a similar disk, but without a gasket, fits outside the hole. A wing nut tightens both halves together. A wire soldered onto the end of the screw with a cord prevents losing any parts.

I disassemble the patch and hand it to Sim. Careful not to unbalance the raft, I turn slowly onto my knees and reach toward the tear. The damage consists of a hole more than three inches long and two inches wide. I can't tell whether both patches will plug it entirely. Sim hands me the first patch with the wire lead tied to a cord. I slide half the patch into the air chamber to cover one edge of the tear, push on the outer cover, and then tighten the wing nut. The second patch fits alongside and covers the hole with a hair to spare.

Sim has pumped constantly while I fixed the hole. Now I lean back and take over. With each push of the pump, the air chamber tightens. I count my strokes. When I reach a hundred and ten, Sim tells me to stop. A slight hiss from the patch confirms that some air continues to escape from the space between the two patches. But it works better than expected.

Sim gets down to the business of housekeeping. She barks like my old sarge at Fort Dix as she orders me to lie down and put my feet up on the side of the raft. Then she piles a mountain of stores on me. The floor of the raft is just a thin piece of rubberized fabric. If we lie directly on it, we'll be cold and susceptible to attack by fish. Or we might tear it. When the far end of the floor is bare, Sim covers it with one of the cushions salvaged from *Siboney*. Atop the cushion, she puts the camcorder, the bucket, and the bag with bedding. Into the bucket go the gloves, the knife, the camera, and several food cans. She clears space for the next cushion, which like the others is three feet long and a foot wide. The second cushion fits easily.

I move again, and Sim repeats the process. Soon all four cushions line the bare floor. The two small cushions go under our bottoms, while the life jackets and foul-weather gear help lift our heads. The canned food becomes part of our headrest. The camcorder case, with the camcorder and the 35 mm camera, lies against the air chamber near our feet. On top of the case, she places the large bucket. The watermaker, wrapped in a jacket, is under my feet. Water, flares, and all our other gear are squeezed in alongside us.

When Sim spreads two comforters under us and I move to my side of the raft, I find it downright comfortable—that is, except for the two water jugs, two and a half gallons each, pushing against my back. Sim has put sharp objects, including two pairs of scissors and a nail file, into the gun case with the .38 Smith and Wesson. But I seem to have missed the bullets. We need to find a home for the six-foot-long fishing rod with its razor-sharp hook. For the moment, I'll hold it between my legs with the tip and hook out over the water.

I've kept a log on *Siboney* since the day I sailed for Hong Kong out of Manila in 1968. This latest logbook is the eighth, and begins in 1987. Its last entry reads:

> 0342 JUNE 15, 1989 DAY 21 OUT OF BALBOA
> POSITION 5 DEGREES 30 MINUTES NORTH
> LATITUDE 99 DEGREES 7 MINUTES WEST
> LONGITUDE—SURROUNDED BY WHALES

Sim hands me a ballpoint pen, and I enter:

> 0430 HIT HARD BY WHALE—OPENED SEAM—
> WATER RISING
> 0445 ABANDONED SHIP
> 0500 *SIBONEY* SINKS

On a new line I continue:

> 15 JUNE 1989 THURSDAY—DAY 1 ON RAFT
> 0800 ORGANIZED RAFT—PUT CUSHIONS
> UNDER US—MAKING INVENTORY

Also aboard is my navigation workbook with all the satellite fixes received since leaving Miami. On the page opposite the fixes are notations with my radio contacts. We have no charts, but later I will construct one from the satellite position data.

It's time now to put our new home together. When I look around for instructions, big bold letters on the side of the raft order us to "Deploy sea anchor before erecting canopy to reduce drift." Giving it no further thought, I obediently unwrap the sea anchor and toss it over the side. It fills like a small parachute at the end of a twenty-foot cord.

Next we inflate the two arches, one on each end of the raft, with the small air pump. These arches, which are ten inches in diameter, run across and over the raft. When fully inflated, a rubberized fabric sewn into the arches covers both ends of the raft. Another flap, also fastened to one of the arches, zips into the opposite arch and forms a roof. Two flaps attached to the long sides of the oval raft zip into the arch and become windows. With the canopy roof in place and the windows zipped partway up, we begin to feel more secure, safer. Our new home has quickly become dark and cozy. Sim, exhausted from her chores, lies next to me and closes her eyes.

Seconds later, she turns my way and asks, "Bill, will anyone search for us? Do you think they'll find us in this immensity? We are miles away from anywhere. Will the raft hold up?"

"I hope so" is the only reply I can conjure. The same quandaries have been twirling in my head, and I haven't found a single positive answer to any of them.

We turn toward each other, embrace, and hold on tightly. We kiss. Tears flow like monsoon rains. Sim looks up at my tear-streaked face and says quietly, "I heard a voice last night, soon after we drifted away from *Siboney*. The voice was low, much like a whisper, and over and over it repeated, 'Forty days, forty days.' I can't get that message out of my mind. What do you think it means?"

Forty days? We'll be dead in forty days. The designed life of this raft is no more than two weeks. We don't have a chance of squeaking out of this one. Sim breaks into my thoughts.

"Bill. Will we live? Will we be found?"

"Of course we'll be found."

"When? In forty days and nights?"

"It'll take a few days, maybe a week."

"I hope so. Bill, I love you."

"I love you too, Sim."

ABOARD THE RAFT
LAST CHANCE
1000 THURSDAY • JUNE 15, 1989

N INETY MINUTES LATER, Sim's mood has definitely changed. She has had time to think, and to see through my glib assurances.

"You bastard. And you are a real bastard. Your disgusting jealousy got us into this disaster. You had to separate me from my children. You forced me on this trip. And here I am, in a miserable miniature raft where I'm certainly going to die with an equally miserable monster."

I try to break in, but her broadside continues.

"You ugly beast. You just lie there and smirk. You want me dead, but you went too far this time. You're not going to get out of this alive, either. I'm going to die, but you will die too. What will my invalid mother do with me dead? You are a criminal of the worst kind, Butler. We must pray we die quickly and without pain, for there is no hope in praying for life."

I start to argue, but it's like throwing gasoline on a raging fire. She goes on for what seems an eternity . . . my madness, my children, her children, her poor mother, hopelessness, death. Exhausted, she slows for a second, and I try for a change of mood.

"Sim, find the EPIRB."

Momentarily distracted, she stops the cannonade, digs in the pile of stores under her feet, and quickly finds our bright-red emergency signaling device. I extend the antenna, then read the instructions. "Keep in a vertical position" is the first thing I see. I turn the switch to

TRANSMIT. A small green light flashes, indicating our signal is now being beamed to any satellites and airplanes in the vicinity.

I can't find a place to hang the EPIRB vertically, so I hold it outside the canopy for almost an hour, until my arm tires. Then I find a strap on top of the canopy that holds it more or less upright. The batteries are designed to power it for three or four days. I stretch out again and glance over at Sim.

She looks up at the EPIRBs and says, "That will get a signal nowhere. It's all we have, so I'll shut up. I've said too much already. I wish I were dumb and unknowing. Perhaps I'd feel more secure."

"Sim, it's transmitting. It should work."

"*Cruising World* said that most EPIRBs don't work. They tested a bunch, and only one or two in ten did the job."

"I heard you before and I hear you now. You must believe this is the one in ten that works."

"And they also said that the system isn't working worldwide. There are many gaps. Considering the desolation out here, we are surely in one of the gaps."

"Damn it, Sim. Can't you think positive? It's working. Help will come."

"You're dense for an engineer. The system needs an earth station. There isn't a chunk of earth within a thousand miles of here. And as far as hoping for an airplane, anyone flying overhead is in worse trouble than we." Sim speaks the last words with a strange smile.

"OK, baby, I know. Maybe it won't work. But what's wrong with humoring ourselves? What do we have to lose? I still think we'll see results. Someone will pick up our signal. They have to. I feel there is a ship heading our way right now." Sim's grin broadens. She shakes her head. I throw up my arms. "OK, so I'm more than a little punchy."

When we try to get comfortable, we quickly find there is not enough room for the two of us plus the stores piled around and under us. A large trash bag full of spare blankets and comforters for use in the higher latitudes has been in the way since we first cast off. Sim pulls it open and finds three comforters, a heavy cotton sheet, and a wool blanket. In a flash, she throws two of the comforters over the side.

While they are still in sight, Sim has second thoughts. "Perhaps we should have kept them," she says. "They were my babies' favorite comforters, and we may have had use for them." We agree to throw nothing more overboard for another day or two. We move the remaining bedding around to soften our headrest and, except for various lumps under the bedding, our raft turns out to be genuinely cozy. Under the canopy, it's dark and cool. We lie on our backs, which is fine for Sim, as she can stretch out, but the raft is eight inches too short for me. I push my head up until it touches the end and put my feet on the air chamber at the other end.

Rain starts halfway through the afternoon. Gigantic drops pelt the raft, yet we and our stores stay dry. The dark-blue coat of waterproofing makes for a snug nest. Our last sleep was before one in the morning, and our exhaustion surrenders to the regular patter of rain.

When I awaken, I notice Sim rummaging through one of her cosmetic bags. She pulls out a miniature set of dominoes. Refreshed, I lose no time in challenging her to a game of double sixes. We must hold the pieces in the palms of our hands, as the raft rocks too much to place them on the cushion that is our playing table. Sim wins the first game and also the second, with the scores duly entered in the log. We call it quits halfway through the third game when our stomach and back muscles complain loudly. Besides, hunger tears at me. We had our last meal aboard *Siboney* before sundown yesterday, more than twenty hours ago.

Sim takes over her traditional role as meal planner, announcing, "We'll ration food and maintain a three-meals-a-day schedule. We'll eat the crackers first, with one cracker in the morning. At lunch, let's eat two with peanut butter, and at night we can go back to a single cracker."

Her plan sounds acceptable, but it's missing an important ritual. "Before supper," I counter, "we'll have happy hour as usual."

Sim shakes her head: "OK, *borracho*. Tomorrow, we'll have a can for lunch. We can't afford to let our bodies go down too fast." I nod in agreement.

Sim digs under the covers and comes up with a can of Keebler's Export Sodas, which have been a twenty-year staple aboard *Siboney*. They stay crisper longer than any other cracker we have tried, even in the humid surroundings on a boat. I gulp down half a cracker and gag. Desperately, I reach for a bottle of water, open it, and wash the cracker down.

Sim watches the entire performance and suggests, "You're taking too big a bite. Look, bite off a crumb at a time. Like this. Then let it melt on your tongue with your saliva and, when it's soft, swallow it."

I nibble on my second cracker. Breakfast stretches out to fifteen minutes. Several gulps of water give me the sensation that I'm full. My eyes close.

Sim sits up with a jerk and brings me out of my snooze. She's rigid, like a hunting dog.

"What's that?"

"What's what, Sim?"

"That bump. Didn't you feel it?"

"I'm not sure. Wait."

I'm jabbed in the middle of my back. Then there's a bump to Sim's bottom and two to her legs.

Sim leans on her elbow and whispers, "What can it be?"

I shrug my shoulders and shake my head. The bumps continue. It feels like we're hitting a log, which could have nails that could puncture the raft. A scratching sound runs down the side of the raft. Sim jumps up, opens the window, and looks out.

She calls out, "Bill, it's a huge turtle."

"A what? Is it good to eat?"

"A turtle. It's more than three feet around. It's going to puncture the raft."

I zip down my window, grab the orange oar, and row the raft around. A huge sea turtle paddles leisurely toward the raft. It lifts its head out of the water to breathe and looks directly at me. Large black rings surround its eyes, producing a menacing aura. Barnacles cling to the light-brown armor plating of its carapace as it heads under the raft. I hit it with the end of the paddle. It kicks with all four flippers, splashes, and dives. Message received.

Small raindrops start to fall from a dark-gray cloud overhead. We quickly zip the two windows closed as the drops turn to a downpour. Under the waterproof canopy, we stay dry. We snuggle, embrace, then sleep. Sim prays aloud, "God, save us, please God." I fail to recall a single prayer. Besides, I can get us out of this without any prayers.

My watch chirps. I find the flashlight next to my head and untie my reading glasses, which hang from the inflated arch. It's midnight. We have been on the raft for nineteen hours. Heavy rain pours down, but not a drop has fallen on us. I pull our cotton comforter up, bunch the pillow, and begin anew the process of falling asleep.

My thoughts return to yesterday. What did I do wrong? What could I have done differently to save the boat from the attack? Why did the whales suddenly turn on us? They appeared friendly and never bothered us as they swam alongside for hours. Our hull, painted a dark red, may have looked like a large blue whale in the black of the night. Did the pod of pilot whales consider *Siboney* an intruder, a menace to their young? In that case, they would have attacked instinctively and not stopped until we lay mortally wounded, no longer a danger. That would explain why they didn't come after the raft.

Or, being carnivorous, did they attack in the belief we were edible? I've read stories of pilot and killer whales attacking large, solitary whales in midocean. Several members of the pod position themselves under the large whale to keep it from sounding. Three or four more attack the tail to cut its means of propulsion and balance as one or two jump over the air hole to prevent the whale from breathing. Another dozen become a collective battering ram and hammer away for the kill.

Once the whale is dead, the entire pod feeds. Preposterous, but true. After all, had *Siboney* been a whale, it would have made dinner for the entire pod. In either case, we should be safe aboard the raft. We haven't seen a whale since we cast off. Hopefully, they will find nothing of interest in our frail craft, as a lunge by the smallest of the whales surely would spell our end.

When I awaken, Simonne still prays out loud in French. The air chamber is reassuringly tight. I turn and sleep anew. When I open my eyes next, I see a rainy dawn. When I stir, Sim reaches over and kisses me. I peek out the window but rain sweeps in, and I quickly close it and lie back down. Sim turns toward me with a faraway look.

We embrace. This isn't all that bad, I muse. Rain falls and the wind blows, but we're dry, safe, and cozy, and I have a lovely raft mate. The comforter feels like a feather bed. I try to perk up Sim.

"Hey, Sim, this is like the Hilton. We'll make it, you'll see. Help will come soon, like in a James Bond movie. What time is it?"

Sim is the raft timekeeper. Instead of wrestling with my glasses, I find it easier to ask her. We have saved two watches, my digital Seiko and Sim's Raymond Weil, the one I gave her when we flew to Venezuela for Christmas 1988. My watch chimes or, better yet, chirps on the hour. Both show dates.

"It's nine Miami time. And it's Friday, June 16." That makes it seven or so local time. On *Siboney*, I had planned to change ship's time to Hawaiian time in another thousand miles. This would have given our biological inner clocks a chance to adapt to a new rhythm before arriving in Hilo.

The time has come to do a little formal navigation. My navigation workbook contains my summaries of course changes and daily distances traveled since leaving Miami. My last entry aboard *Siboney* was the 0342 satellite fix. Thirty hours ago, we were safe and secure. Ah, better not to dwell on that. That last sat fix put *Siboney* twelve hundred miles west of Panama. The Galápagos Islands lie six hundred miles to the southeast, upwind, unreachable. To the west, there are four thousand miles of empty ocean, the nearest bits of land the lonely island outposts of Christmas and Fanning islands.

With the good position fix at the point where we sank, I can calculate where we are. As of noon today, June 16, we have been adrift one day plus seven hours—thirty-one hours. At three-quarters of a knot, our easterly drift is about twenty-five miles for these thirty-one hours. I can't measure the effect that the current has on the raft, but I can feel its push. It's like riding one of those escalators that aren't set right and jerk along. An inexorable, invisible force holds the raft so firmly that neither wind nor waves alter our course.

The rain has stopped, allowing us to open the windows and expand our horizon from the two to three feet we have in the tightly closed raft. The clear weather will allow me to measure the drift caused by wind and waves. I cut a two-inch-square piece of paper and drop it to windward, where it quickly wets and floats under the surface. Sim has her watch ready as I call out, "Mark."

I wait until the paper is ten feet away from the raft and again call, "Mark."

"Thirty seconds," Sim answers.

"Sim, check wind direction." She digs the compass out from under the bedding, holds it up to the wind, and calls out, "South, 180 degrees."

A little mental arithmetic: Ten feet of drift in thirty seconds means twenty feet a minute. That's twelve hundred feet an hour. There are 6,020 feet in a nautical mile. The drift caused by wind and waves is a bit over one-quarter mile per hour. In the thirty-one hours on the raft, we have drifted north seven miles. Of course, my calculations are rough, but I will try to keep them up until we're found.

Light rain begins and again forces us to close the windows. The wind increases. We play dominoes. I win six games to Sim's five and enter the results in the log. Larger waves break on the raft. Spray splashes over the window and onto us. We tighten the window ties and cover up.

Sim sops up the water that has collected in the bottom of the raft with a small sponge. She then squeezes the sponge into the pail. My job is to hold the pail and dump it when full. Sim reels, seasick. We have pills in the raft emergency kit if she gets worse.

At one in the afternoon, Sim opens a can of diet Veg-All. "Diet" of all things! Just what we need. We have no eating tools and quickly master the use of the toothbrush so as not to lose a single tiny piece of our precious veggie food. We save half the can for supper.

The wind dies toward late afternoon and the rain stops. I open a window in hopes the fresh air will dry us out before night sets in.

"Bill, what's that?" Sim's in her hunting dog pose.

I don't hear a thing. "What do you hear?"

"A noise. Listen. Let me look."

Sim opens the window a little farther.

"My God, Bill! There's a freighter coming straight for us! Oh my God! They found us!" she shouts. "Your little red EPIRB works. We are saved! Oh, thank you, dear God! Thank you!"

"Let me see." I struggle up and look to where Sim is pointing.

A large freighter with a dark-blue hull and white topsides steams straight for us at high speed, pushing a wave before it that curls, breaks, and crashes on both sides of the bow. Never have I seen a more magnificent sight. I rejoice and call out, "Oh baby! We are saved! Quick, put some clothes on."

The heat has kept us naked from our first moments on the raft. Besides, we're short of clothes. We saved the clothes we were wearing plus a small plastic bag with two pairs of shorts and two T-shirts that belong to Sim. Last night, we wore T-shirts to keep warm. Sim throws on a pair of shorts and a shirt. I open the windows and zip back the canopy.

The ship, less than three hundred yards from our raft, heads directly for us. We embrace, laugh, and cry, unable to believe our incredible luck. I raise my hands in thanks and shout. Simonne wraps one arm around me and cries with unrestrained joy.

The huge propellers bite into the churning sea in what appears to be reverse gear. "Sim," I cry out, "look, he's slowing down."

We scream with glee. Castaway in the depths of the Pacific, one moment we're alone, and suddenly, straight out of the deep-blue sea, life heads for us. We're going to live after all!

"Wow, something really worked. The Mayday got through. No, they're homing in on the EPIRB. We'll be saved!"

Sim doesn't take her eyes off the ship. She nods and says, "They're coming for us. There is no question they've seen us. Otherwise, what would they be doing out here? What phenomenal luck."

The bow of the ship is two hundred feet away. The air chambers throb from the thundering boom of the huge diesel engines. The sides of the ship rise high off the water, neatly painted. When it stops and comes alongside, how can we make it up to the deck? What will they throw down for us to grab?

The ship's bow pushes tons of water before it, a sea of froth, rolling and breaking toward us. The raft deftly rides the crest of the bow wave. It pushes us away from the fast-moving hull. Our eyes are on the door to the pilothouse. Someone should emerge any second now and wave to us.

The bridge approaches. We see no one on the bridge, but then it's hard to see through the glass windows. Have they not seen us? We scream for help. Sim waves a white shirt. With the bridge abeam, we yell even louder and wave frantically. Something is very wrong. The sides of the ship are barely fifty feet away. The bastard almost ran us down. I look toward the fast-approaching stern. Are the engines in reverse? They *must* be. I can't tell.

Sim breaks the spell. "Bill, it's not stopping."

The confused propeller wash indicates reverse. I try to explain, "Sim, it takes miles to stop a big ship," but then cry out, "Where is everybody?"

The deck of the ship remains empty. The bridge passes. Nervous and desperate, I command unnecessarily, "YELL, Sim, YELL!" She is already screaming louder than I am. I call out desperately, "Where are the flares? Get them quick!"

Sim digs under the covers, finds a flare, and hands it to me. I look up. The bridge has passed. It's too late. No one looks out the stern. With only three flares, we can't waste one on a long shot. I shake with nervous desperation and plead, "Sim, yell!"

She needs no prodding. She has been screaming and waving her shirt since the bow passed. The stern comes into view. Large white letters announce the *Ter Eriksen*, out of Oslo.

"Norwegians. Wake up, damn you! HELP!"

"Sim, they're turning, aren't they? They must be."

"Why don't we fire off a flare? They're still so near."

The ship turns ever so slightly to starboard. It's getting darker now. I'll try to signal. Sim hands me the lantern, and I flash "S-O-S . . . S-O-S . . . S-O-S."

Sim signals with her shirt and continues to yell as I blink SOSS. A mile past us, the *Ter Eriksen* shows its starboard side in what appears to be a wide turn. Minutes later, the ship is but a blur on the eastern horizon. The turn was an illusion. They did not see us. When I look again, the sea is empty, and once again, we're alone.

We refuse to accept the obvious. Sim continues to scan the horizon for signs of the returning freighter. Jagged waves create constantly changing patterns against the lighter sky. I wrap my arm around Sim to pull her closer. With night closing in on us, it is obvious that rescue will not arrive today. We must now prepare for our second long night adrift.

Sim remains on her knees, staring at the darkening horizon in hopes the ship will return for us. Long minutes pass until she falls, totally disheartened, into my waiting arms. We remain embraced.

Tears pour from our eyes. Darkness swallows both the ship and our little world. I cannot speak or, for that matter, comprehend this new event. Slowly, night shuts out day. Once again we are alone, much more so than before. I struggle to fathom all that has occurred in so few hours. Our latest narrow escape has shattered what little hope remained. How could the *Ter Eriksen* not post a lookout? Any lookout could not have failed to see our bright-orange raft drifting less than a hundred feet from their deck.

Simonne is the first to search aloud for an answer. "Why didn't they see us? We were so close. My God, they almost ran us down. If a ship that close fails to see us, what hope do we have of ever being rescued?"

I too despair and say, "I really screwed up. I should have fired a flare when we first saw it."

Sim puts her right arm around me and pulls me closer. "We were so sure they were going to stop. It wasn't dark enough for the flare, and besides there was no one looking. Anyone on the bridge looking out would have seen us. Particularly with all the fuss we were making."

We hadn't seen a soul on board. They probably had a radar similar to the one on *Siboney*. They set a ten- or twenty-mile guard zone around the ship and need not worry about collision. Land or a ship would make the radar beep. That's why, whenever we sailed, one of us or the radar was on watch. We were convinced that large freighters do not maintain lookouts.

Sim's eyes drop as she edges deeper into my arms. The cool night air makes her tremble. "It's hopeless. The Mayday messages didn't get through. The EPIRB is trash. We're twelve hundred miles from help. When help does arrive, we're invisible. God help us. Let us live. I don't want to die, please God!"

I zip the canopy closed and lie back down. I put my arms around Sim and pull her closer. We hug and cry. Sim calls out to God as tears stream down her cheeks. "Oh Lord, help us, send us another ship. Give us another chance. Please send help." We feel more alone now than yesterday, after *Siboney* sank. Humans, safety, so very, very close, yet beyond reach.

Her cries of anguish pour out: "Cris, Alex, my babies! Do something! Sally, call the Coast Guard. Do something! Anything! God save us; let me see my sons again. I am not ready to die. Bill isn't either. We have so much yet to do." She looks up and cries out, "Why, oh why did this have to happen to us? What have we done, dear Lord, to merit this punishment? We are not evil. Forgive us our sins! Help us!"

"Calm down, sweetie," I say, trying to be reassuring. "We'll make it."

With that, she turns. Her eyes flash lightning, and her voice thunders. "*You. You* are the one who got me into this! *You* pushed me into this. I didn't want to leave Miami. I was happy in my house. You were obstinate, mad, blind, stupid. We should have sailed the Caribbean for a year. This long trip could have waited until we arranged everything onshore. No, we had to leave now. We had to hurry, and for what? Butler, answer me. For what? To have whales almost kill us, and now, in this junk raft, lost in a desolate ocean, surely to die?"

"Desolate? May I remind you a ship full of people almost ran us down just minutes ago?"

Sim shoots me another seething look. "Those bastards. But you are the evil one. You insisted on separating me from my children before I was ready. My mother is sick and I left her alone. Suppose something happens to her? She knew we were going to have an accident. She told me over and over to be careful, not to go. When we don't report in on the radio, she will be the first to worry. She knows the boat sank and she knows we're barely alive. The worry could kill her. And it will be all your fault."

This argument is going nowhere. What can I say? That we're going to make it or, better yet, that we've *got* to make it? I try to reason with her. "We've patched the raft and it's holding air. We have water and we can fish. We sent messages. . . ."

She cuts me short. "None of that is worth a damn if some big shark comes along and starts chewing on the raft. Then we will be dead. Butler, do you know what dead is, or are you a zombie? Through. Finished. No one will ever know what happened to us. I'm praying. Why don't you try? It may do you some good. Or don't you remember how to pray? You certainly don't. The Lord sent this tragedy to you as a warning. You'd better start soon, or it may be too late."

"I received the message, but He really didn't have to go this far." I search for a way to calm her and say, "Let's examine our mistakes. Haven't we led good lives?"

"I'm not that sure. When we divorced, I hurt my husband, and your wife was heartbroken by the whole affair. We hurt them and we hurt our children."

Sim continues to stare out her window. "It was such a difficult situation. As much as we tried not to hurt our loved ones, we ended up hurting everybody, including ourselves, because we couldn't be together. Then, when we got together, we couldn't be happy because we knew our exes weren't. It was traumatic for the children. They all suffered—mine, yours. Had we been closer to the church or had we received counseling, we could have resolved this situation in a smarter way. It was a catch-22 situation. It was either them or us. We chose us. We had glorious moments, but we paid dearly for it. It's hard to rebuild on ashes, and ashes are what we left behind. The worst part for me, and I think it was the same for you, was leaving people behind: my husband, your wife. People that we still love in a certain way, and it hurt to see them hurt."

Sim remains inspired, and I let her rattle on. "Yes, but for both of us, life as it was couldn't go on. I couldn't function. I felt caged. Something had to give."

She's right. What a strong feeling had swept over us. It was like a tidal wave, a monster tsunami. Nothing could stop it, and God knows we tried, both of us. I thought again of the Tamanaco Hotel pool, late on that sunny afternoon. The attraction between us was instantaneous. Because we were both married, we fought the intense captivation. How often after that did we try to stop seeing each other? Always, always, this indescribable obsession drew us back together. "Love is crazy," I mutter.

"Love is crazy and a two-edged sword. It's hell and heaven at the same time. Every little piece of heaven is paid in hell. But I don't regret being with you. What I do regret is what it cost to get here. If I had the choice again, I'm not sure I would have the guts to go through with it all. For us, it was everything—passion, desire, and an all-consuming obsession that swept me away. Too bad I didn't meet you when you were young, free, and single."

"Yes, except that when I married at twenty-one, you were only twelve years old. A little young to marry, wouldn't you say?"

"Yes, but you could have waited for me," Sim sighs wistfully, not without a tear.

The sun drops under the horizon without a sunset. While some light remains, I ask Sim to read the cards. Yesterday, she found in her toilet case a half-dozen cards printed with prayers, parables, and psalms. She read them for the first time last evening, and for a brief moment, while she read, I escaped into a world of hope and light and beauty. Tonight, as she finishes reading, the shadows of night deepen and close out our second day as castaways. Sim takes a last look around, and I do the same out of my window. Low, dirty clouds cling close to the sea. Deep in thought, we hug, and so embraced, we fall into a deep sleep.

When I next look at my watch, it's just before midnight. In the near-total blackness, I find Simonne, rosary held tightly between her hands, eyes closed, lips synchronized to her prayers. When I push the air chamber, I find that the raft needs air. Sim has seen this but let me sleep. I screw in the pump, fill the chamber until it's tight, close the valve, and remove the pump.

As I lie on my back in the complete blackness of this quiet Pacific night, my mind begins again to try to make some sense of our misfortune. I see little hope of rescue from either an organized search or a random find by a freighter. Someone must first miss us enough to stir up a search. And when they search, where will they look? We will be impossible to locate unless the EPIRB works. I must give some thought to turning it off and saving it for another day. I dare not betray any of these thoughts to Sim. I must keep her hopes up. It'll be better that way. Simonne hasn't slept at all, so far as I can tell. Too many worries. I watch her pray and feel better for it.

Waves jostle the raft as the southwest wind picks up. When I look out, clouds hug the sea and have turned blacker. Sim pumps air. I apparently nap, for when I next open my eyes, the air chamber is again limp. We're losing air much too fast. I must locate the leak and try to stop it or at least slow it down. When I finish pumping, a faint gray glow overhead tells us that Saturday, June 17, will soon dawn. Heavy rain greets us on our third day adrift. The wind speed increases to fifteen, then twenty knots, then up to thirty. The waves build proportionally, until mountains of water whisk under us at no less than twenty miles an hour.

In the ocean, far from land, swell height is of no real significance to a small craft such as ours. Much like *Siboney*, the raft floats easily from the top of one thirty-foot swell down into the trough and up again to the next crest. Swells the size of small hills approach from windward, careening tons of power, relentlessly rolling toward us, ever steeper and larger. Most waves approach from the south, but a few approach from the east, and yet others from the west. The distance from crest to crest is well over one hundred and fifty feet. On each swell, four- to six-foot wind-driven waves add power and confusion.

Waves that ride the top move faster than the swells. When a wave crests at the top of a swell and then breaks, it submerges the raft in up to a ton of water. The roar of an approaching wave prompts us to grab hold of the internal lifelines. The wave breaks and collides with the raft with a sonorous boom. I lie poised to jump to windward in case we start to roll. Will our tiny vessel take the beating? Will the ballast bags do their job? We have so much to learn about the heavy-weather performance of our new vessel. Other waves, flush with unspent energy, glide beneath us and speed away on their journey toward land.

Each minute turns into an hour as we hang onto the safety straps. The roar of the sea drowns out all words. The wind screams in our ears. Simonne, on her back, eyes closed, hair soaked and matted, rosary held tightly in hands joined on her chest, prays incessantly. The driving rain stings my eyes whenever I blink them open. I lie on the windward side and receive the full force of the breaking waves. My mind races. What can I do to get us out of this predicament? How could I have created this disaster? To be lost at sea in a small plastic raft is tough enough, but to be lost more than a thousand miles from shore stacks the odds against us. Damn it. I've got to come up with a solution. Meanwhile, I remain prepared for a possible rollover.

Hundreds of miles to the south, tempests that will never reach us generate the seas that pound our fragile raft. These towering multi-story mountains of water arrive confused, their journey interrupted by the Galápagos Islands now more than five hundred miles to the southeast. Waves out of the west, not as large or powerful as their southern brothers, have a fetch of more than four thousand miles. Some may have been heading our way for more than a week.

When the two wave systems meet at the point where our minuscule vessel floats, the mighty collision creates a ten-foot-high breaker that slaps the raft with the force of a car crash. We are thrown, soaked, and quite often spun 180 degrees, which puts the leeward window, kept open for ventilation, toward the fury of the ocean. I must quickly zip down my window to row the raft back while keeping an eye on a new breaking wave. One moment we're at the top of a swell and can see over the horizon. The next moment walls of water surround us. Minutes later, another wave smothers us and the raft spins around yet again.

Hours pass. Every eighth or tenth wave is twice as large as the others. Whenever tons of water dump on the canopy, it collapses and sends a shower of salt water through both windows. We can find no way to escape the soaking. As each wave breaks, we slide down the swell like a roller coaster. We jump to windward when the raft heels perilously, threatening a roll. A wayward wave could lift the windward edge of the raft, allowing the wind to catch the bottom. We remain tensed, awaiting that split second when our world will turn upside down. The deafening noise keeps us braced. Three out of four waves roaring in break and pass ahead of or behind us. Each blow on the raft resounds inside the air chambers with a cavernous boom. Every breaking wave sends us surfing.

Yet the waves are not really our nemesis. They push us toward the shore and home. We need high winds, strong waves, and heavy currents to reach shore. Time is against us. The longer we are at sea, the higher is the chance of meeting some unknown hazard. Or we could become ill or weak from lack of food. I feel like crying out: Let the wild wind blow! Let the breaking waves take us quickly toward land.

The ballast bags that hang under the raft have kept the waves from overturning the raft. There are four bags in all. Two small ones, two feet long and black, are at the ends. On each side, a bag four feet long and light blue provides most of the stability. All four bags are a foot and half wide and deep and have three-inch holes punched along their sides near their point of attachment to the raft. Eight inches of chain are sewn into the bottom corners of each bag.

When we launched the raft from *Siboney*, the chain pulled the bags down and they quickly filled with seawater. Whenever a breaking wave hits and threatens to roll us over, it must overcome the weight of the water in the bags. When the full force of a breaking wave smashes against the raft, the holes in the bags let some of the water out, reducing stress on the fabric. Yet most of the water ballast remains to provide vital stability to our tiny vessel.

Each wave smashes the raft with sledgehammer force. We cringe as we hear the approaching roar, sounding much like an oncoming freight train. When the wave hits, the raft, caught in its swirling waters, skids ten feet totally submerged, pops back out, and quickly resumes its previous course. We've secured the watermaker, air pump, and water bottles to the raft just in case we do flip.

It is before dawn when Sim throws a bolt out of the blue. "Bill, how could that freighter not see us? He came so close."

I banter back. "They had a satellite antenna. They were relaxing, eating, or drinking beer or schnapps. God knows."

"Not schnapps, aquavit."

"Whatever."

"Norwegians. I thought they were good seamen. No one was looking. How can a ship travel at that speed and have no one looking out? What's going to happen to us? Will anyone find us in this watery desert?"

"We'll be OK. The raft will make it. We have water. It's just a matter of time. They'll be looking for us soon."

"Who will be looking? Where will they look? Bill, only we know where we are. Nobody else does."

"Help will come," I declare as forcefully as I can. "We can survive for many days, even a week or two. The EPIRB is still sending. I checked it first thing today. There is a chance the Maydays got through. Besides, someone will soon miss us. When a week passes without a call, that will be a strong signal."

"I sure hope so." Sim remains quiet for a moment, then her face breaks into a smile. "Guess what. I heard 'Alma Llanera' on the radio. It was beautiful." "Alma Llanera" is the Venezuelan equivalent of "America the Beautiful"; it's a song we learned to love in our nine years in Venezuela.

Sim has turned on her little yellow radio, tucked near her head, sparingly every night to conserve our only set of batteries, the ones Sim had put into the Walkman a day or two before our shipwreck. This is our only contact with the outside world, and how lucky we are to have it. We have tacitly agreed, without really discussing the matter, that only Sim will listen to the radio. I hope it helps her get through the long nights. Pleased she is distracted, I ask, "When did all this happen?"

"You were asleep. It was three or four in the morning. I picked up a lot of stations. I heard the news from the Voice of America. Eight Chinese have been sentenced to death because of the riots. Your old buddy Mr. Marcos just had emergency surgery. Storms knocked out power in Washington, D.C. And tomorrow is Father's Day. Congratulations."

"Every day is Father's Day, don't you know? And though I lived nine years in the Philippines, Marcos is not my pal." It was an old joke of Sim's. In fact, the general economic downturn brought about by Marcos's policies was the main reason I left the Philippines. "Anything else on page one?"

"I heard mostly Mexican music, which means Mexico is closest. I get nothing as soon as the sun comes up, which means we're far from land. My best reception is between one and three in the morning. I picked up a station in Oklahoma, but it faded out right away."

While I ponder how long the batteries will last, I notice the raft needs air again. I ask Sim for the pump, which she pulls out from under my head. The bellows-type pump, four inches in diameter, is our only means of putting air into the raft, for I have not discovered a way to blow air in by mouth. The raft has two valves, one at each end, plus a valve in each of the arches.

I screw the pump into the valve closest to my head and turn it to the right to open it. My fingers hold the bottom of the pump. I move the bellows in and out and count strokes by tens. At one hundred and twenty, the air chambers are tight. When I try to remove the pump, the valve won't close, and I must work the pump continuously or the raft will quickly deflate.

I need pliers, but we have not one tool on board. Oh to have taken a few before we sank. *Siboney* had every tool imaginable for any type of repair. I was ready to tackle any job: mechanical, electrical, refrigeration, engine, rigging, or carpentry. I had spares for everything. Here we have nothing except a knife, two scissors, tweezers, and the can opener. With a sudden twist, I force the pump loose, but the valve remains open. I quickly plug it with my finger and call out to Sim:

"Sim, look for the can opener."

She plucks it from the pail and hands it to me. Using the two legs as a pair of pliers, I am able to close the valve, though I can still hear some air leaking. We need to find a way to plug it. Sim digs through the parts bag supplied with the raft and comes up with a yellow plastic knob with threads on the bottom. It looks a lot like a yellow mushroom. I try it, but the threads are too small.

"Wait a second," says Sim. She pulls a pair of scissors out of the dark-green suede gun case and cuts a strip from her T-shirt. I wrap it around the threads and screw the assembly into the valve. Sim returns the scissors to the case and zips it closed. The valve holds air. For now.

The raft, when fully inflated, is an oval five and a half feet long by less than four feet wide on the inside. The total floor area is under sixteen square feet. I am six feet long by almost two feet wide at the shoulders and, when I lie down, I need at least eleven square feet. Sim takes up eight or nine square feet, so without counting stores, we are missing four square feet. We've tried lying on our sides, but then our knees and bottoms don't fit. We've tried head-to-foot and head-to-head, and honestly I can't tell which is best or worst. We just do not fit. If Sim finds out that a six-man raft was but a hundred dollars more, I'll be a dead castaway. But what the hell, we're as good as 85 percent dead as it is.

The damn bucket is always in the way of my feet, as are the two containers of water. The camcorder case, also under my feet, is full of the larger sharp objects, like the fishing reel, can opener, and camera. The two life preservers and the two large cracker cans are part of my headrest. If I could only stretch out. Just for a minute.

A printed nameplate on the side of the raft glares at me boldly: "SWITLIK-FOUR MAN COASTAL RAFT." I keep asking myself: Where are the two other people going to squeeze in when they arrive? A couple of mermaids . . . well, that would be something else. Four people could be squeezed in—for about an hour. I've been aboard with a naked Sim for almost fifty hours, and I'm ready to abandon ship.

A southerly wind has built twenty-foot seas. The roar of breaking waves is the only sound we've heard since *Siboney* sank. Except, of course, for the *Ter Eriksen*, and for the racket Sim makes when she chews me out. In another day or so, those damn Norwegians should be transiting the Panama Canal. Damn!

Sim prays aloud in French. I try putting together a prayer but can't get started. I can't recall the Lord's Prayer or even remember when I prayed last. It was probably forty years ago. Now, lost in the vastness of the Pacific Ocean, I feel terribly alone. Sim, rosary in hand, has found company, someone to communicate to, someone to lean on for support.

A tear runs down Sim's cheek as she says, "Bill, this rosary is a miracle. My mother gave it to me last October when we visited. I didn't know I had it with me. I was looking through my toilet kit, and there it was."

She continues. "This is my rosary from my childhood, from my first communion. I can still remember how pretty we were, dozens of little girls, all dressed in white. My mother and I spent days shopping for my dress. It was so pretty, all white. When we filed into St. Michel Church in Menton, we looked like a bunch of little angels."

Misty-eyed and choked up, she continues to reminisce. "Until I was twenty, I went to church all the time. I was very close to God. As soon as I left home, I began to drift away. I have missed church so much over the past thirty years. Why, oh why, did I wander away? Things would have been so much easier. And different."

A massive wave breaks over the raft, interrupting Sim's musings. A bucketful of water pours through the closed window and soaks us once again, with Sim getting the worst of it. As she spits out salt water and wipes herself dry, she says, "We've got to make it. I want to change. I want to go back to church. I now understand what has been missing in my life."

"We'll make it, Sim. And we will go to church."

Her thin smile tells me she well knows the nearest church is more than a thousand watery miles away, miles that we must inch across propelled by nothing but wind, waves, and current. If we only had a sail or some way to increase our speed. To really speed up, we would have to remove the ballast bags or at least press them flat against the bottom of the raft. We'd reduce drag, but then the first breaking wave would turn the raft upside down. On the other hand, the drag of the ballast bags helps keep us moving at the same speed as the current. As our raft continues its slow journey, I reach for Sim's hand and squeeze it tightly. It will take a mountain of miracles to see us through this one.

I glance at the message on the air chamber that reads "Deploy sea anchor before erecting canopy to reduce drift." Reduce drift?! What we need to *is* drift—drift to safety. I reach way around the back of the arch, find where the sea anchor is tethered, and pull on the line. The sea anchor is gone! Something must have bitten it off.

The raft is just too heavy. Its freeboard is under ten inches, less when it's rougher and when the air chambers need air. The lighter the raft, the safer we will be if we hit a storm or if the raft suddenly loses air. I suggest that we inventory what we have on board. Simonne readily agrees.

Sim starts at the far end of the raft under my legs and calls out each item as I make entries in the log: two (two-and-a-half-gallon) plastic water jugs, seven bottles of Evian, and two big bottles of Perrier (a good French girl never leaves a sinking boat without them), watermaker, one and a half cans of saltines, eight cans of veggies, five beers, half a jug of cognac, compass, barometer, ship's clock, two watches, camera, camcorder, two life preservers, the full set of six cockpit cushions, can opener, knife, gun, two sponges, two sets of foul-weather gear, one big trash bag with bedding, a large blue sailbag, Walkman radio, EPIRB, two flashlights, a lantern, logbook, writing material, three flares, five small cartons of juice, two pairs of shorts (both Sim's), four T-shirts, fishing rod and reel, one hook, three of Sim's toilet kits with odds and ends, and a large white bucket.

We also compile a list in the log of the important items we missed, things we should have brought on board the raft to help us survive. When I last saw them, thirty flares in a sealed plastic container were on top of the trash bag with the bedding. The bag made it to the raft, but the flares did not. The flares should have floated, but I don't recall seeing them.

I kept a full case of charts next to the logbook. I missed the air horn. With it, we could have signaled the *Ter Eriksen* and, at this moment, have been on our way to Panama. We have virtually no clothing. I have no pants. The shorts I was wearing when we sank met a sudden death when, hours after we sank, my bowels exploded. The shorts had to go. We had a full inventory of medicine on board *Siboney*. None of it, not even a bottle of Merthiolate antiseptic, made the raft. We have no shoes, but then who has ever seen a castaway with shoes?

The empty Veg-All can has been transformed into what we've come to call the "pee-pee pot." It's so much easier to use than the large pail. The pail is always stuffed with the knife, gloves, and gun, all of which we must put in a safe place while using the bucket. Besides, Sim creates quite a scene when she climbs onto the bouncing bucket to empty her bladder, me holding her and the bucket from impending disaster. When nature calls, Sim struggles to her knees, which, at three in the morning in twenty-foot seas, is a real undertaking. A real trouper, she sticks her head out the window while urinating to look around for the one ship that will come to save us.

It's time for formalities. Every vessel I've sailed has had a name. I announce: "Sim, let's christen the raft. What shall we call it?"

"It should be significant. Do you like *Second Chance?*"

"How about *Last Chance?*"

"Good name. That's it! I'll get the cognac."

With two drops of cognac for the raft and two drops each for the crew, we are in a properly christened vessel.

I propose a toast. "May the stout raft *Last Chance* see wild west winds and rough seas."

Sim glares at me and says, "What are you saying? You're crazy!"

"Do you want to make it to the coast or not? A strong west wind will blow us to safety. Wind, current, and waves are our allies. Time is our enemy."

I love the passage in James Michener's *Hawaii* where the Polynesians, in their catamarans, were set to sail for legendary lands to the north. Many people were aboard. Food and water were limited. They had to speed to their destination or die. The high priest invoked the gods to send them the "wild west wind." We now need the wild west wind. To push us to shore before . . . an uncontrollable shiver cuts my trance short.

When I embrace Simonne, another bout of tears and wailing grips the two of us. The utter hopelessness of our situation is so real we dare not think too deeply or talk about it. There is no point in fooling each other. We face so many variables and countless unknowns. My enjoyable pleasure-sailing—and our retirement cruise have become a deadly nightmare.

Simonne, who has been pensive, suggests we lighten ship, and I jump to agree, as the lack of room has me in a constant cramp. Without a second thought, the camcorder goes over first. As we watch it sink, I think back to how proud and happy we were when we bought it in Miami, and of our plans to film an around-the-world video. So far, we had shot just twenty minutes while passing through the Panama Canal.

Next goes the 38-caliber pistol. I still cannot explain how I missed the bullets. We kept them right next to the gun. I cleaned everything out of the locker, or so I thought. The gun would have made a terrific signaling device. A couple of shots to the topsides of the *Ter Eriksen* would have brought everyone aboard on deck. Or if that hadn't worked, a shot to the pilothouse would have brought the troops out. But then, irate, they might have decided to run us down. Or shoot back.

The ship's clock and barometer are the next to go. I find it laughable when I recall how, in water chest high, I pried them off their places on the bulkhead near the galley aboard *Siboney*. The ship's clock, when we were not at sea, always hung on a wall in our bedroom, where it chimed away the hours and half hours. On sleepless nights, I could keep track of exactly how sleepless the night really was. Otherwise, I never heard it.

The barometer would be handy to have on board except that the glass cracked last night and the needle fell off and disappeared. Sim collected all the glass and threw it over the side. She's looked all day for the sharp pointer with no luck, but will continue tomorrow, for we need no new holes in the raft. Besides, why worry about future storms? We'll find out about them soon enough, and there's no safe harbor in which to hide and no way to get there if there were.

Sim breaks into my musings. "Bill, quick, we're filling with water. Look."

"I don't see any water. The raft isn't leaking. Take it easy, baby."

Still excited, she points. "See, here, look. There it is." Sim runs the sponge under one of the cushions and squeezes not more than ten drops into the can. "Where's it coming from? We must have a leak. The raft is falling apart. We are going to sink!"

Exasperated, I suggest, "Taste it, Sim."

She looks at me quizzically, makes a face, then dips her finger into the bilge and confirms, "It's not salty."

"That eliminates the leaking, sinking, falling-apart raft."

Sim searches under the bedding and finds we've lost water from one of the large water jugs. "You squashed it," she says, without looking up.

After Sim rests for an hour, I propose, "Madame, do you not think it is time for a repast? Yesterday we lunched at one and dined at seven. Breakfast today was at nine. Let's keep those hours. I feel like I digested all the meals quite well. You are a first-class raft cookie. Stir something up real quick." She glances at me and quickly adopts my mood.

"Whatever you say, *mon capitaine*. Let me look into the cupboard to see what we have on the menu. Perhaps a cracker with peanut butter with a raisin on top?"

"Dish it up, cookie dear. Let's eat two crackers for lunch. What a shame we missed all those jars of jam and peanut butter and the cans of sardines and tuna."

I take four crackers out of the can under my head while Sim digs into the peanut butter with the handle of the toothbrush. As I chew small bits of my cracker, my thoughts go to shore. Today is Saturday afternoon. What are our children doing? Sally, Joe, Cris, Alex . . . do something . . . call the Coast Guard . . . call our friends . . . we're in trouble . . . your parents are going to die!

Sim's right on her analysis of the EPIRB. The Mini-B is trash as far as doing us any good out here. My Mayday signals did go out on a live band, but there was no one tuned in. During the daytime, the bands are dead, made so by the presence of the sun. A dead band gives just that impression. There is nothing, not even static, unless there is a thunderstorm around.

Though the band I tuned to was live, I found not one station on the air. I ran from one end of the twenty-meter band to the other. The time of the day was against us. It was four in the morning Eastern time. The Americas were asleep. Even the most ardent amateur radio operators had gone to bed. The sun would have killed our signal to operators in Australia and the Far East. No contact means just that. No one heard my signal. My only hope is that someone was tuned to the Coast Guard weather frequency and heard my plea for help.

Our single best hope lies with family and friends. When will they miss us? I know that my children, who have sailed with me on most of my voyages, consider *Siboney* unsinkable. The single-sideband radio is new to the boat, and they have no idea how powerful a tool it is. Besides, *Siboney*, in most of her thirty-five thousand miles, was known for her lack of communication. We never engaged in VHF chitchat. I turned on the VHF radio only for short periods when approaching a marina. The boys probably think I am rejoicing after the single-sideband radio died. They know I like a quiet boat.

Between Miami and until ten days after leaving Panama, I was too busy with boat chores to spend much time working the ham bands. Single-sideband radio contacts are often tedious unless atmospheric conditions are just right. It takes time to scan the band to find the kind of contact I'm looking for, and then I must wait to break in to place my call. Many calls go unanswered. When sailing in close contact with shipping and land, I'm too preoccupied with navigation, course changes, traffic, sail changes, and boat chores to have the energy to chase around the shortwave bands.

At six in the afternoon on June 2, with *Siboney* settled into a two-thousand-mile leg to the west, I had tuned the radio to the ten-meter band and listened for traffic. I heard a CQ, which in amateur radio talk is a request for a contact. I made my call and, to my surprise, back came my call sign from a ham radio operator in Georgia.

When I looked over to Sim, she was misty-eyed with joy. We were in live contact with the outside world. I gave my new friend a rundown of our round-the-world trip and then requested that he put through a collect call to my son Joe in Miami to find out if his wife had made me a grandfather for the seventh time. In seconds, Joe was on the telephone listening to my voice booming off the speaker. The

Georgia ham relayed Joe's messages to us. The baby was not yet born, but time was short. Everyone else was fine. We sent our hellos to all, gave our position, and promised to call back in a couple of days.

After that first contact, I tuned to the ten-meter band at six every evening and each night talked to an amateur radio operator in a different part of the United States. The radio signal on ten meters skips off the ionosphere, and where it lands depends on sky conditions on that particular day. I was never able to renew my contact with Georgia, for my signal dropped the next night into the Oklahoma-Texas border. On following nights, I made contact with radio operators in Washington, D.C., Indiana, and Connecticut, and with a man on a sailboat anchored off Puerto Rico.

On June 11, eager to talk directly with our children, I switched to the commercial marine frequencies. I tried to reach the AT&T high-seas operator in San Francisco on a dozen different channels with no luck. WOM, in Fort Lauderdale, was constantly occupied with calls from passengers on the dozens of cruise ships plying the Atlantic. When I was given a chance to break in, my signal did not get through. In desperation, I tried one of the higher commercial frequencies. A surprised shore operator, unaccustomed to receiving a call on such an unusual channel, answered right back, though rather perplexed. Our first call went to Susan in Texas, and the second to Simonne's boys in Miami. I gave both of them our position, our projected course to Honolulu, and our expected ETA. Susan told us that Joe's baby, a girl, had been born the previous day, June 10. I told Sue that I would call Joe in two or three days to congratulate mother and father.

Cris said Sim's house had not yet sold, but he had someone interested in renting it. Were we interested? We told him to hold off for a couple of days while we thought about it. I told him we'd call back with an answer later in the week. Cris was to call Sim's mother in France and tell her we were fine.

My nightly contacts on ten meters continued. Sim beamed whenever I chatted with hams in faraway places. On June 14, the night we sank, my signals landed in southern California. My last contact was with Jesse, N6SBV, in Hemet, a town near Los Angeles. He was eager to maintain contact with us as our sail progressed, and we set up a schedule for future nights. I thought about asking him to call home but decided to wait one more day.

Today is June 17. Our last contact with the children was a week ago. How will they react when they receive no further calls? Perhaps it's too early for them to worry. In another week, when fourteen days have passed, they will know something happened. A search should follow soon after. We will have to wait another week. Unless, of course, the EPIRB or Mayday does its job.

Sim announces the start of her menstrual period and begins to search for protection. With a jerk, she pulls the heavy cotton sheet out from under my head, as it is the driest item on the raft. I hold one end while she cuts long strips about four inches wide, then cuts these into pieces about a foot long.

An increasing rate of air loss forces us to pump every half hour. Sim searches around and soon finds not one but two leaks. The patch that covers the tear leaks between the two patches, and air leaks out of the valve. Sim hands me a piece of white tape she salvaged, and I wrap it around the valve, then tighten it with a length of cord. An hour later, the air chamber is still tight. Something positive for a change. I'll work on the patches if the leak gets worse.

One question keeps running through my mind: How long before someone starts looking for us? Another week? Two? By the time we're off the scope for two weeks, our children and friends should conclude that something has happened. I voice my thoughts, and Sim nods, hopeful. "Exactly what I was thinking. Nothing will be done this week, though you told Joe and Cris that we would call. They'll surely think we are having trouble making a contact." Her face falls, and her lips droop. "I really miss my babies. I should never have left them. Why did I ever let you talk me into going on this mad adventure? I was crazy to leave my beautiful home. You always get your way. Nothing I could have said or done would have changed your plans. You're crazy and a self-centered egoist of the worst kind."

"Wait a minute. We talked about it for two years. You never said you didn't want to go. You really amaze me. Last October in France, you were as excited as I when we shopped for dried food to take on the trip. Why didn't you at some point say, 'Bill, I cannot go'? Something that simple?"

Sim nods. "We didn't talk enough about this trip. We were always so busy. We never had a quiet moment. Every time I broached the subject, you became uptight. You did not want to listen to me. You had your plans and projects all set. You had all the details worked out, and anything I said met your disapproval."

She continues, "I don't know when you changed all the plans. If you remember, we had talked about going to the Caribbean for a year. We would hop from island to island. You know them all, but I don't know any except Barbados and Martinique." She pouts and goes on, "We were going to socialize at exotic anchorages, make new friends, relax, have fun. No. It couldn't be. You wanted it your way, although you know how much I hate long passages. Panama to Honolulu has to be the longest ocean passage in the world."

Sim barely takes a breath before continuing. "You are a monster of egoism. As long as you are satisfied and your needs are met, everything is fine. Who cares if you trample everybody's feelings? Mine, my family's, your family's. I gave up my beautiful dog, Seda Linda, my house, my furniture, and my children to follow you on this miserable trip. I must have been out of my mind."

She keeps hammering away. "Look where we are now. It's time you get a hold on your life. If we ever make it, you will have to make some drastic changes. You got away with too much until now, Butler, but your luck is running out. If God lets us live, I swear I am not going to listen to you blindly in the future. No, sir. That is over. I refuse to be your slave, your toy, your tagalong."

Sim again begins to boil over. "Don't you realize that you went too far? That we are going to die some horrible death? A stupid and useless death. You, the big hero. Superman. Show me how you are going to get us out of this one. Try to squirm out of this one, Butler."

I attempt to distract her. "Come here, baby, let's squirm together."

"Don't touch me, you monster. Keep your hands off me. Use your energy figuring out how to get us saved. How could I be so dumb as to fall for your crazy round-the-world cruise in your old boat? Oh Lord, have mercy on me." Tears fall, and I squirm. She's right, up to a point, but then, she could have stayed home. The long silence that follows is a relief.

Heavy, low, ashen clouds sweep overhead. To the west, a low, black cloud line rings the horizon. Night envelops us. I close the window, then rearrange a corner of the bedding around the cracker can as a pillow and settle down. Poor Sim. She is so right. We should have talked more to better synchronize our hearts, our dreams, and our feelings. Adventure it was, and the dangers were there. We both knew that. She, being more of a realist than I, surely saw the negative side more clearly. For me, this was to be the realization of my life's dream. I was on a high, blinded with excitement and joy at having readied my vessel to become a circumnavigator.

Never had *Siboney* looked so beautiful, so prepared, and so ready to roam the seas. Was I an egoist? Probably, but how could I not be? Soon old age will cut my wanderings down to near-shore day sailing. This was my last chance.

I take Sim in my arms and hold her while she cries out her frustrations, her fear, and her homesickness. I cry with many of the same feelings. When Sim regains her composure, she reads, then prays quietly. Her mind wanders to her home in France. "What can my mother be thinking? Is she worried? She has to be. My poor mother, old and sick and alone. What will she do when I don't return?"

ROQUEBRUNE-CAP-MARTIN, FRANCE
0200 (FRENCH TIME) SUNDAY • JUNE 18, 1989

Madame Marie Saissi knows something is wrong. Three candles burn in her bedroom. Unable to sleep, she strolls out to her balcony. Monte Carlo, engulfed in its usual haze, is off to her right. The Mediterranean stretches below. Evenly spaced swells roll onto the shore and break on the sandy beach. Her thoughts go to Simonne. "My baby is out there. She's in trouble. I know it. In my dreams, I have seen danger. I have known for at least six months that her trip would end badly.

"Whenever she called, I warned her not to go on the trip. 'Simonne,' I would plead, 'get Bill to postpone the departure. The year 1990 would be better.'

"No, they had to go. They wouldn't listen. And now, something terrible has happened to them. Tonight, I'll light another candle. I will pray constantly for their safety. There is nothing else I can do."

ABOARD THE RAFT
LAST CHANCE
0000 SUNDAY • JUNE 18, 1989 • DAY 4

M Y WATCH CHIRPS. I shine the small white flashlight on its dial. It's midnight. Or should I say, it's only midnight. Nights are eternal. I'll sleep through half of it, if I'm lucky. The other five or six hours turn into endless attempts to sleep interspersed with long silent sessions of speculating on what tomorrow will bring. If we live through tomorrow, will we see the next day? Will the raft hold up? That is the key unknown. If the raft loses its buoyancy, how deep will it sink? Will the inflated arches keep it from going under totally? How long can we survive chin deep in water? So many unknowns, but I must try and prepare for each and every possibility.

The endless night creates within me a deep despair, made even more penetrating when I glance at Simonne lying by my elbow, forlorn, her eyes closed, so utterly vulnerable. I peer past her sleeping, naked body through the open window to a world full of nothingness. There is no moon, not one star. I play games with my eyes. Open or closed, there is no difference—the darkness is absolute. The ocean appears as a sinister black monster waiting to claim two new victims. Specks of light from minute phosphorescent plankton dance below the surface, their light sources triggered by the splash of waves. Life surely abounds around us, but so far we've seen neither fish nor bird. What monsters lurk below us? I dare not speculate.

I think back to the *Ter Eriksen*. That was a close shave. A hair's difference in its compass course, one one-hundredth of a degree, and the raft *Last Chance*, complete with its two-man crew, would have been chopped into pieces by those huge propellers. I can see them clearly—twelve feet in diameter, the three blades hungrily biting water much like a starving great white shark. Had the hand that put the course into the autopilot turned the setting knob to starboard the width of a sheet of writing paper, the large freighter would surely have run us down. I shudder once again when I picture the ship's bow aimed directly at us as it plowed a giant path through the seas. The displaced water, as it climbed up the steel knife-edge of the bow, formed a comber that rose high until the force of gravity made it curl and then break furiously ahead of the ship. Had the ship been heading for us, we could never have rowed clear. I can't erase the picture of the raft bouncing down the hull, huge clinging barnacles first ripping the raft, then tearing into Simonne and me. As the stern approached, the powerful pull of the propellers would have sucked us in and minced us. Despite our misfortune, we've had a huge dose of good luck. Someone appears to be looking after us.

Scattered drops that turn into incessant, heavy rain break my incubus and lull me closer to sleep. Sim prays incessantly, rosary in hand. Again I try to pray but cannot. I can now remember the first part of the Lord's Prayer: "Our Father, who art in Heaven, hallowed be thy name." But that's as far as I can get. Sim mumbles on in French, barely audible over the pounding deluge.

The wind picks up and the weather worsens. Waves build quickly under a light-gray overcast. Clouds, low and ugly, scud ever faster to the north, indicating worse weather to come. Large seas roll us around inside the raft like cement in a mixer. We are fortunate to be in a small raft and packed in tightly, else we'd tumble around like a loose barrel in the back of a truck. The roar and slam of a wave jostle me awake. The wave washes the entire raft as it passes overhead to spend its energy in a sea of foam. Soon, seas will build in strength and break again and again on their journey to land. How I wish we could lasso the crest of the largest wave and charge with it toward shore. In two days, we would be on land, safe and sound. Another impossible dream.

Wind whistles through the canopy as heavy, continuous rain pummels the raft. The raft loses air faster. Sim never sleeps for long, so I wait until she stirs to pump air. I pump while Simonne prepares the paper for the plug. I've tried doing it alone several times, but I always lose most of the air and must start again. When the chamber is tight, I remove the pump, Sim plugs the hole with her finger, then screws in the plug. She never misses. She's terrific and a good crew, if she didn't rag me so much. Every day so far I've received a two-hour barrage, always the same old themes.

On top of that, I've been getting increasingly dizzy, and now I can't turn or get up without losing my balance. I've probably lost a lot of salt through perspiration since the sinking. Once or twice in the past hour when I moved my head, I got the sensation that the entire raft had rolled over and over. If a ship were to find us now, I couldn't possibly save myself. I've had horizontal vertigo before, but never this bad. I usually got rid of it by taking salt tablets, but figure seawater could fill the same purpose. I rinse out our can, fill it with seawater, and take a sip. Wow, is it salty! I mix in a bit of fresh water and manage to drink the rest.

I look over at Sim and cannot see her although she's inches away. I reach for her hand. It darts into mine. Her squeeze tells me she is happy to have me close by.

Seas strain to destroy the raft. The roar of an approaching wave cues us to tighten our grip on the support straps. One, two, three waves miss the raft. When we relax, a ton of water slams into us. Breakers roll our way in an endless parade. The ballast bags, with hundreds of pounds of seawater, hold us steady. But for how long?

Should the raft capsize, the arches might help us through a complete roll. How would it happen and how would we react? Capsize could be sudden and catch us unawares. A wave crashing against the windward air chamber could lift it until a gust of wind slipped under the flat bottom of the raft and blew it over. By then, we would be falling off the crest upside down. A new wave would crash into us as it and the wind pushed the raft through a full roll. Inside, our weight would be on the canopy and arches, with our gear piled on and around us. Would I have to leave the raft to bring it around, or would the wind and waves do it alone? In any event, we've tied the water-maker and bellows pump to the raft. If we keep the windows closed, most of our water and stores should stay with us. Yet we're bound to lose something. We could even damage the raft or hurt ourselves. I rehearse repeatedly how I must react to this dreadful scene, until, truly fatigued, I sleep.

At long last, our fourth day on the raft dawns dark, cloudy, and rainy. Where has the sun gone? I haven't seen it since we've been adrift. Salt water has soaked everything aboard. The strain of the day's long, vicious storm has left us sore and worn out. Sim is seasick, and I remain terribly dizzy. Whenever I turn, I sense the raft spin, and topple over. Simonne supports my every move. In an emergency, I would be useless. I drink two more cups of seawater followed by two gulps of fresh water. The repugnant salt taste stays with me. Many experts claim that drinking seawater can be deadly, but I can think of no other solution for my dizziness.

A caravan of hissing mountains of water pummels the raft all morning. Waves break constantly around us. One in four scores a direct hit. We keep the raft pumped up so it is tight and rigid, and hang on. Sim sponges the floor of the raft every half hour in an attempt to keep our stores dry. In the early afternoon, wind and waves ease.

Sim notices I have my eyes open and says, "Bill, today is Sunday. Let's do something special on Sundays. We'll eat a can only on Sunday. We have four cans left. Rescue will come by the time we get down to the last can."

"I like the idea, except let's skip today since we had a can yesterday."

Sim shakes her head. "No. We're both weak, and you're dizzy. We need to help our bodies adjust gradually to less food. We'll open a can today. Besides, it's Father's Day. The children must be thinking of you. Cheers."

"Thank you. Thank you. We'll have a can of chickpeas. Can you figure out which one it is?" I move my head as Sim digs under my headrest. She pulls out a can with the right shape. "I'll open it," Sim volunteers.

The can opener was one of the first items Sim loaded onto the raft. She opens the can, and it does have chickpeas. We sip the salty broth before it spills.

"Bill, let us give thanks," she says, and recites the Lord's Prayer in French.

Balancing one pea at a time on the end of our only toothbrush, we finish half the chickpeas. Since the weather is relatively cool, the other half will stay fresh until this evening. The rain has not stopped, and monster waves continue to punish us as we drift along. Bored and tired of just hanging on, I dig out the log and my navigation workbook.

I have always maintained a detailed log of my activities at sea. Whenever *Siboney* left the dock, even for a one- or two-hour sail on Biscayne Bay, I entered a one-line summary of the weather, distance traveled, and time away from the dock. Each of the thirty-five thousand miles sailed by *Siboney* under my command are recorded in eight logbooks, all but the current one safely stored in Miami. In all logs, I have summarized at year's end the nautical miles sailed, hours underway, and days at sea.

With time on my hands, I leaf back through the log to my last totals, which are for year-end 1988. I add the jaunts around Miami, then add on totals for the leg from Miami to Panama, and from Panama to where we sank. From March 1968, when we sailed to Hong Kong to race in the China Sea Race, to the moment of sinking, this produces totals of:

NAUTICAL MILES SAILED: 34,794

HOURS UNDERWAY: 8,020

DAYS AT SEA: 582

Over time, I developed my own system for tallying my logs. If I sailed six hours to an anchorage thirty miles distant, stayed three days, then sailed back in six hours, I logged sixty nautical miles, twelve hours underway, and three days at sea. I now follow the same procedure as on *Siboney*, with a day running from midnight to midnight, except for day one, June 15. The boat sank at five in the morning, so we were on the raft for nineteen hours on that fateful day.

Today is Sunday, June 18, day four on the raft. So far Sim and I have taken turns making entries in the log twice a day. On *Siboney*, I made my first entry whenever I first awakened after midnight, usually between two and three. Now, given our snail's pace and the need to conserve the batteries in the flashlights, I enter the new day as soon as the sun is up and we're both awake. I update the log at four or five in the afternoon, before night sets in.

In my navigation workbook, which we saved together with the logbook, I set up a table with columns for the day number, the day of the month, the speed and direction of the drift created by the power of the wind and waves, and the current set (speed) and drift (direction). The last two columns are latitude and longitude and begin with day one at 5 degrees 30 minutes North latitude and 99 degrees 10 minutes West longitude.

Whenever I can look out without getting soaked, I try to get a fresh feel for how fast the wind and waves are pushing us north. I hold the compass up into the direction of the wind and find that the wind and the waves come from the south. The wind was light on our first day. It picked up on the second and has blown hard for the last two. With a scrap of paper, I've just timed our speed to the north at a bit less than twenty seconds to cover ten feet. That comes out to more than eighteen hundred feet per hour, about a third of a knot. I enter a set of eight miles to the north for the last two days, with four miles for the first day and six for the second. My estimate of our overall set to the north is eighteen miles.

How fast the current is pushing us along is anyone's guess. It must be close to a knot to keep us on an easterly course, though wind and waves pound us from east and west of south. I enter an easterly set of twenty miles per day for all four days. With this dead-reckoning data, I come up with a position at midnight tonight of 6 degrees North and 98 degrees West. We've drifted more than a hundred miles to the east-northeast since we sank. With shore now eleven hundred miles to the east, we'll be there in forty-four days if wind, waves, and current hold up. That'll never happen. Besides, if the raft receives the same ferocious pounding for another week or two, it'll be trash.

Sim returns the log and workbook to its dry place in the white plastic bag. The pen goes into a small yellow plastic case with a dozen others she bought in Panama. Sim watched me prepare the dead-reckoning table and then read my log entry. Looking out the window at a distant cloud, she talks as if to herself. "Lost. We are lost. Even if anybody among our family or friends worries, even if the Coast Guard is willing to search for us, where will they start? We are so far away, so far away."

"You need faith," I say, hoping to instill some of my positive thinking and make her feel better.

Sim looks at me with fire in her eyes. "Look who's talking about faith! You? Butler, you are the most faithless person I have ever known. You don't even know how to pray."

I fight back. "Knowing how to pray helps, but it isn't the key to faith. You have to believe we will be saved."

Sim looks out into space. "Look who is preaching. My God. The devil incarnate himself. I have never seen you even kneel, in church or for that matter, anywhere, much less pray. Give me a break."

I look her straight in the eye. "We'll be saved, Sim. Get that through your dense head. We aren't the first to be adrift in a raft. Many others, like us, have had their boats sink from under them and have been saved after many days at sea. So cheer up."

Sim's eyes brighten. "*Cruising World* ran the story of a man who drifted seventy-six days in a raft in the Atlantic. I think his name was Callahan. I wish I had read his book. He was alone."

"And you're not alone. You have this gallant, jovial, and handsome raft mate for company who'll whisk you to safety."

"Phooey! I can't swallow either the gallant part or the handsome part. Have you seen yourself in the mirror? Your hair is matted, you're unshaven, your T-shirt looks like you pulled it out of the bilge, and you are dirty, you smell . . ."

"OK, skip the handsome portion. How about witty?"

"Butler, get serious. We're in deep trouble. And we can't do anything to help ourselves."

A cramp has me search for a new position that will yield a semblance of comfort. Most of the time—and that means up to 80 percent of the day—we lie on our backs because it is the most efficient (space-wise) and comfortable position. Sim has done a great job making up our "bunks." My bottom lies on one of the four boat cushions placed laterally on the floor of the raft. One of the smaller cushions is under my back. Under it, Sim placed a life preserver to raise it higher so that my head, resting on the air chamber, is more or less in line with my back. Under my neck, she has piled the binoculars in their case, a large can of crackers, and the spare-parts bag. Her bed is made up about the same. On top of the cushions, she has spread the large striped comforter, and under my head I have the wool blanket we bought in the Andes. She detests the feel of wool so she uses the cotton spread. My feet are also raised by the multitude of stores she has stuffed under the comforter, things like the watermaker, the foul-weather gear, and the other life preserver. My feet rest easily on the opposite air chamber.

We have drifted two days without sighting human life. Next time we do, we must be ready to signal instantly. Sim must keep a sharp lookout, particularly at night, when flares are most effective. She keeps wondering when someone will look for us. Will it be two weeks? Three weeks? I try to infect her with my optimism and insist that our stay in the raft will be short, saying, "Every day that goes by increases our chances of someone finding us. Today is the eighth day since our last radio contact. One of the children will react soon. They must be worried now, and soon they will do something."

"I pray every minute for that," she sighs.

Sim bleeds heavily. The soils go into the empty cracker can. Slowly, the stormy weather eases. Seas lessen. A breaking wave hasn't struck us for almost an hour. Clouds lift and the rain stops. We turn back-to-back and quickly fall into a deep sleep. When I again look out, the sun is an hour from setting.

Unable to stretch out fully, I complain to Sim, "My knees hurt. Could it be arthritis?"

Sim, lying on her side, shoots back. "If you've got arthritis, it's in your brain. What you have is simple. Your muscles are rigid from lack of movement. I have the same problem. We have to lie on our back and exercise our legs. Bicycle in the air."

"What we need is to relax. You've been too uptight since the first night on the raft."

Sim turns toward me, a wild look in her fiery eyes. "The great captain says to relax. Relax. How in hell can anybody relax? I'm afloat in a sinking raft, a thousand miles from anywhere, packed in like a sardine, and punched all night as if in a bout with Muhammad Ali. Read my lips, you dummy. WE ARE GOING TO DIE. Do you understand me, you no-good zombie? Nothing is going to save us. The expensive radio that didn't get your Maydays through. The EPIRB that never sent a signal. When I think we paid five hundred dollars for that worthless piece of junk. We should sue those guys who sold it to us. The crazy skipper who doesn't know where he is or where he is going. And the big macho says 'relax.' You are hilarious, Butler. Relax. You're going to die and you don't even realize it. You've got the great habit of always saying, 'relax' whenever you have no solution to a problem."

I shrug. "What can I say? I am a failure. How about a game of dominoes?"

"Dominoes. Throw them overboard. Stick the dominoes up your big ears."

"Pass them over. I'll check the fit."

"*Bruto.*" But Sim smiles and says, "OK. Let's play. What else is there to do? I get tired of listening to your bull." With a groan, I inch to a semisitting position. I take my place on the starboard side as I move my legs across the raft. It feels so good to sit up and not have my head spin, thanks to my daily saltwater cocktails.

We refer to the end of the raft with the patch as the "stern." It has been facing west for the past three days, away from the full force of the breaking waves. Facing east or toward the bow, I am on the right side of the raft, and Sim lies on the left. My side faces south, the direction from which the waves approach. Though the ballast bags have worked perfectly, my weight on the high side offers an added margin of safety. Besides, Simonne can't stand the wham-bang force of the waves that break with vicious blows against the air chamber to then catapult over the canopy. On the other hand, the person on the low side, away from the waves, often gets soaked. When a roller breaks and hits the raft, water squirts between the canopy and the window with such force that it shoots over me and onto Sim. How do the French say it, *c'est la guerre?* Every time she receives a bucketful of water, I turn my head to hide my snicker.

In today's domino game, we play points. We both hate to lose. Sim plays a determined game and easily takes me to the cleaners. I hope it improves her disposition.

"You've won first prize, baby, here I am."

"I won YOU? Take a look at yourself in my mirror and come back to the real world."

"Perhaps a little kiss instead. It's still Father's Day."

"I don't trust your kisses."

I banter back. "Me? Just because you're naked and lovely and scrumptious doesn't mean I'll take advantage of you. My intentions are purely platonic, uh, therapeutic."

"Butler, you've taken me on your platonic voyages before. I know how little platonic they end up, and I know all about your cure-all therapy. Stay away. Besides, I've made promises."

"What sort of promises?"

"It's a secret. Hold onto me. I'm going to take a look around." Sim turns over on her knees, opens the top part of her window, and sticks her head out. The swells are still well over thirty feet, but they're long and the crests aren't breaking. Sim gives a weather report. "We have better weather ahead. Seas are down. Wind is between ten and fifteen knots from the south. I'm coming back in, hold me."

"Hold you where?" I say, as I run my hand up her thigh.

"Ayyy, not there, *bruto*. Try to be serious, Butler."

"Just trying to help a damsel in need. It beats having you fall over the side. What, I get no thanks?"

Sim settles back in and says, "Let's read before it gets dark." Sim takes the set of cards with psalms and prayers from a small ziplock bag that has snapshots of her children and other family. Tears roll down her cheeks as she stares at the faces of her mother, her sister, and her boys. Slowly, she regains control and reads.

When darkness engulfs our little world, Sim's menstrual period gets heavier. We don't dare throw anything over the side for fear of attracting sharks. The flashlight helps us settle down in this darkest of nights. We pump as much air into the raft as we dare and doze off.

Sunday night turns out to be rather peaceful for a night deep in the Pacific Ocean on a thin plastic raft. Our bunk remains warm and comfortable. Sim and I synchronize our turns at the same time, and no arguments over space erupt. We pump three or four times and sleep well between pumpings. The night passes quickly. If they all pass at this speed, we'll be out of this predicament in no time.

Waves today, Monday, are higher than fifteen feet. I make my daily estimate of drift: twenty miles east, eight miles north. I can feel the push of the strong current as it grips the ballast bags. It nudges the raft with a gentle jerking motion, much like a car with an ignition problem.

Meanwhile, Sim is still bleeding heavily and is now dizzy as well. Eyes closed, she prays for help in getting our message through to God that we are in desperate need of His hand. Sim has tied several medals to the canopy with images of Mary the Miraculous, St. Michael, and Our Lady of Lourdes. She touches them all the time. Poor Sim. Her hair is matted and dirty, and her drooping lips betray her deep despair and hopelessness.

A thump announces the arrival of another turtle. It first bumps Sim in the middle of the back, then hits me. It's Sim's bottom next, later my legs, and on and on for over twenty minutes. Sim, her head and shoulders outside the raft, waits for it to surface. With the small paddle in her right hand, she's ready to strike. When the green sea turtle emerges for air, Sim swings for its neck and hits. The turtle kicks and dives.

It quickly returns, but Sim is ready. "Take this, this, this, and this, you monster!" she calls out in fury.

"Sim, cool down," I insist, for I fail to see the need to get so worked up.

"I'm going to kill it."

"Sim, baby, the turtle isn't doing all that much harm."

"That's because you are a blind zombie. That turtle is going to sink us."

"How can it sink us? The top of his shell is round and smooth. It's just hitting the ballast bags. It can't do any damage. Relax. I think it's a male and has fallen for our raft."

At that moment, the turtle surfaces, and Sim swings madly as she yells, "Take that, and that, dumb bitch. Go away! Leave us alone!"

She hits the shell with a dull thud. The turtle swims ten feet away from the raft and turns again toward us. It lifts its ancient head out of the water. Its two large, black eyes stare at Sim with a curious, quizzical look. This must be the first time it has encountered our species. It promptly swims back toward Sim.

"Ay! I'll fix you this time!" she screams.

Sim hits the turtle. Again it swims six feet away and returns. The scene repeats itself until Sim, exhausted, excitedly passes me the paddle. "Here, Bill, quick. It's on your side. I can hear him scratch the raft. It's full of barnacles. It's going to puncture the raft."

The turtle has its shell half under the air chamber and paddles wildly, taking us with it. I try to hit the turtle, which attempts to swim away, but I miss. I swing again, then see that it has a flipper tangled in the raft's boarding ladder. I lean over the side of the raft and turn the shell, laden with moss and barnacles, until I can reach the tangled flipper. The turtle strikes back with its beak, narrowly missing my fingers. I unwrap two turns of the webbed nylon boarding ladder from around its front flipper. Once released, it dives into the deep.

"Hold the paddle, Sim. I'm going to tie the boarding ladder so this doesn't happen again." I roll the red straps of the ladder into a ball and use two ties to hold it closely to the raft.

Minutes later, the turtle is back under the raft. Sim simmers. I lie back and try to relax. We're bumped ten times in a row. Sim boils over. She's ready to jump overboard and wrestle the beast to the end.

"What is that monster doing with us? What does it want? It's going to tear a hole in the raft. Why doesn't it go away? Butler, answer me! Why am I surrounded by dumb males?"

"Which question first? I really think he's in love with you now, not the raft. Perhaps you should cover yourself when he's around. Why get all worked up over one turtle? Let's only worry about turtles with broken edges or barnacles. A turtle with an even, round shell can't damage the raft."

"Butler, you live in wonderland. Can't you hear it scratching right now? How many scratches can this junk raft take? This turtle is going to work its way right into this raft!"

"A shame it's not a female. Maybe there'll be a little action on this raft."

"Is that some sort of complaint?"

"No, of course not. What would make you believe that? It couldn't be your conscience because you have none. Besides, I'm considering taking up a monastic life when I get to shore. I'll lead the simple life."

"We had the simple life. Then you got restless and cooked up this crazy around-the-world excursion. And here we are."

"This is the simple life. We relax, lie back, float, and make mad passionate love until we're found."

"Get that out of your head. The raft is too shaky for funny things, and I'm not in the mood. Besides, I made promises."

"Let me try to get you into the mood, my little bonbon. Come to zee *capitaine*'s exotic Pacific waterbed. Perhaps a leetle keess? You still haven't told me what your promise is all about."

She quickly changes the subject. "It's one o'clock, the turtle is gone, and it's time for lunch." Our usual cracker with peanut butter tastes like a filet mignon dinner. A crumb at a time, then two gulps of fresh water, satisfies my hunger. Five raisins for dessert round out an exceptional meal.

"Madame, I challenge you to a game of dominoes." Today we play games, not points. I win the first four rounds. Sim smiles when she wins her first. We're forced to stop when large seas again pound the raft. The wind had begun to build late in the morning and is now blowing more than fifteen knots. Waves are picking up, too. We're surprised how quickly seas build and how long it takes them to settle back down after the wind stops.

The crash of a violent wave jolts us as water cascades over the window and drenches us. A quick look outside reveals mountainous gray seas rolling in from the south. Clouds race overhead, dense and gray. They speed toward the northern horizon, toward the doldrums, where they will collide with that perennial weather wall to create formidable climatic towers. We tighten the windward window as today's torment begins. Sim reads early.

Sim's reading before the onset of night again fills us with an aura of peace and tranquillity that bolsters our will to survive another fearful, eleven-hour night. Again, I try to contact Sally. I close my eyes, concentrate on her apartment, and transmit my pleas. "Sally, help us! We are in danger; we are going to die. The boat sank. We're in a raft in the middle of the Pacific. We need help. NOW!!!"

With my eyes still closed, I strive to reach my twenty-eight-year-old daughter in Mount Vernon, New York. Of all the children, Sally is the most likely to receive my messages. She and I have made contact before. So many times, back home in Miami, I would call her, and she'd pick up the phone on the first ring and say, "Hi, Dad, I knew it was you. I knew you were thinking about me."

Besides, she is the one least burdened with outside activities. She spends most of her day at home taking care of her year-old baby, Cody. Her husband works hard to hit the big time as a drummer. If I can get through to anyone, it will be Sally.

I concentrate. "Sally, listen . . . your daddy is in deep trouble . . . call the Coast Guard . . . call friends . . . we need someone to start searching . . . HELP . . . HELP . . . Sally . . ." I distinctly feel contact. It's nine P.M. in New York. I picture Sally in her large stuffed chair watching TV. Cody is on her lap. I try again and again to reach her. I feel I am getting through. "Sally, you're my big hope. Do something. Send help . . . now . . ."

MOUNT VERNON, NEW YORK
2130 MONDAY • JUNE 19, 1989

Sally Smith is in her favorite recliner. Baby Cody suckles busily while Sally watches TV. Sally finds her mind drifting away toward the deep Pacific Ocean. Dad and Simonne last called Susan and Cris more than a week ago. Joe had a baby on June 10. It's now a week later. Why hasn't Dad called Joe?

"There's no need to worry just yet. I do wonder how it's going for them. They left Panama three weeks ago. Dad said he expected a sixty-day trip from Panama to Hawaii. He should be calling next week."

Sally's eyes begin to close, lulled by the drone of the TV. A new picture forms in her mind. She sees an immense black void. Far away, she hears her father call, "SALLY, HELP! HELP! YOUR DADDY IS IN TROUBLE! WE ARE GOING TO DIE! HELP! GET HELP!"

Her eyes pop open. What was that? It was so vivid. Has something happened to Dad? What is going on?

ABOARD THE RAFT
LAST CHANCE
0900 THURSDAY • JUNE 22, 1989 • DAY 8

THE STORM LASTED two days. Mountainous seas hammered our minuscule floating home, each single wave of such size that it could have easily capsized and swallowed the raft and its contents. I remained constantly on alert. When I heard each thunderous roar of an approaching breaking wave, I leaned way over to windward seconds before the avalanche of frothing water buried our floating home. The raft slid deep down into the trough and, just when it appeared we could not emerge from a watery grave, out we would pop, soaked but safe. Two or three waves would miss us before the product of another midocean collision caused by opposing weather systems buried us anew.

It is inevitable that sooner or later one monster wave, much more powerful than the others, will roll us over and over, then drive us down into the deeps, to release us only after expending its awesome power. We cannot possibly survive this type of punishment much longer. We keep both windows tightly zipped, hoping that when we do roll, Sim and I and the watermaker will stay on board.

Yet our lucky star still shines. The blow passes us by. The ride over smooth rolling waves after the seas flatten out provides a surprisingly quiet night's sleep. We even sleep right through our one-week anniversary. When we have to pump air only every three hours overnight, I am in castaway heaven. The comforter is dry and the air temperature perfect. Sim sleeps bare, which gives me a chance to give her plump torso a full examination. She looks like an angel. Another couple of weeks on our three-saltine-a-day diet, I think ruefully, and she'll have a knockout figure. I keep an edge of the comforter over me to keep my cold blood warm. Neither of us has been sleeping longer than an hour and a half at a stretch. When I awaken, it's only long enough to pinch the air chamber, take a quick look around, and sense that all is as I left it. Then I doze back into a castaway slumber.

The raft has performed first-rate during our latest blow. Not once did it become unstable and threaten to flip. The morning dawns clear and bright. Of course, what we now call clear is considered quite cloudy back in Miami. Low-lying clouds no longer press us into the ocean but are higher, light gray, and not so dense. Sim points to a sliver of blue sky, the first we've seen while adrift. We greet the sun as a long-lost friend. It's not a perfect day for an air search, but it's the best we've had yet. We scan the skies and genuinely expect to hear a faraway hum signaling that help is on the way. Soon after, a glistening Coast Guard Falcon jet will make a low pass overhead. It'll dip its wings in recognition, and our ordeal will soon be over. We will be safe and on our way home in no time.

Sim's voice cuts into my fantasy. "Don't tell me sleeping beauty's awake. You've missed half the day, Butler. I've been pumping, cleaning, beating off turtles, and you've slept through it all."

"Good morning, sweetie. I've been busy dreaming. Did you see the Coast Guard jet that flew over this morning?"

"You may be joking, but I did dream about a plane waving its wings at us. It made several passes before it flew off. Let it be true, oh God, let it be true."

I am sure they will launch at least one search flight today. But will they look in another part of the ocean? Susan and Cris had our position on June 11. What have they done?

I gave the ham operator in California our coordinates as of eleven hours before we sank. He will surely send the usual acknowledgment card to my address. Will the children sense its significance and call him?

Perhaps Karl can. Karl, my neighbor in Miami, installed the single-sideband ham set aboard *Siboney*. He would have to transmit an emergency CQ on the ten-meter band. That is, if he can, for his

Collins radio may not have crystals for that band. Even so, it would take days for a net to form to trace the station in California with whom we had our last contact. Too many ifs.

I turn toward Sim and ask, "Were you able to pick up any news on the radio?"

"Lots. A Russian cruise ship, the *Maxim Gorki*, with nine hundred and fifty people aboard, hit an iceberg in the North Sea and is sinking. I hope the children make a connection. They sink and we sank. I shouldn't say this, but it's luck for us. Now they should get worried. They are bound to put two and two together and conclude they have no news from us because the boat went down."

I voice my agreement. "They should definitely make the association. Come on, gang. Think! Think! Get your brains in motion. Call our friends. Act! Now!"

Simonne continues to escape the confinement of the raft by touching the landborne world with her little yellow Walkman radio. Careful not to drain the batteries, she listens just minutes at a time, beginning after midnight, when reception is best. As the signal skips off the ever-changing ionosphere, she must continually retune to new stations or let a minute or more pass until her original station reappears. Mexican stations come in strongest, for Acapulco lies only seven hundred miles to the north. If we're out here another week, I'll have her track the strength and source of the many stations she picks up to help me verify our drift toward shore. Though every sign convinces me we're drifting to the northeast, I'm hard-pressed to prove it to Sim when she casts doubts on my navigation plots.

I add our last day's run to my dead-reckoning log and total our way made good in the week since *Siboney* sank. I find we've drifted to the east with the current a total of a hundred and thirty-five miles, and we have been pushed forty-five miles north by the wind and waves. I jot down our new latitude and longitude in my workbook. But what I really need is a chart to better visualize our progress. I decide to make one. I draw a half-inch grid on a page of my navigation workbook and label the coordinates for latitude and longitude at intervals of 1 degree for each square. Longitude will run from 80 to 100 degrees West and latitude from 0 to 20 degrees North. We're in there, somewhere.

In my navigation notebook, I find the exact position for Balboa and for Punta Mala, both in Panama. Balboa is the Pacific Ocean terminus of the Panama Canal, and Punta Mala is a cape south of the canal that all ships going north must round. I enter both positions on the chart. I remember that Acapulco is right on 100 degrees West and close to 17 degrees North. I enter a dot on the chart and label it. As I remember it, the coast between Punta Mala and Acapulco is almost a straight line, and I draw a line between the two points. The Gulf of Panama goes north from Punta Mala to Balboa and drops in a semicircle to the southeast.

With Sim's help, I locate the borders of the Central American countries. Costa Rica is north of Panama, of that we're both sure. Then it's Nicaragua. We know Guatemala is next to Mexico. We can't remember if Honduras or Salvador is next to Costa Rica, so we leave the entire area blank for now.

I put an X on the chart where we sank, which is twenty squares from the coast. Each square is a degree, sixty miles; thus we sank some twelve hundred miles from Panama. We're eleven hundred miles from the nearest Central American coastline to the east. Seven or eight hundred miles north to Acapulco. Sim watches my every move.

"How far are we from the coast?"

"Oh, about nine hundred miles." I always knock a few miles off my estimates to keep my customers happy.

Sim knows this and adds 20 percent to everything I say. She asks, "Where are we headed?"

"This current will take us right into shore. We're at 7 degrees North now. The current will push us east until we approach the coast. The wind and waves will push us north."

I can't remember what happens to the current near shore. Does it swing north, or does it go south? But why worry about reaching the coast? Help should be on the way soon. We need several clear days, and we'll be out of here.

Sim runs her fingers along the crease between the floor and the air tube in search of anything sharp. She has repeated this precaution every day, afraid that abrasion might open a hole in the air chambers. She still hasn't found the barometer needle. She also watches me all the time to ensure I don't leave scissors, a file, or the hook near the plastic tubes. She keeps the scissors, the nail file, the hook, and the knife in the leather gun holder. When I use the scissors, she keeps her eyes on me until they're put safely away.

We have drunk the last bit of water stored in both two-and-a-half-gallon water containers and have tossed them over the side. Now we have only the large plastic bucket to contend with. We've almost drained two of the seven bottles of Evian, which means I had better check out the watermaker and see how it works. Sim retrieves the machine from under my feet and removes the foul-weather wrap that protects it and keeps it from damaging the raft. The device has three plastic tubes. One of the two larger ones, the saltwater intake, has a mesh filter fitted to the end. Waste salts wash out of the other large tube. I drop both large tubes over the side. Sim hangs onto the third tube, from which we hope fresh water will emerge.

The body of the pump is almost two feet long and has a two-foot handle attached to one end. As I stroke the handle and salt water is sucked in from the sea, the pressure needed to move the handle increases. After a dozen strokes, bubbles and finally water drip from the small tube that Sim holds over the side until the water is clear.

I put the tube in my mouth while I continue to pump. The water is salty at first, but ten strokes later it becomes sweet and pure. Sim puts the tube into an empty plastic bottle and holds both until the bottle is about a quarter full, then takes over. She's a sight pumping, naked as a centerfold. I ogle, whistle, and get a dirty look. Sim and I trade the watermaker back and forth after six or seven minutes, when our muscles start to ache.

Each liter takes twenty minutes to fill. We do thirty strokes in thirty seconds, or one stroke per second. Twenty minutes has twelve hundred seconds, so a liter needs twelve hundred strokes. We'll keep trim and toned, at least from the waist up.

Sim has the first sip and announces the taste first-class. "As good as Evian," she declares, which, from a Frenchwoman, is the ultimate stamp of approval. If the machine continues to work, water will not be a problem. We fill our day's supply in forty minutes.

Sim once again gets into a "reorganize the raft" frame of mind in hopes of gaining a few extra inches of floor area. The food and liquid inventory yields one can of vegetables, four cans with unknown contents, one can of juice, two beers, one can of clams, one large bottle of apple juice, two bottles of Perrier, one half-filled bottle of cognac, one half-liter of Coke, one small bottle of Sprite, two bottles of Evian, one can of crackers, seven liters of water, and three boxes of raisins. Sim makes it all disappear under us in what we now call the bilge.

The day continues sunny, and the breeze is light from the south. Seas are six to eight feet but calm enough for me to open my window. Sim also opens hers and part of the canopy, and we hang a corner of our bedding out to dry. What joy we find in again being part of the world after seven days hermetically sealed inside our tiny raft. I tighten my hold on Sim's hand as we gaze out the open window at passing clouds and at birds that circle the raft in search of a meal.

No landlocked aquarium approaches what we have below our raft. I can see more than a hundred feet down. Dorados are everywhere, and they jump and splash in seeming glee. Schools of brightly colored fish similar to parrot fish dash around followed by what look like yellowtails. Among them swim small sharks. Four orange tripletails swim within an arm's length. They barely move and stay inches under the surface, swimming not upright like other fish but on their sides. One eye looks straight up at us. I could snag one if I had a harpoon. Perhaps I can make one.

I untie the fishing rod from the air chamber where we secured it that first day right after *Siboney* sank and, with the large knife, cut the rod in half. With four feet of monofilament fishing line pulled out of the reel, I secure the hook to the end of the thin half of the rod.

I watch my prey as they circle closely. With one eye up, they appear to watch me. Before the gaff was ready, they swam right up to the raft. Now they come no closer than ten feet. I wait. Minutes go by. Three tripletails slowly coast in. I jab the hook under the closest fish, pull, and miss. All the fish vanish into the depths. I wait, but I know fish. They're gone. These will not be back. I'd love to catch a dorado, but how do we land it without damaging the raft? One small hole in the air chamber, and the party is over. We've used up all the patches, and the emergency inner tube has been deployed.

If I had had a net when the tripletails first arrived, I could've caught one. How do I make a net? What knot do netmakers use? I decide to give it a try. I know that the first item all netmakers and menders need is a longish spool. I pull more line out of the fishing reel and wind ten feet onto one of Sim's ballpoint pens. I hang the small half of the fishing rod between the arches and wrap a dozen loops of the nylon around it stretching from one end to the other. Then I practice making knots. When young, I watched Cuban fishermen mend their nets. Sim, back in Menton, sat with the fishermen on the old breakwater as they worked on their nets. We take turns practicing, but the right knot continues to elude us. An hour later, with nothing but a tangle to show for our efforts, we give up and throw the odd pieces of nylon over the side. What a shame. I'm sure I could catch a fish if I had a net.

When I look out again, the yellow fish are nowhere to be seen. In their place, dozens, possibly hundreds, of dorados swim playfully under the raft. These are the Atlantic sea dolphin, the fish Hawaiians call mahimahi. They dart in schools of six or more below the surface. Their blue and yellow colors enliven the underwater world. Some dorados, with bright, phosphor-blue pectoral fins and yellow tail fins, skirt inches from the raft and tempt us to catch them. Suddenly, a dorado will shoot out of the water to land flat with a slap and a splash, done, I have no doubt, out of sheer happiness. They celebrate life with exuberance and joy, so pleased to be in their element. Our element is so many miles away, among green fields and fat cows and trees with long, leafy branches. Will we live to see land again?

A flying fish takes off in a frenzy, chased into the air by a hungry dorado. Flying inches off the ocean, its progress is followed closely from below by a fast-moving blaze of gold and blue. Flight energy expended, the flying fish hits the water with a slight splash, vanishing into waiting jaws with a flurry of foam.

I inch around onto my knees and lift my head over the canopy. Twenty-foot swells, graceful now and far apart, roll under us on their way to some distant shore. Skies are clear to the north and west. Clouds ring the horizon to the south. A few hours of sunshine is all we ask.

Birds fly and feed all around us. Boobies sweep the crests of waves in search of surface fish. Their large wings help them soar effortlessly in their quest for food. I count thirty-two boobies, mostly young with light and fluffy feathers and fuzzy markings. At any one time, half are in the air. The others perch nearby on the water, either squabbling or preening.

Simonne calls out, "Here, pretty boy. Bill, look at this beautiful booby. He's my friend. He came yesterday and the day before that. He spends the night with us along with another dozen or so birds. The others aren't as pretty as this one. Look at his black body, his white chest so rounded, so soft. Have you seen his eyes? They look straight at me. Agate eyes. It's a male, and the brown and beige ones are females. Why is it that in the animal kingdom the males of the species are always the most striking?"

"Pretty Boy" swims closer. "Is he good to eat?" I tease.

"Don't you dare joke about it. Isn't he gorgeous?"

"He looks more delicious to me than gorgeous. He has me salivating. Here, pretty bird, here. I bet he tastes great, and he'd make super bait."

"Bill Butler, stop your eternal dumb talk. You're not going to touch one of my birds. Here, sweetie, come to me. Look, he isn't afraid. He loves me."

Sim continues. "He's really pretty. And look below. Look at all those dorados and other fish. We're in wonderland, above and below the surface. But what are they doing this far from shore? There's nothing out here but water. The nearest land must be the Galápagos, and that's more than five hundred miles away."

Sim remains excited. "Look, next to Pretty Boy there's a beauty of a young female. Her eyes are black, and she looks like she's wearing makeup. Her beak is blue, and her face is mauve and violet. She looks like Elizabeth Taylor in *Cleopatra*. I'm going to call her Cleopatra. And there's another but not as pretty as Cleo. Won't the sharks eat them?"

When we first saw the birds, we wondered whether they would be shark bait. A shark, when hungry, will eat just about anything. As days passed, it became obvious that cohabitation on the high seas is a natural phenomenon sorted out millennia ago. The birds watch everything that's going on and, although alert, do not act overly preoccupied. Sharks swim among them just feet away. The boobies dunk their head into the water to stay abreast of action under the surface and then continue to preen and cackle. My guess is that sharks choke on feathers.

Meanwhile, our sea family grows. More than forty seabirds swim with us. They sleep and scuffle nearby and drink salt water. The boobies discharge excess salt through special nasal glands. When they shake their heads vigorously, the salt flies. A dozen birds swim lazily near the raft. At first when they dipped their beaks in the water, I thought they were drinking, but they'd pop if they took a sip with every dip. Now I'm convinced they're just checking out what's going on below. Pretty Boy and Cleo approach within several feet of Sim, who has them entranced with her running chatter.

The boobies are forever busy preening. When perched on the sea as they ride the waves, they work on waterproofing their feathers. We watch as they bend their head around and push their beak into a spot near their tail feathers. There, with their bill, they squeeze droplets of fatty oil from their preen gland and convey the oil to their feathers in nibbling and wiping actions.

Twenty birds float alongside, all busy waterproofing their feathers, not one interested in Sim or me. That is, except for Pretty Boy, who has definitely fallen in love with Sim. He watches her every move and cocks his head when she talks. Sim says Pretty Boy is her guardian angel in disguise. I hope so. We need all the protection we can get.

On the way out from Panama, we saw very few birds. Every day or two, one would fly with us for an hour, and once in a while a booby would rest on a spreader, but I'd shoo them off before they messed up my sails. Three or four days before we sank, I woke up in the morning to find the mainsail stained with a heavy dose of droppings. I threw several dozen bucketfuls of water on the spots and scrubbed for an hour before the sail was white again.

High overhead, heading into the wind, soar the keen-eyed, always watchful frigate birds, their great wings spread to their full six-foot span. Their flight is at times motionless, stability provided by distinctive twin tails that act as rudders. I haven't seen one yet come near the surface. Do they stay up there all night? If not, where do they go?

Simonne so loves the boobies. She leans over the side and says, "The males have such striking markings—white and black or white and brown. The color of brown is the most beautiful I have ever seen. It reminds me of a monk I saw once in Assisi in Italy, who prayed alone in a church where I had wandered in search of shade and silence.

"It was summer outside. As I knelt, a ray of sunshine shone through a high stained-glass window. It gave the monk's robe a glow that appeared to come from inside. The color of the booby reminds me of that moment.

"Whenever I see birds," Simonne continues, "I always think of St. Francis and his boundless love for all life on this earth. Birds flocked to him. They sat on his shoulders, ate from his hands. Animals obeyed him. I respect people who love animals, because God gave these to us and we have a responsibility toward them.

"I learned from the old fishermen in the south of France to preserve and respect the environment. They gave their prey a chance. My brother Serge, a good underwater hunter, caught most of his meals—octopus, sea urchins, and squid—with his bare hands. He never used gloves or a knife. If they were what he wanted, he kept them. Otherwise, he threw them back."

With Sim's steadying help, I turn from my back to my knees, then stretch myself up to take a look around. I'd love to stand, to test my legs, but that's impossible. I would surely damage the raft. The full majesty of the deep-blue ocean spreads before me in every direction. Swells big as low-lying hills roll in formation from the south to lift us gently until we are at the apex of our watery world. Whitecaps dot the oceanic swells that raise us to their crest until I can see over all other waves. Each time we rise, I focus on a small part of the horizon, hoping to spot help on its way. The sea remains eerily empty.

When a crest passes, we drop slowly, often thirty, forty feet down into the abyss of the trough. When I look up, I see towering peaks of water surging toward us, giving me the sensation we may never emerge from the deep trench. But we do rise, soon to stand again atop the pinnacle of our water world. I breathe in the vast vista, constantly changing, ever on the move, powerful, punishing, yet sustaining, both friend and foe, a soothing balm, a dedicated killer, yet our only hope.

I stay on my knees long after they begin to ache, for I can't get over the feeling that a ship is nearby and will come to our rescue. The small light on the EPIRB continues to blink and could bring us help. We have been at sea seven full days without sighting human life. Today makes eleven days since our last radio contact. Our family must soon miss us and activate a rescue mission. I repeat my mental signals to Sally. She's my big hope. "Do something, baby. Call everyone you know. Involve our friends. You won't find us easily, but the pieces to the puzzle are in place." Simonne concentrates on Cris. She has a special bond with him, her eldest. When Sim hears a whistle in her ear, she's sure it's her mother thinking of her. Her mother knows we're in trouble, but she's so far away and sick. What can she possibly do?

As daylight wanes, boobies come in to roost. Our raft becomes a bird port. To leeward, a dozen birds, lined up in formation much like planes approaching an aircraft carrier, close in on the raft with wings slightly curled, webbed feet extended. Their approach is perfect until they collapse their wings and put their weight on the canopy. No doubt it looks mighty solid from the air, but it's only thin cloth suspended between the inflatable arches. Under the weight of a bird, the canopy folds, and the booby slides right off and lands in the water with a fanny-flop and a surprised look, its hope to spend a quiet, dry night perched atop our canopy dashed. Sim and I explode with laughter as each booby slips off and lands with a splash in the sea. Their antics keep us entertained until we tire and I wave them off with the pole. Undaunted, some go around for a second try. Others quietly swim away twenty feet to windward. They stay close, providing companionship for the long night ahead and reassurance that we are not alone in the world.

We eat a cracker each for supper, followed with a long drink of water. Sim reads the prayers. Overall, this has been a great day. The start was a bit hairy, but I can take many more days like this one. Perhaps we may survive after all.

A red-orange sunset tops off our best day so far. I prop my head up with a life preserver to see the bright-scarlet western horizon. Sim gazes out the window, pensive, dreamy, until the darkness is total. Our flock of boobies are all bunched together. They quack at one another as they float easily on the breaking waves. I check my watch. Total darkness is at eight forty-five, which I enter in my log.

The seas have flattened further. The raft loses less air, and the turtles have gone elsewhere to scratch their backs. The gentle breeze lulls us to sleep. I'm ready for another dose of raft heaven.

"Bill, look, there's the Virgin Mary."

"That's Venus."

"I know it's Venus. We call it *Stella Matutina*, Star of the Morning. It's my favorite star. It's always been there when I need her. She is the first star in the sky and the last to disappear. A guardian of souls. Our guardian."

"It's not a star. It's a planet."

"Whatever. Look, there are some more stars. And the moon. Oh, it's so beautiful. We won't be alone tonight. And the seas are much calmer. This should be a pleasant night without those awful waves."

A violent jolt shakes the raft. My heart almost leaps out of my chest. What in the hell was that? My mind races as my hand finds Sim's. Another sledgehammer-like blow sends the raft spinning. I lean into Sim and put my index finger up to my mouth. Sim is wide-eyed and whispers, "Shark." It must be. All four sides of the raft receive hard blows in rapid succession. It feels like Babe Ruth is out there slugging homers, our raft the ball.

We remain immobile as we clutch each other tightly. Whatever it is, has it left? My heart pounds. Waves lap against the side of the raft as if counting time. We wait in silence, powerless. Death has knocked. Is this the end? The shark must be huge. What does it want with the raft? If it's a mako or a tiger shark or a hammerhead, this cruise will soon be over. If it's a great white, we have only seconds left. In three passes, it will swallow the two of us and half of the raft. Our lives will soon be over. How stupid of me. I sailed away for pleasure and now I will die. Damn.

Another powerful blow freezes my blood. Sim squeezes my hand until it hurts. Poor Sim. She didn't want to go on this trip. I talked her into it. Her children and mother need her desperately, and here she is, where she will die with me. My mind has been running through every experience I have ever had with sharks. There must be something I can do. I inch up to a sitting position, zip the window down partway, and lean over the side. Twenty feet away, shooting at high speed toward the raft, is a torpedo-shaped trail of phosphorescence. It slides by my side and, when abreast, hits the raft with its tail. The plastic of the raft is paper thin. I lie back down and whisper to Sim, "It's just a small shark playing with the raft."

I lie.

"Small shark!" Sim exclaims, much too loudly. "It feels like an express train. What do you mean by small? Twenty feet?"

"Shhh. No, baby, four or five feet." I chop a couple feet off our predator. Why scare her any worse than she already is?

The raft receives another ferocious blow on Sim's side. It's another shark, or is it the same one? We hold still as Sim prays with a new intensity. What is it they want with the raft? Minutes turn into hours as I lie in cold sweat, unable to come up with a defense or an escape. We are again held hostage. First, by the whales that destroyed *Siboney*; now, by sharks, an invisible menace and a force fully capable of instant destruction. Lord, have mercy on us.

I can't describe the panic that grips me. I have lived most of my life close to sharks. One of my fishermen friends in Cuba lost half his face to a shark he had caught and thought was dead. His deformed face was testimony to the destruction these primitive animals can cause. We have absolutely no protection. We're at their mercy. I know their habits. First, they'll play with us, and when they tire of that game, they'll get down to serious business. This banging is part of their sensory testing. They will very soon know exactly what we are.

The shark attacks stop when a light drizzle turns into a downpour. Perhaps the decrease in salinity caused by the rain or its noise made them leave. For more than an hour, I try to catch rainwater. I pull the canopy down into the shape of a funnel and hold an empty bottle outside under the bunched-up cloth. Water pours everywhere except inside the bottle. The bottle slips out of my hand. The canopy flops in the wind. Sim complains when water drips off my elbow and onto her cover. After an hour, I have filled only a quarter of a bottle. I offer Sim the first taste. She gags and exclaims, "Pure rubber."

I take the bottle from her and take a full gulp. She's right. The rubberized canopy must be washing off, and who knows what chemicals it's releasing. Now we have a choice. We can die poisoned or die eaten. I give up catching water when the rain starts up again. The shark or sharks do not return. Perhaps it was just a curious, lone shark, a onetime occurrence.

Simonne prays. I listen to her murmur, then doze off. Morning finds us rested, which is a miracle considering how the day started. The shark has not returned. The wind has shifted to the west. The raft heads north and south, which means we're out of the current. At least the monster waves are behind us.

Living to see and breathe this new day is no less than a miracle. Never has either of us lived with such deadly fear—fear and the overwhelming conviction that our next breath would be our last. Fear of a lingering death. Fear of mutilation and a painfully slow death by bleeding or drowning. When my eyes find Sim's, I sense she is as filled with gratitude as I for having been spared from this latest threat. When she suggests we read the psalms and prayers, I readily agree. We must heal and strengthen our hearts for what lies ahead.

Simonne starts with a psalm that so aptly fits our situation. It reads:

> *They that go down to the sea in ships, that do business in great waters; These see the works of the Lord, and His wonders in the deep. For He commands, and raises the stormy wind, which lifts up the waves of the sea. They mount up to the heavens, they go down again to the depths; their soul is melted because of trouble. They reel to and fro, and stagger like a drunken man, and are at their wits' end. Then they cry unto the Lord in their trouble, and He brings them out of their distresses. He makes the storm a calm, so that the waves are still. Then are they glad because they are quiet; so He brings them into their desired haven. Oh, that men would praise the Lord for His goodness, and for His wonderful works to the children of men.*

Tears stream down my cheeks. How weak we are. How could we ever make this trip alone? We need help, and only God can help us now. Simonne next reads my favorite parable, the parable of the lost sheep. I am a poor lost sheep, in so many ways. Is it too late to be saved?

ABOARD THE RAFT
LAST CHANCE
0130 TUESDAY • JUNE 27, 1989 • DAY 13

HAMMERING SEAS and howling wind have bored into our pith like augers the past three nights. Cold, lonely, scared, and miserable from the incessant thrashing of wind, wave, rain, and shark, I cling to Sim and search my inner senses for an answer as to what yet awaits us. Hours ago, when the last rays of light yielded to the murky darkness that now envelops us, the wind started to increase. Blustery gusts soon screamed at us as if questioning our right to exist. The seas quickly responded. Great seas lifted the raft as they roared past us, foaming and frothing like so many angry lions. The resounding boom of waves against the air chamber reached into the marrow of our bones. We embraced, in search of mutual reassurance. With respite from no quarter, I gasped for breath, waiting in our jail cell for that one wave that would ultimately destroy us.

Now, an hour into this new day, one wave after another still attempts to overwhelm us, to do away with this unwanted intruder, this orange-and-yellow blemish on its blue-and-white frothy mantle. Hundreds of tons of water propelled by the wind at more than twenty miles an hour hurtle at us. Fresh sheets of spray bury our fragile vessel. Gallons of cold water spill inside and onto us. We remain naked as wind-driven rain and spray fly under the canopy. Under the saltwater-soaked comforter, we fold into each other to search for and draw out each other's warmth. Will this be the end? How close are we?

Simonne's cries reach out to the heavens. She pleads with God to listen to her, to please open His heart and forgive her, her sobs broken only by the thunder of another breaking wave. Tears pour down my cheeks as I dwell on the hopelessness of our plight and the thought that we may both soon die, never to see our children and their babies again, never to be found, to vanish off the face of the earth, our lives unfulfilled. I damn myself for insanely barging ahead on this trip and for my hardheadedness, which took us so far out to sea, outside of shipping lanes and probably out of range for the emergency radio beacon.

Minutes turn into eons. With the roar of each avalanching wave, we tighten our hold and squeeze toward the windward side of the raft. The night is so black I see nothing. Each time a moment passes without a breaking wave and we relax our grip on each other, a wave larger than the rest buries us once again. When will this punishment end? When will we have a moment's peace? When will the Lord bring us out of our distress?

Simonne's prayers are at last answered. The rain slows and then stops. I look at my watch. It's two thirty. The wail of the wind and the rumble of the waves no longer drown out all other sound. I hold Simonne's hand tightly as the raft rocks along. The wind has died, but the waves still sweep over us. When the wind dies, the waves take a day to reflect the change. When the wind starts to blow, wave action picks up in an hour. That's not fair. But the whales sinking our boat wasn't fair either. My eyes close and stay closed as my mind fills with savory sleep, Simonne's mumbled prayers my last conscious impression.

A violent jolt, as though a fifty-foot breaker has collided with the raft, jars us back into consciousness. Sim leans closer and whispers, "He's back." We embrace tightly. Lest our visitor detect the presence of a meal, I shush, unnecessarily, and hand signal Sim, "Not a word, not a move." The next strike spins the raft around 180 degrees, my side now to leeward. Five more blows in a row bring panic. Neither of us moves. Not a word is spoken. I hold Simonne tightly, my mind wildly trying to sort out this new situation.

Whack. Whack. Whack again. Sim whispers, "Pray." I search in vain for a prayer. Dear God, help us. The shark leaves. I wait, immobile except to feel for Sim's outstretched hand. She squeezes mine.

Then four successive blows rock the raft. These are followed by more than a dozen raft-spinning slaps at machine-gun speed. Time stops as we are punched, shoved, and knocked around until we have no doubt our existence will soon be over. Unable to defend ourselves or escape, we brace ourselves for the worst. In the dark, I visualize hundreds of razor-sharp teeth set in jaws wired to the brain of a wanton killer, jaws open, row upon row of teeth thrust ahead of a powerful body traveling at high speed. The shark first bumps its prey to better sense what it is. Then it attacks. I look up to the heavens and plead for help.

Between attacks, minutes turn into hours. We rest on our backs, eyes fixed wide, hearts pumping wildly, and we gasp for air and wait. I play out many different scenes in my head. How big an animal is it? The bash to the raft felt like Muhammad Ali swinging a two-by-four. This shark must be twice as big as Ali. What type of shark is it? I dare not guess. They're all deadly. Mako, tiger, hammerhead—all highly efficient predators, purpose-built machines. Why do they beat on our raft? Is it curiosity? Are they testing this strange floating object to plan a final attack? With my free hand, I feel for the air chamber in search of reassurance but find only a thin layer of rubberized plastic. We are definitely going to die. Only a miracle or divine intervention can save us now.

Two hours pass without a whack. We have at least an hour to go before we can expect relief from this infernal darkness. When the first vestiges of dawn creep across the sullen sky, we are utterly exhausted yet exuberant. We have been born again. We never expected to make it through this fearful night.

I have kept a brave facade for Sim's sake, but I think I know sharks. I have fished and fought them all my life. I have more than a dozen true shark stories and a wall full of shark jaws. Just a thin wall of plastic fabric separates us from rows of saber-sharp teeth. One strike and we are through. Is this some species revenge for all the sharks I have slaughtered?

Sharks are skilled hunters, their senses sharpened through four hundred million years at the top of the food chain. More than twenty-five species of sharks have been known to attack man and boats, though most sharks are scavengers or hunt smaller prey. Tiger sharks eat everything from a wide variety of fish to other sharks and turtles, birds, seals, squid, garbage (including plastic rafts), and carrion. But the shark that attacked wasn't a tiger; we would be dead by now if it had been. All sharks love warm water except the great white, which will go anywhere for a meal. The water temperature here is about 80 degrees, perfect for sharks. Our shark problem may just be beginning.

I can hardly wait for full daylight to see what we're up against, but I do know there may be more than one shark, since they mature in packs. Mature sharks then segregate by sex and come together only during the mating season. When parturition is imminent, the female moves to a nursery area, gives birth, and abandons her offspring in company with other newborns. Sharks have a slow rate of growth, about one to three inches per year. Males of the same age stick together because if they mix with larger sharks, they will become part of the day's menu. If we see many sharks, this will signify immature animals. A single shark will signify a mature member capable of a predatory attack.

Dawn greets us with dense rain. I sit up, stiff from the dampness and our tense night, and look out the window into a deep-blue ocean wild with motion. Clouds scud overhead, heavy with rain. Sheets of water in changing patterns tumble from black squalls that dot the horizon. Upwind, a dense black fringe covers 90 degrees of horizon. I smooth out lumps in my bedding, bunch a part as a pillow, and lie back down.

"Weather forecast," I call over to Sim. "Storm fast approaching from the west. More rain. Residents on raft to get soaked."

As Simonne serves up our breakfast saltine, a bright flash is followed by a loud crack of thunder. A second bolt lights up the inside of the raft. Much louder thunder follows. I count the seconds between the flash and the crash. The next one is forty seconds. Sound travels at seven hundred feet a second. At forty seconds, the storm is thirty thousand feet away, or under six miles. Soon, Sim calls out twenty seconds. The squall moves in. We are being attacked from all sides. Sharks below. Now lightning bolts from above. What next?

We close both windows and fasten the canopy to the top of the window. A flash brighter than the midday sun followed by a thundering boom brings Sim into my waiting arms. "Ten seconds," she whispers. I know Sim ponders as I do. Could lightning strike a raft?

The storm breaks with a blast of cold, moist air. Thirty-knot winds push the raft at over a knot. Stronger gusts threaten to flatten the canopy as it strains to become airborne. Sim throws her weight to windward. Rain beats onto the raft and mixes with the wind-driven salty spray flowing over the window. The last bits of dry bedding soak up drips too many to count.

Sim lashes the watermaking machine and water bottles to the inside of the raft and tightens the window tie-downs. A wind gust heels the raft over to leeward. Waves grow steeper. Sim edges farther up on the high side to add her weight to mine. We brace for capsize while I play out in my mind how to recover. Is this what hell is like? We remain immobile, exhausted and bewildered by the continual punishment. Hours pass until the worst of the storm is behind us. Sim lowers the window, allowing the moisture-laden breeze to reach our sodden bedding.

When will help arrive? Seventeen days have passed since our last radio link with our family. Cris awaits our decision whether to rent the house or not. We haven't called to congratulate Joe on the birth of my new granddaughter. I wonder what they have named the baby. My failure to make contact should generate a strong signal. Airplanes and ships must be looking for us at this very moment. Today we should keep a sharp lookout for an airplane.

Our radio silence should bring action. Or will it? If we don't call, no doubt they will conclude that the radio isn't working. If the single-sideband radio on *Siboney* had failed, we would sooner or later have contacted a passing vessel via VHF radio and asked them to relay a message home. It may take another week for the family to be fully convinced we're in danger and to get a rescue mission in motion. Or will anyone really worry?

The waves are so high that we experience the characteristic lull when we're deep in each trough, then gusts when we ride each crest. If anyone is out looking for us today, the monster breaking seas will make our raft invisible from the air, as we're deep in a trough most of the time. We couldn't be seen even in a direct flyover, and to top things off, the orange coating on the outside of the raft is turning light yellow. Soon, we'll appear like just another breaker—a small one at that.

Where in the hell are the planes? My last radio contact was on June 11. We've been off the scope for sixteen days. What better signal do they need? Where do the children think we are? What do they think we're doing? Isn't anyone thinking about us? I yell out the window with a "C'mon gang, we need help. Now!"

If we had a handheld VHF radio on the raft, we could have signaled the *Ter Eriksen*. I left ours behind on *Siboney* because it was trashed. In the storm that pushed us off course three days before we sank, a huge wave had soaked it. I rinsed it off with fresh water and put it aside to dry before charging. When we sank, the VHF radio was still wet, the batteries uncharged.

The waves ever so slowly abate. The bedding dries, and I turn in hopes of finding a softer spot. "My captain," says Sim when she notices I am awake, "would you like the morning news with your breakfast?" I grunt and nod, and she continues. "Everyone got off the Russian ship before it sank after it hit that iceberg. The leaders in China shot seven more men. Someone found the battleship *Bismarck* that went down in the Second World War. And in Cuba, there is a big flap over a bunch of officers involved in drug trafficking. The ringleader is a friend of Castro called Ochoa." I still find it incredible that we can stay abreast of world events even while lost to the world. Strange, but it helps me feel a mite less lost and alone.

The story of the Russian ship sinking should get one of our children or a friend to think about *Siboney* and the possibility that our ship may have gone down. Or will it? In several days, we'll have been incommunicado for three weeks. Surely, an air search will be launched in a matter of days, and very soon we'll be found and on our way home.

A scraping sound that runs from one end of the raft to the other brings Sim's hands shooting into mine. When I sit up, I see a large shark racing for the raft. Inches away, it dives, then surfaces on Sim's side. A quick spin and back it darts to pass alongside, its white belly up inches below the surface. The shark skims along my side of the raft and, when abreast, whips its tail against the air chamber, no doubt the source of the violent blows we felt all last night. The shark then sweeps along the other two sides of the raft and gives each a mighty whack. I hold the pole outside the raft, pointed end down. If the shark follows the same pattern, it should approach from my right. A light-gray shape shoots my way. I plunge the pole at the fast-moving shadow and miss. The shark pummels Sim's side, then the bow. I wait. It shoots under me before I can react. On its next pass, I jab it in the middle of its stomach. Its tail flips high and sends water all over me.

Two more sharks circle below. One approaches a foot below the surface and within reach. I poke its head. It jerks and swims away. The next hour passes quietly. To my dismay, a shark twice as long as the raft swims by the window, not ten feet away. I glance at Sim to be sure she isn't looking.

The monster circles but maintains its distance. I close the window and hide behind it. If that shark were to attack, it would be all over in seconds. The large black mass circles, its huge dorsal fin slicing the water. The top edge of the fin has a white spot. My Lord, a white-tipped shark, the most deadly of man-eaters.

Sim asks, "Did you see anything?"

"Nope. Rain is letting up."

I lie. The four- to six-foot sharks that are our constant visitors worry the devil out of Sim. If I were to tell her that we have a twelve-foot shark ten feet away, she would sleep even less. I zip both windows up all the way to make sure Sim cannot see out. We both lie quietly. I fall asleep. Sim prays most of the night. After midnight, the smaller silky and lemon sharks return, whack the raft, then leave.

I fall back asleep until another whack makes me jump. I lower the window and ready the pole. I see nothing. I lie down. We're whacked. I'm up again and wait. We're struck on Sim's side. Mine should be next. I see it move in, then lunge with the pole and connect.

"Did you hit him?" Sim asks.

"One hit. Zero misses. I can't understand what they're after. It's as if they're playing with us."

Sharks batter the raft all night. When they stop, a turtle arrives. It bumps us from head to foot and gets caught in a strap; I release it, and it swims away without even a thanks. In between all the action, I nap whenever I can. Whenever I doze off, the sharks return. I bounce up, pole at the ready. They are invisible. I score not one hit. I lean back, take a deep breath, and close my eyes.

Sim shakes me violently. "Bill, quick, pump! There's no air in the raft! We're sinking!" I awaken from a deep dream. We were back on *Siboney*. Whales were furiously pounding the hull.

"What time is it, Sim?"

"Two." Rain pours down as I pump vital air back into the air chambers. I had hoped it was closer to dawn. I'm so stiff I can barely move. On the positive side, the canopy keeps us dry. I pump until Sim gives me the usual OK. If I stop before she checks the air chamber, she will invariably find it limp and I'll have to start again.

"Bill, where's the flashlight? Quick, I lost my rosary." This is the third or fourth time Sim has fallen asleep holding her rosary. When she tosses in her sleep, the little metal loops that hold the beads pull apart. She tears around under the cushions until she finds all the little pieces.

Fear and apprehension keep me awake for hours. Is the white-tipped shark still around, and will it attack? Sharks are cautious; they'll circle an object until their sensitive sensory glands confirm it's safe to attack. Vibrations, minute electrical charges, smell, taste, and appearance are fed into a central sensory databank compiled over the past four hundred million years, which will decide whether it's safe or worthwhile to attack. If it receives a "go" signal, our death will follow within seconds. I cannot think of a thing I can do. I dare not splash with the pole or make any movement, for that may be the signal that triggers the final attack.

Motionless and cramped, I wonder if we will live to see the dawn. The night drags on into what seems an eternity. The sodden bedding lumps and the hard edges of the life preserver push into my back. I must remain immobile, since any movement upsets Sim. My salt-water-soaked shirt needs to be aired, but I can't turn on my side or my knee will poke into Sim's liver or some other part of her anatomy. Anyway, it's better to wait until the sun is up to dry the sores that have formed on my back. I feel like a piece of salami. Sim will chew me out if I move, and the shark will chew me up. Butler, how did you ever get into this predicament?

In the east, pale clouds slowly turning crimson announce the coming of a new day. Gingerly, red skies extend farther north and south until our little world comes to life. How wonderful to be alive and to again witness the vanquishing of darkness by the light of day.

We now have thirteen new hours of hope and possibly of salvation. If the day turns out to be clear, search planes should be flying. Realistically, it may take them a day or two to locate us. Perhaps they've been searching. We've made no contact for eighteen days. On the other hand, there's a lot of ocean out here. If they could focus one of those super spy satellites this way or one with an infrared scanner to pick up the higher temperature of the raft over the surrounding sea . . . dream on, Butler!

As the first warm rays of the newly risen sun strike the raft, we burst out of the cage that has held us prisoners for this longest of nights. We will be more careful today when we drape the sodden bedding over the arches to dry. Several days ago, as we engaged in a game of dominoes, we didn't notice that one end of the cover we put out to dry had dropped into the water. To make it worse, it was Sim's end, the part she bunched up to make a pillow. Sim had to turn the comforter around to place the wet part near our feet. That was one hell of a drill, as was the recrimination that followed. On the positive side, time does fly by as we argue over trivialities, though the constant nagging is working into my marrow.

Sim sounds the alarm. "Whale, a big whale! My God, he's coming our way!"

A gigantic black whale aims directly for the raft, its huge dorsal fin purposefully cutting the water. Thirty feet away it blows, sounds, and we never see it again. I call out, "Hey Sim, didn't you send a donation to the Save the Whales fund?" No answer. I could strangle her. I continue with, "I have a feeling the whale you saved is probably the one that sank *Siboney*." The bastard! This whale could have cut the raft in half in one pass. I should have brought the fiberglass sailing dinghy; it would have provided great backup. As *Siboney* filled with water, I had debated the pros and cons of cutting it loose and bringing it with us. We could now be sailing on the course of our choice and at two or three times our present speed. On the other hand, the savage seas that engulfed us over the past two weeks would have sunk the dinghy. Full of water, it would have created a dangerous pull and could easily have torn our raft. No use rehashing past decisions, Butler. The dinghy is gone, sitting on the bottom.

I can see my Dyer dink still tied to the cabin of *Siboney*, suspended upside down in two miles of water. *Siboney*, sails set, flags flying, embedded in the mud in an unnamed Pacific canyon. If she could jettison her lead keel, she would pop back to the surface. There's no chance of that. The eight new one-inch bronze keel bolts I put in will yield only long after the hull has rotted away.

The lead keel that holds *Siboney* to the bottom kept her upright through the worst of storms. In 1967, caught out in a typhoon off Manila in the Philippines, giant waves broke on *Siboney* and flung her over, mast down. The top of the mast, forty-five feet off the deck, touched the water. A second wave followed suit. *Siboney* bounced back each time, erect, the lead keel doing its job.

Sim breaks into my musings. "Bill, why do the sharks come at night? They petrify me. The fabric on this raft is so thin. I've been looking at it during the day when the raft is low on air and, really, it's nothing. A dull shark tooth could cut through it. What happens if the main air chamber goes? How can we swim with all those sharks around? Oh Lord, help us."

"We'll survive, Sim. The boat cushions will float. The two arches are full of air, and they will keep us up. We float, too. The only heavy item on board is the water pump. We'll be sitting in water, but we won't go down."

"Not go down? May the Lord protect me from your stupid naïveté. If we lose the raft, it's over. We will be swimming. We will die. There's no other way."

"You can give up if you want, but I'll struggle until I draw my last breath. And I know you'll battle all the way as well."

I turn my back on Sim to get away from another needless, endless argument and gaze out the window. Tripletails swim up to the raft. They are so close that I put on my gloves and try to snag one. I touch one, but that's as close as I come. Perhaps I could make a spear, straighten the fishhook, and tie it to the end of the pole. That might work. I put the barb end of the fishhook into the hollow end of the fishing rod and slowly take the bend out of the hook, careful not to break it. The hook is tough, made by Mustad in Denmark. I lash it to the pole with nylon line, and now I have a spear.

The fish must have watched my every move. There isn't one in sight now. I wait. I nap, then look out again. Still no fish. Toward evening, three tripletails approach. I let them close in on the raft; then I raise the harpoon, plunge, and miss.

"Bill, a turtle. This is a big bad one."

That's it. I've got it now. The tripletails follow these large sea turtles. The turtle scratches the bottom of the raft as Sim cries out, "Barnacles!" I get the heavy pole ready, and when the turtle comes up for air, I swing, miss the neck, but hit the shell. The turtle turns and dives.

Sim is right. This turtle has a heavy load of barnacles and a torn shell to boot, either of which could damage the raft. The monster emerges ten feet from the raft, takes a breath, and then paddles lazily alongside until it lifts its ugly head out of the water, looks me straight in the eye, and heads my way. I hit it again, this time on the back of its neck.

I can't help but chuckle. These antediluvian creatures are on the endangered species list, but I have never seen so many turtles in my life. There must be hundreds out here. We see four or five every day. What in the devil do they want with the raft? To make love to it? Seek shelter?

The turtle's eyes remind me of Dracula. Expressionless, dead, round, and black, surrounded by a black circle three inches in diameter, they appear to have a perpetual hangover. The eyes make the turtles look dumb, and dumb they must be. No matter how hard I hit them, they come back for more. I must devise a better method of battling them.

Tonight I close the windows before dark. I can't let Sim see the size of the two sharks that us. They're easily twice as long as the raft. Unexpectedly, she opens the window and looks out. I pray the monsters are not around. "Bill, look at that sunset. We haven't seen one for several days. It's pretty. See, there's a cloud that looks like Mara. Do you see it?" I sit up and look down, not up.

"Yes. It even has her eyes." Mara was our schnauzer. She died two years ago while trying to deliver pups. At that moment, a twelve-foot hammerhead shark circles, its dorsal fin fully out of the water.

"Sim, come on, lie down. Read the psalms."

"In a minute. I want to enjoy the sunset and watch my birds. We've never had this many spend the night with us. I can count over fifty boobies."

I sit back up. There before us swims our monster. I can no longer divert her attention, and I wait for Sim to react.

"Bill, oh my God, there he is! What kind of shark is that? A hammerhead?"

"I, I think so." My game is up.

"It's been with us for a week," says Sim. "It comes every night at this time. It swims around the raft a dozen times and leaves. It probably waits for one of us to fall overboard."

"Do you mean you've seen it and haven't told me?"

"I didn't want to scare you. You have enough problems."

"Sim, baby, I've also seen it for the past week, and I didn't tell you because I didn't want to scare you. That's a laugh. If it hasn't touched us for a week, it probably won't. Let's forget it. Why don't you read?"

Sim reads our evening prayers before night sets in. We have two flashlights and a lantern on the raft. One flashlight, which came with the raft, is fully waterproof and heavy duty. The other flashlight is a cheap one I carried as a spare. The lantern is heavy duty and waterproof. All three work fine, but we use them as little as possible since we have no spare batteries. My entire stock of batteries, neatly packed in ziplock bags, now lies at the bottom of the sea.

At five this morning, we passed our two-week mark on the raft. We missed the big event, sleeping in after our all-night battle with turtles and sharks. I have a new theory: a turtle under the raft keeps the sharks away. Who knows, perhaps we should be gentler to the turtles. Anyway, the night was a drill until three in the morning, when all predators left and we slept a dead man's sleep for a couple of hours, which is as long as the air leak will let us.

Thursday, June 29, dawns clear and bright. Waves are down. The raft traveled little all night, heading in no particular direction. The birds are nowhere in sight. Every other morning when we have awakened, we've enjoyed watching the boobies skim the waves in search of a meal. Two lone boobies fly in the distance. Perhaps the others are out fishing far off and will return tonight. Last night they formed a tight group fifty feet to windward and preened and pecked at one another as they bobbed on the waves, gently paddling with their big blue feet to remain headed into the wind. They have not met in such a large group before. Normally, they form small groups of five or ten. If they are gone for good, where did they go?

The always-present frigate birds remain. Aloft, a young bird follows its mother. Both soar with their giant wings outstretched and head into the breeze without perceptible motion. The larger frigate collapses its wings and drops like a bomb. The smaller one remains motionless high above the raft. The frigate plummets a hundred feet in seconds. A dozen feet above the ocean, it opens its wings, slows, and turns, still at high speed, in pursuit of a booby. The booby spots the frigate bird and, squawking loudly, struggles to escape.

An aerial pursuit—Sim calls it a ballet—ensues. We have not witnessed before such speed and mastery of flight. The booby uses its high speed and maneuverability to escape. The frigate, wings now fully extended, stays on the booby's tail. The frigate's attack is merciless. The booby's desperate squawks drown out all other sounds. It's exactly what the frigate bird waits to hear, for the pitch of the squawk tells the frigate if the booby has a fish in its crop. This booby has a muffled squawk, which confirms the crop is full. The frigate gives the booby no respite and lives up to its other name, the man-o'-war bird.

We've watched frigate birds catch fish honestly. From way up high, they drop to the surface and run at high speed over the waves to scoop up flying fish and small school fish that venture too close to the surface. But they do appear to get special delight out of harassing boobies. This frigate chases the booby until it regurgitates its catch, the fish falling freely toward the sea. The frigate, in a swift maneuver, swoops the carcass out of the air, flaps its wings, and heads up to its young. After a casual climb, mother feeds baby, much like in-flight airplane refueling. Soaring at mom's wingtip, the youngster avidly nibbles every handout.

While we enjoy the morning aerobatic show, the skies cloud. The western horizon is black, a portent of another heavy storm. The current is moderate and the raft barely swings. I try to fish, without success. I should have grabbed a bird while they were still around, except Sim would have outsquawked any booby. We make water, eat our cracker, then nap.

Minutes later, a flash of lightning is followed by a long, growling roll of thunder. "Eleven seconds," Sim calls. Again, we button up the window against the canopy. Isolated raindrops turn quickly into a major downpour. This squall doesn't have the high wind gusts of the last one. Heavy rain falls until midmorning. Sharks stay away throughout the shower. Rain, rain, please don't go away.

Sim spots it first. "Bill, the raft has turned around."

We remain motionless. The horizon spins in a full circle. I open one side of my window, and water drips in as I poke my head into the rain. A huge green sea turtle flaps lazily, one flipper caught in the boarding ladder. The pounding by the sharks loosened the nylon mesh boarding ladder from where I'd tied it. I grab the tangled flipper, careful to stay clear of the gaping, viselike jaws, and unwrap the webbing. The ladder has caused more problems than it's worth, yet should either of us land in the water after a rollover, we might need it to get back into the raft in a hurry. On the other hand, we've been in several major storms and the raft has always proven stable; the ladder is really not worth the trouble, so I take the knife out of the pail and cut it away. That's the end of that problem, unless of course, we end up going for a swim. If I were to reduce our situation mathematically, how many unknowns would we have, a zillion? Way too many. The answer is not in mathematics but with a higher authority.

Raindrops filter in through the canopy, but wrapped inside our comforter, we are dry and snug. And sharks don't attack while it pours, so let it rain. Bump. Sim lowers the window, sticks her head out, gets soaked, and sees nothing. The turtle is under the raft. We're bumped a dozen times, gently, never in the same place. Sim fumes as she shakes her head like a dog coming in from the rain, then explodes:

"I can't take it any longer! I'm fed up with turtles, with sharks, with the situation, and most of all with you, Butler. It's all your fault. I hate you. I could strangle you. And don't laugh, you wretch. You look awful with your beard. I hate beards, I hate turtles, I hate sharks, and I hate you! DO YOU HEAR ME? HELP! HELP! SOMEBODY HELP!"

I cringe as she screams out the window. Every mako and hammerhead shark within miles will soon home in on us. She continues. "I hate this raft; it's too small, too slow. It's unbearable torture. Why, oh why, did you have to be such a scrooge and buy the cheapest, smallest raft on the market? I saw so many good rafts at the boat shows we went to, but no, you miserable cheapskate, you are always going for the bargains. What is all that money you left in the bank going to buy you now? You must want to take it with you! I'm going to die, but you will die with me, you horrible bitch!"

I break in. "Sim, in English, women are bitches. Men are bastards."

She screams right back, "You're still a horrible bitch, you bastard!"

She runs out of breath and I grab at the chance. "You forget you couldn't even lift this raft when we were sinking. This one is only fifty-five pounds. How would you have handled a hundred-pound raft?"

"You could have helped, you nitwit. We would have such a better chance to survive." She continues, and I try to tune her out. Some of her points are indisputable, but others are best left lost in the Pacific. The word *Pacific* is such a misnomer. It doesn't even rhyme with *sinking, whales, sharks, turtles,* or *pissed-off wife.*

Sim and the rain ease up in the late afternoon. The turtle swims on. Sharks return. I bonk a couple and get sprinkled in the process. Several booby birds are back. One perches on the canopy. It's such a terrible night that we decide to let it sleep with us. We huddle together, angry words forgotten. Honestly, when it comes to basics, we only have each other. It's us against all the predators in the Pacific Ocean. Who will win? And what are the odds?

There's a new leak in the overhead canopy. Sim puts a can under it and catches many of the drops. When I change positions, I turn it over and it spills. Sim grumbles and sponges what she can out of the bilge. Nothing is dry any longer—that is, except for me. A good shot of scotch would work wonders right now.

As night falls, we pray. Sim reads early, as the heavy overcast will hasten night. The reading soothes my mind and body and helps ease the transition from daylight, where we can see and fend off our predators, to darkness, when deadly invisible forms intent on our destruction surround us on all sides. We are two souls adrift in a watery hell, lost to the world in every sense imaginable.

Finished reading, Sim muses, "What a shame, Bill, that we didn't get the missal Dick Lloyd gave us at our going-away dock party. It would be a blessing to have it now. I'm ashamed we never opened it on the trip out from Miami. We were always so busy. His gift meant so much to me. I wish we had saved it. I never want to be so busy ever again that I have no time for God."

"Yes, I know. I didn't see the missal in your locker, nor did I see the bullets."

"That's a great association, Butler, missal and bullets. Oh Lord, give me patience with this man. Besides, sixteen days are enough punishment. Sharks, turtles, thunder, lightning, high waves, rain, and you, Butler. All at the same time. And I do not know which one is worse. Often, Butler, you are even more despicable than the sharks. Enough is enough, Lord. Save me; do something. Do you hear me? I WANT TO BE SAVED! NOW!"

"I can't believe what I'm hearing. You presume to tell God how to run His shop? He will decide when and how He will save us. You can bully me, but be careful how you handle the Main Man."

"I hope it's soon. I can't take any more of this. Help me, HELP ME! PLEASE!"

I tighten my hold on Sim's hand, and she begins to cry. I fall asleep to the murmur of her prayers.

Sim jolts me awake and calls out, "Two turtles this time. And they are doing it. The male is chasing the female. Oh, Bill. They're back under the raft."

"Relax, Sim. They're only doing what comes naturally. Besides they're endangered. They need all the babies they can make."

"Endangered? We're endangered! At least they are in their element. Get out of here, you perverts."

Sim jolts each of the turtles and off they swim, the female trying desperately to escape from the faster-swimming male. There is no question what's on the male's mind. But what's her excuse? A headache?

Heavy rains, pushed by a strong wind out of the west, force us to lock ourselves in once again. The current must be light, as the raft swings wildly. Rain seeps in through the canopy. We use the pole to push the canopy up like a tent. Rainwater rolls off, and less leaks in. I don't know why, but the canopy is disintegrating. The blue water-proofing on the inside has cracked and begun to peel and fall off.

Even the birds aren't airborne. One booby spent the entire night perched on the canopy. It defended its space from intruding birds with loud squawks. With all this rain, I don't understand the difference. They're soaked no matter what. Three boobies paddle nearby. But the large group has never returned. Where did they go? To Isla de Cocos? I have been looking for signs of Cocos to the north, but could it lie to the south? The best I can recall is that it lies around 90 degrees West. Whether it's 5 or 7 or 10 degrees North is beyond me. We sank at 5.5 degrees North. In two weeks adrift, we have been pushed perhaps a hundred miles to the north, which puts us near 7 degrees North. The current has propelled us steadily east at fifteen to twenty miles a day, or an average of a hundred to a hundred and twenty miles a week. That puts us near 95 degrees West, still a long way to Cocos. The birds most probably flew off to the Galápagos, now three-hundred-plus miles to the south. How long would it take them to get there? Ten hours, or maybe fifteen?

Between rain showers, we make three liters of water. Why didn't the people who made the raft think of putting a hole in the middle of the canopy with a small rubber funnel to catch rainwater? When I try, most of the water either drips into the raft or misses the bottle, or the bottle slips out of my hand and spills. I get soaked, our bedding gets even wetter, Sim gets out of joint, and we end up, after an hour, with less than half a cup of water. Unless it really pours down, I catch nothing but drops. From now on, I'll rely on the watermaker. Sim agrees. After all, it cost a bundle, and I risked my life to grab it from the sinking *Siboney*.

The lovers are back at it under the raft. She hides between the ballast bags. He chases after her, probably whispering sweet nothings. She strains to escape.

"Hell, Sim, I can hear that female turtle now . . . listen . . . she's repeating over and over, 'Not now honey, later. I'm not in the mood. I have a horrible headache.' . . . or did she also make a promise?"

Sim wallops me with the paddle.

A full morning of turtle foreplay wears us down. First they are under the raft, then out fifty feet, then back under, then around, then out, later back. When they draw near, Sim defends us. When the orgy moves on to other waters, the sharks return to slap the raft without mercy. I beat some off, but more come. More than twenty sharks circle ten feet under the raft. One or two surface for a shot at the raft. I hit one on the right and another from straight on. A third shoots out from under the raft. I land dozens of direct hits. Then rain starts up again, and I close up our home and rest. Is there anything out here except sharks, turtles, and rain? I make a mental note never to venture out into this part of the Pacific again. Of course, first we have to be saved.

Rain has fallen steadily for the past two days. The increasingly leaky roof adds to our misery. The outside coloring of the raft has gone from bright orange to pale orange and now to light yellow. The miserable weather depresses us. We don't feel like playing dominoes or word games or even talking, and remain ensconced in our inner thoughts.

Sim breaks the silence. "Bill, do you realize that, if we disappear, nobody will know how we died and what happened to the boat? They'll never know that we made it this long, only to die stupidly because no one searched for us."

"I've been thinking the same."

Sim continues. "Three weeks have gone by since our last call. If someone were going to look for us, it would have happened by now. We've had some clear days, enough chance for an air search."

"We must think of how to signal. We must get a message through. Perhaps a bottle . . ."

"A bottle? Who would ever find it?" She pauses, then explodes with enthusiasm. "That's wild. It's great; let's do it."

She continues, "Let's at least give it some thought. We must do something. My mother will die if we disappear. We are now almost forty days out of Panama. In another two weeks, we are due in Hawaii. Ten days after that, we will be truly behind schedule. People will surely launch a search. If they do, it'll be closer to the Hawaiian Islands, not here. I'm sure my mother knows we are in danger. She knew there was danger even before we left. Why, oh why, didn't I listen to her? My children will never know what happened to me. Do you know how difficult it is to go through life not knowing what happened to a loved one who disappears without a trace?"

I've never seen Sim so sad. I agree. "That's why we must send out a message of some kind."

Sim's despair builds. "And how will my babies ever get along if I disappear? Will the bank continue sending them money? Will the life insurance pay them? Meanwhile, what are they going to do? It may take years before they see a cent. And my mother, how is she going to survive without knowing about me? How? How?"

"Ease up, Sim, before you blow a fuse. Your babies are eighteen and twenty-six and need to start looking out for themselves. I left instructions at the bank to take care of your sons. The instructions stand until we return."

"I really don't understand you. You act so relaxed."

"And I don't understand what good it's going to do to get all worked up. There's nothing we can do about anything onshore. If we never show up, the bank will certainly go to court to declare us dead. I have no idea how the laws of Florida treat people who disappear. It could be seven years before they can settle the estate. Meanwhile, the bank will disburse money to our dependents per my instructions and their best judgment as to real need."

Sim continues. "How will they pay the mortgage on the house? Will the mortgage insurance pay if we're not found? They'll probably lose the house to the bank. Oh my God, why is everything so complicated? Why can't we die in peace and without worries?"

We hash the same subjects around for another hour until I suggest, "Why don't you read? It's almost dark." A semblance of peace settles over the raft, but Sim's apprehensions are far from over. I can almost read her mind, and I can feel new fears build in her stubborn head.

The easterly current picks up again after sunset. The raft moves steadily after swinging aimlessly all day. The wind is out of the southwest. Rain continues as we doze.

Simonne, with night upon us, speaks quietly in her corner of the raft, buried under the comforter.

"When are we going to see the sun, to be dry and warm again? Will someone find us? When will God have mercy on us? When is He going to take us to safety, to our children, to our old life? Will we have an old life to go back to? Will this experience change us? If so, how? God will become the key to our lives. We have learned to pray again. We have cleansed our souls before God. We've spoken candidly to each other for the first time in years. We try not to make future plans. How can we plan in these conditions? Death is our constant companion. Life as we knew it a few months ago, on land or on *Siboney*, is but a sweet dream. Whatever happens, we have made peace with each other and with ourselves. We ask God to forgive our sins, to accept our deep-felt repentance, and we accept His will. We place our hope in His merciful heart."

I snooze away.

ABOARD THE RAFT
LAST CHANCE
0800 TUESDAY • JULY 4, 1989 • DAY 20

THIS HAS BEEN the darkest, most dismal, and most horrid night so far. Rain fell in sheets, and sharks smashed the raft nonstop, tossing my shark-rain thesis into the deep. Heavier rain started shortly after midnight. It soaked us, our bedding, and everything in the raft not wrapped in plastic. Water leaked through the canopy in torrents. We covered up with the striped comforter and spread the sailbag over it to divert part of the deluge. The trash bag sits over the sailbag to funnel much of the rainwater into the bilge, which Sim periodically empties with the sponge.

At two this morning, a shark pounded the raft so violently and with such savage intensity that we were positive our end was close at hand. At twice the speed of the others, this shark darted fiercely from one side of the raft to the other much faster than I could follow. A phosphorescent wake followed its every turn, yet whenever I plunged at where I thought it would be, I failed to connect. How much more pounding can the raft take before it's holed and sinks?

Not one of my antishark ploys worked. Time and time again, I plunged the fishing rod ahead of the ghostly illumined shape hurtling toward the raft. I never even came near to touching the beast. Ten, twenty, thirty violent blows made the raft spin like a top. This shark seemed intent on destroying our little vessel. Petrified with fear, unable to deter the onslaught, we prayed as never before. Sim clutched her St. Michael medal throughout the attack and prayed so loudly at one point that I had to quiet her lest the shark pick up her vibrations and come after us.

Never have these two castaways welcomed the dirty-gray dawn more devoutly than on this Tuesday. As though in pity for our plight, the wind wanes as the sun begins its climb, hidden behind thick masses of clouds. Sim's eyes remain closed. Rosary between her hands, she has to be deep in prayer. I have no idea at what time I slept, but I have awakened to a marvelous surprise! A blue sky with a sprinkling of white clouds lifts my spirit out of its soggy low. And today is the Fourth of July. What is the gang doing back home? Picnics? Fireworks? Parades? And here we are, deep in the Pacific Ocean, alone, forgotten, and lost. We are surely going to die. What is the U.S. Coast Guard doing today? Is anyone thinking of us? That we might be lost? In danger?

It's Tuesday, our twentieth day on the raft. Eighteen days have passed since we have seen a sign of human life. We desperately need bait to start fishing. I'll grab one of Sim's birds if it comes within reach. We have lost a lot of weight. Sim is trim. So far, we have been burning excess fat. Before long, we will start losing essential muscle and, even worse, energy. Lethargy scares me. What if I am unable to make water or become too weak to fish?

During the past two weeks, I have tried to catch a fish with absolutely no luck. After my harpoon idea failed, afraid it would slice through the raft, I bent the hook back into its original shape and connected it to the line at the end of the fishing rod. I have used everything imaginable for bait: paper, crackers, mussels. Nothing worked.

Sim notices I'm awake. "What a horrible night. I thought our time had come. In my prayers, I prepared to die. I was sure we would not see daylight." I can only agree, for I too had my doubts about the outcome of last night's vicious attacks. How can this raft withstand such punishment? How much more can it take?

On the positive side, the current is strong. I can feel it. The raft jerks along, inches at a time, on its relentless set toward shore. I have not the slightest doubt about our course. And the sky is blue. Hope is blue, hope in the sky. A few days of decent weather would do wonders for our spirits. We lunch on a cracker with a touch of peanut butter. Three raisins make dessert. I savor each as I would an ice cream bar.

Sim watches me eat. "We have some twenty crackers left. In three days we'll be out of food. You've lost a lot of weight. I'm getting to like your beard. You have a full meal caught in it. There, let me clean it."

"Nooo! Leave my beard alone! I may need a snack in the middle of the night. I'll be fishing soon, but I warn you, I may have to catch a bird. The key to catching the first fish is bait. We'll wait another day but no longer. The longer we wait, the weaker we become. It's risky if we get too weak, and we're nearly at that point now." The truth is that I don't feel that hungry any longer, which is a worse sign than hunger.

Sim is serious. "I'm sure something will come our way. Let's wait a while. I don't want you to hurt one of my birds. Did you see, Pretty Boy is back? This morning he perched next to the raft and looked at me with those big yellow eyes. He is trusting and so sweet. He even pecked at my hand. Please think of something else for bait. Don't touch my birds."

Sim has found so much solace with her flock of birds. She continues, "If you kill one, all the others will leave. I can't stand the loneliness. This wretched emptiness. The birds are my only company and entertainment. The birds are God sent. They are my friends, and Pretty Boy is so perfect and so special. My own little guardian angel in disguise. You will leave them alone, won't you, Bill?"

She is so earnest, yet she knows that if nothing else comes our way, she'll have to look the other way while I wring one of their beautiful necks. Our priority is survival, and to survive, we must stay strong and healthy even if it means I must kill a bird.

Our sunny day drags along. We play a half-hearted game of dominoes until I'm called away to do battle with a dozen or more sharks. I then beat off the same two turtles, who are still at it. How long do these dumb turtles mate? They've been going for a week. "OK, fellows, enough. Beat it!" I scream as I beat the water with my pole.

How do these monsters find our noiseless, minuscule raft in this vast ocean? We have drifted more than three hundred miles in the past eighteen days. The turtles and sharks always find us. What kind of homing signal do we emit? Is it my and Sim's eternal bickering? Or their insane curiosity? Do they realize there's something edible aboard?

Sim, who has been watching the water, says, "Bill, have you noticed there is an oil slick around the raft?"

"Yes, there is one right now. What's your point?"

"It has something to do with the arrival of the sharks. In the morning, after the first few slaps with their tail, the slick suddenly appears. It's not the raft. And I've looked carefully. We haven't floated into anything oily. The sharks must secrete it, like tomcats."

I have seen it too, and frankly I'm inclined to believe sharks, like tomcats, instinctively mark their territory. What else could they be doing with this belly-up display and whacking of the tail?

When the sharks leave, Sim hands me the watermaker. I drop the prefilter into the water a foot under the raft, and with the body of the machine hooked under my right armpit, I pump the twenty-inch handle with my right hand. In this way, I rest one arm while the other works. I do twenty strokes with my right hand and ten with my left. When I tire, I hand the machine over to Sim. She makes water in a sitting position. She takes the handle in her left hand and holds the body of the machine against her bent knees. Sim is one of those lefties forced at school into becoming a righty and still suffers from it. Often—such as in traffic—she has to stop and think where right or left is. It drives me crazy.

We ignore the constant slap of sharks on the side of the raft, as these are the smaller ones that reside under the raft. Suddenly, the saltwater filter jerks and I heave it out of the water. Shark teeth have scratched the black tube. We stop for a few minutes, then continue, ready to haul the filter up at any moment. In forty-five minutes, we have two liters of clear, fresh drinking water. The Evian bottles have ridges, about an inch apart, which help us measure our progress. We each do three ridges per turn. Two turns each and a bottle is full.

I chuckle quietly when I think of a couple of nights ago. In one of our pitch-black, rough, rainy Pacific specials, Sim had started to pee when I heard a loud oath in French. The can had been bottom up and she had wet her bed. I played the deep sleeper to stay out of that one.

We celebrate the Fourth of July with a quarter can of juice, one half of a cookie, and three drops of Hennessy each. We sing the "Star Spangled Banner" and follow it with "America, the Beautiful." When we sing "from sea to shining sea," anguish overwhelms us with such force that tears drown out our little celebration. The party ends prematurely.

Our thoughts go to shore and to how each of our family members is celebrating the day. Are they watching fireworks at Miami's Bayfront Park? The greatest Fourth of July we ever experienced was in 1986, aboard *Siboney*, in New York Harbor. We sailed from Miami to Cape May, New Jersey, in nine days, stopped a few days in Atlantic City, then motored up to Sandy Hook. On July 3, we took *Siboney* through the Narrows, into New York Harbor, and to an anchorage off Ellis Island. With thousands of other boats, we witnessed one of the most incredible two-day shows the harbor has ever seen.

While reminiscing with Sim, I have been scratching a large number twenty on a full sheet of paper. Sim looks over, but I manage to hide my artwork. She burns with curiosity.

At last, I'm ready. "Sim, make yourself pretty; it's picture-taking time. This is day twenty and also the Fourth of July. A picture for posterity."

"Posterity. Do you really think there's any posterity for us? This is the end of the road."

"Bull. Hand me the camera." Enclosed in a ziplock bag, my Minolta has so far remained dry. I find a place for it on the opposite air chamber. We settle on a pose. I spring the timer as Sim holds the page with the twenty on it in front of her bare bosom. The camera flashes. Our raft-bound Fourth of July celebration is complete, and I settle down for a nap.

Sim startles me out of dreamland with a gentle nudge. She whispers excitedly, "A turtle. Just the right size. There."

I lift myself up. She's right. A turtle with a shiny, light-brown carapace, about twenty inches in diameter, swims toward the raft. We don't make a move, so as not to spook it. While it approaches, I thread the fishing cord through the eye on the rod. At the end of the cord, I make a noose.

As the turtle comes alongside, Sim grabs a flipper, then holds it firmly by its shell. I lean over her to put the noose around the turtle's neck and draw it up tight as Sim pulls the turtle out of the water. Flippers flail and its jaws reach out at Sim. She passes the flapping turtle through the raft and drops it in the water on my side. This is the first small turtle we have seen, and the break we need to survive. Our prayers have been answered.

All four flippers thrash as the turtle struggles fiercely for its life. I push the pole deep into the water to keep its claws from damaging the raft. The slightest mistake on our part could make the difference between food and hunger. Worse yet, between life and death. As I wait for the turtle to die, I look up.

Skies are clear blue. A perfect day for a parade. It's now around three. The barbecue back home is going. Hamburgers, sweet corn, apple pie. But we'll have our own feast. Our first fresh food in twenty days. God has provided. He must intend to save us.

Thirty minutes pass, and the turtle continues to struggle violently. With an inexplicable force, it twists and snaps the pole in three pieces. I manage to catch one of the pieces and hang onto the line. Killing it is going to be harder than I thought.

"Sim, quick! Hold the turtle while I get the other pole ready."

Simonne leans over me and holds the animal. I prepare the larger pole. As Simonne holds the wildly tossing turtle, I put the other end of the cord through the eye on the larger pole, make another noose, and put it around the turtle's neck. I draw the cord up tight and push the turtle down. I've got it this time.

Another half an hour passes. The turtle has been inert for ten minutes. It appears to be dead. But the instant I loosen my grip on it, it thrashes madly and tries to escape. I know turtles don't drown easily, but I thought an hour should do it.

We are both tired, not to mention hungry. Funny, we have spent three days with almost no food and we were not all that hungry. Now, with food at hand, we can't wait. It's time to cut this exercise short.

"Sim, let's bring it on board."

"Are you sure? It's still alive."

"Put the sailbag on my lap. I'll lift it up and put it upside down on top of the sailbag. You hold the line around its neck taut. Stay away from the beak. Cover its flippers with the bag. Ready?"

I flip the turtle onto my lap. It struggles wildly for air and life. It must weigh all of twenty pounds. Sim holds the bucket with one hand and the line around the turtle's neck with the other. I lift the turtle over the bucket with one hand. Claws at the end of its flippers flail wildly. I reach for the knife and saw away at its throat.

The turtle jerks and exhales air-filled blood with a gush followed by a long gurgle. Blood sprays the inside of the raft. A whistling sputter surges from its windpipe. Sim flinches but holds the turtle firmly. Strength ebbs from our prey as its blood drips into the bucket. The intensity of its struggle lessens. Its laborious breathing weakens. A spasm shakes the entire shell, and it dies.

I wanted to save Sim from this mess by drowning the turtle, but if we ever catch another one, we'll cut its throat right off. It's obvious now that turtles don't drown or asphyxiate easily. One of the world's more primitive animals, they've got to be tough to have survived through the ages.

Sim calls out, "Bill, watch out! Look, near the tail. What are those?"

"Remoras!" I hadn't noticed two three-inch, black, eel-like remoras fastened to the carapace near the turtle's tail. At the precise second when the turtle died, the remoras released their hold and wiggled free. They search for something alive to attach to with the suction device on top of their head.

"Quick, hand me the can!" I call out as the remoras slither on my lap in search of flesh. I push them into the can with the knife. "I'll keep them for bait." They squirm out of the can and head for Sim. She screams.

"Get rid of them! They'll grab onto one of us." I scoop them back into the can and throw them over the side.

Head down, the turtle remains over the bucket. Blood drains as Sim and I catch our breath and recover. I have never killed a turtle before. In fact, I've never seen a turtle butchered. General Electric stationed me at the naval base in Key West, Florida, in 1952, on an assignment testing torpedoes. Most of the local eateries advertised turtle burgers. They were good, but that's as close as I've ever been to a dead turtle.

When blood no longer drips out of its slashed neck, I turn the turtle bottom up on my lap. I saw through the soft bottom carapace, lift one half of the shell, and cut away under it. I saw around the outside edges of both halves, lift away the entire bottom shell, and am met with a horrible-looking array of vivid green, orange, blue, and red organs. The turtle is nothing but intestines and lungs! There is nothing to eat.

Baffled, I question, "Sim, where's the meat? All I see looks terrible."

Sim once helped her brother catch and clean turtles in the Mediterranean. She leans over to me and says, "Here. Try cutting there in the muscle that moves the flippers."

I follow Sim's finger and find dark-pink meat, not unlike the dark meat of raw turkey. I slice off a piece and hand it to Sim.

"Ladies first." She takes the piece with hesitant fingers, looks it over with a skeptical expression, shrugs, and puts the piece into her mouth. I wait for her reaction. Her face explodes in delight. "Delicious," she says, turtle blood on her lips.

"Really? Let me try." I bite down. It has the texture of rabbit. Mmmm! I can't believe it. It's so good. It has a sweet taste, not fishy at all.

We slice more pieces and eat without restraint. The meat is tender and tasty. Our hunger is such that we cannot stop. We slice and eat until we can eat no more. We rest, then eat more. I keep the last few pieces for bait. One of the two empty cans becomes the bait can. The other can is still the pee-pee pot.

Sim considers keeping the shell, but it's so heavy, and I know in this heat it will soon stink. How do we dispose of the shell and blood without arousing the shark population? I look into a clear, ripple-free sea for sharks. There are none around. Strange.

I'll dump the shell and the blood and then we'll row downwind as fast as we can. I look again for sharks, then ease the shell over the side to windward without a splash. It sinks like a rock. I slowly pour out the blood and pieces of turtle from the bucket so as not to splash the raft. I give the bucket a quick wash and signal Sim to start rowing.

We row steadily for fifteen minutes. We are exhausted but content. I look back to make sure no monster of the deep follows our trail. Our undersea world teems with life. All is clear. We put away the oars and drift on. We feel a sense of pride and achievement. We made it. We have taken a major step in our pursuit of survival. We now have bait.

We relax after all the excitement to enjoy the beauty of the day. The day is so clear, the sea so calm. It's great to be alive. The hot sun bores in on us. It really feels like the Fourth of July. We open the canopy. The sun and breeze will remove the dampness from our covers and clothing. Sim sponges the turtle blood from the arches and canopy. With our appetite satiated, we nap.

We awaken to a rare Pacific sunset, a perfect end to a spectacular day. The turtle not only has nourished our bodies but has lifted our spirits. With bait, we can fish. I can hardly wait to begin.

I update the log with some basic arithmetic in my navigation workbook. Tomorrow we will pass the five-hundred-hour mark aboard our raft. If we have drifted at one knot, we will have traveled five hundred miles. That's too fast. At half a knot, we would have traveled two hundred and fifty miles. I am confident we've done better, particularly in the storms when each wave pushed us ten or more feet. We're somewhere between the two. I show my plot to Sim, who graciously agrees.

My best guess is that we've moved at an average of three-quarters of a knot. In five hundred hours, our run comes out to three hundred and seventy-five miles. This puts us seven hundred and fifty miles from the Central American coast, or another thousand hours if we maintain our speed. That's forty more days. But we're sure to be found by a freighter or a search party before then. Someone, somewhere, right now, must be out looking for us.

Outlined by the last embers of a dying sun, a huge hammerhead shark circles the raft. Its dorsal fin cuts the water a raft length from the boat. We lie quietly until darkness is complete and we can see the predator no more. No doubt it and others still circle the raft long into the night. We close the windows at sunset lest these monsters of the deep recognize a movement or receive an instinctive signal to attack. The raft is so fragile that their slightest strike would mean death.

Help has to be on the way. Today was a perfect day for an air search. Seas were calm, skies clear. Where is everybody? We fully expected to hear the welcoming hum of engines. But then, today is a holiday, one of the Coast Guard's busiest days. What form will our rescue take? But will they search this far from the United States? Never!

Our positive feelings are cut short by a rough scrape followed by an abrupt smash to the raft. The raft spins. Another blow follows. Did the turtle blood lead them to us? How much more punishment can this raft take?

I fight back by punching at them with the pole, for surely the sharks will destroy the raft in short order if we allow them to batter it at will. The savage attacks ebb after a couple of hours, and I look out to one of our most beautiful nights adrift. The sea is a mass of phosphorescence. Uncountable stars twinkle and flicker in the dark velvet dome of the sky. They appear to be so close. As Sim reaches out to touch them, they bring back thoughts of her childhood, which propels her into a whispered monologue.

"We were in Opio, in the south of France, in the days following the war. We would spread old blankets on the garden in front of the old farmhouse and stretch out close to one another to gaze at the stars.

"We looked in wonder at the heavens, sprinkled with so many millions of stars. There were as many and as near as tonight. My grandfather, a man of deep faith, became pensive and then said, 'On nights like this, if you watch the stars long enough, your soul melts with the universe, and you'll see the face of God.' All of us children believed him. On other nights, he would point out the stars and planets and call them by name. We made friends with them.

"We got to know Orion with Betelgeuse and Riga, the Dippers and the bear around them. Sirius and the planets became our companions. Their names danced in our heads. We marveled equally at my grandfather's knowledge and at the mysteries of the universe.

"And after much soaring among the star-studded universe, we would come back exhausted, to fall asleep cuddled up near my grandparents. The smells of jasmine and fresh-cut grass and the heavy fragrance of our beloved fig tree, heavy with fruit nearby, surrounded us."

Sim's reminiscing tapers off when the clouds obscure her stars. Since dusk, the wind and current have pushed us eastward, but now we're starting to lose both current and wind. The raft swings and heads more southerly. Soon, light rain lulls Sim to sleep. I continue to ponder.

Is it possible that not one of our loved ones wonders where we are and what has happened to us? If we die—and death is never more than seconds away—nobody will know how or where we died. They will guess and wonder about us for years to come, yet none will know the full story.

It is obvious that my Mayday messages did not get through. The

EPIRB signals weren't picked up either. Our children will never know how we met our fate. What can we do? Long after three A.M., I sleep fitfully.

The night passes endlessly, as so many other nights have passed. Hours mean nothing. Minutes are the real measure. Each night becomes seven hundred minutes of terror. Each minute a lifetime at the edge of death. I don't toss or turn seven hundred times during the night, but I'm sure I come close.

When I open my eyes, Sim smiles. She says, "I'm going to give you the morning news with your breakfast. Sometimes I don't understand why we want to go back to our crazy world. There was a big shootout in Caracas between labor and the government. Carlos Andres Perez called out the troops and is killing people in the streets. Gromyko died, and Bush is calling for the Soviets to get out of Poland. Your buddy Reagan got thrown off a horse, and Gorbachev is in Paris. Everyone is calling him Gorby. '*Vive* Gorby!' they cry. Of all the stupid things."

"Spare me the details," I answer. "I'll have another cup of coffee and a doughnut. You're not wearing out the batteries, are you?" What a difference that little radio makes. I'm glad Sim spotted it before it floated away or sank in the cabin. Why didn't I grab the two ziplock bags full of batteries that were under the bunk? She could have listened all night every night.

"No. I listen only five or ten minutes at a time. It's so consoling. I thought about home this morning. If we make it back, I want to make some changes in the house. On the other hand, the house may have sold. After all, it's been on the market more than four months. Well, whatever. It would be a blessing if it hasn't sold."

She's right. Now that we have lost the boat, where will we go if we get back and find the house sold? We would be homeless. But then, Cris would never sell the house without his mother's OK. All we can do is hope for the best.

Are any of our children or friends concerned? They've heard not a word from us for twenty-five days. Could they find us if they searched? This ocean is immense. Where would they start? Of course, nobody knows that the boat sank. They probably think our radio broke. No one at home, neither our family nor our friends, can possibly imagine the worst. They are probably thinking that the wind has been contrary or that lack of wind has us becalmed. Not one of them would conclude that *Siboney* sank and that we are adrift.

The time has arrived to test my fishing skills. My dolphin hook is three inches long and almost an inch wide. I position the yellow plastic skirt on the leader, tie the leader to the heavy parachute cord supplied with the raft, then feed the cord through the eye at the end of the pole.

I put a piece of turtle meat on the hook and then cast. The line jerks and pulls tight. A tripletail shoots under the raft. I keep pressure on the line until Sim spreads the sailbag over my lap and the raft's air chamber. I pull the fish within three feet of the end of the pole, heave, and the fish is on board and in the bucket. Sim throws a cushion on it. We look at each other, hug, cry, and laugh, amazed. We did it! Our first fish has been caught and boarded.

Wow, that was easy. Maybe we are going to live after all. If only we didn't have the sharks to worry about, we might have an even chance. The fish struggles and almost escapes from the bucket. Sim puts all her weight on the cushion. We are so happy that we can't stop crying.

When we lift the cushion many minutes later, the fish flops out, the sharp spines along its dorsal fin barely missing the air chamber. The fish is as slippery as an eel. We struggle and catch it before it perforates the raft, and shove it back into the bucket. A long hour later, the tripletail is at last dead. I put it on top of the camcorder case and move the plastic lid to my lap. Its three-quarter-inch lip keeps the blood and scales from running into my crotch and the bedding beneath. I'm ready to fillet our catch. Sim prays in French, giving thanks to the Lord for His mercy.

The dorsal and anal fins of the fish are as large as its tail—thus its name, "tripletail." I put one of our oars under the camcorder case top to stiffen it and then cut along its dorsal fin. I free one fillet and run the knife along the skin to remove it. The meat is white and firm. I hand Sim the first piece. I eagerly eat the second.

The taste is terrific. We gobble down each piece as quickly as I fillet it. We are hungry, yet one fillet fills us, so we keep the other for supper. As I am ready to throw the carcass over, a shark whacks the raft. I hit one with the pole as it comes around the end of the raft and bonk another as it swims straight in. In the distance, a turtle lifts its head out of the water to breathe. Will these monsters ever leave us in peace?

I enjoyed my fishing interlude. It gives me a sense of accomplishment. I am the provider. With a little help from above, I will sustain my life and Sim's.

The log entries have become more succinct. Will anyone ever read them? We are alone. The odds for survival are slim, yet I believe in keeping tradition alive and well. To the very end, I will keep up my entries into the log. We will also maintain a semblance of decorum. We brush our teeth, comb our hair, and, of course, partake in the daily happy hour.

And now it is happy hour and time to celebrate. Today is special. July 5 is Independence Day in two countries we love, Venezuela and the Bahamas. We first sing the Venezuelan national anthem, "Gloria al Bravo Pueblo." We enjoyed many good moments in that beautiful country. *Siboney* sailed nine years through most of the Caribbean with the Venezuelan flag flying proudly from its stern. And Venezuela is where I met Simonne.

Together with my sons, we often celebrated July 4 and 5 off Green Turtle Cay in the Bahamas. No Independence Day celebration is complete on Green Turtle Cay without a sip of ale at Miss Emily's. How far are we now from Green Turtle Cay and Miss Emily's? Oh, to be granted but a few minutes of the past.

We pop open a bottle of Perrier after we savor two drops of brandy. The Perrier bottles have been high on our list of expendable items because of their high weight-to-content ratio. We finish the leftover tripletail fillet and tidy up. At last light, Simonne reads one of my favorite stories.

> *One night a man had a dream. He dreamed he was walking along the beach with the Lord. Across the sky flashed scenes from his life. For each scene, he noticed two sets of footprints in the sand; one belonging to him and one to the Lord.*
>
> *When the last scene of his life flashed before him, he*

looked back at the footprints in the sand. He noticed that many times along the path of his life there was only one set of footprints. He also noticed that it happened at the very lowest and saddest times in his life.

This really bothered him and he questioned the Lord about it. "Lord, you said that once I decided to follow you, you'd walk with me all the way. But I have noticed that during the most troublesome times in my life, there is one set of footprints. I don't understand why when I needed you most you would leave me."

The Lord replied, "My precious, precious child. I love you and I would never leave you. During your times of trial and suffering, when you see only one set of footprints, it was then that I carried you."

As more days pass, I get the feeling that someone is caring and carrying us along during our most critical moments.

Last Chance has held a steady southeast course all afternoon. Dark clouds blanket the sky as night approaches. The wind increases and seas build. We make good progress, probably close to a knot. All my dead reckoning is pure guesswork, and only if we make it to shore or get picked up will I ever know if my estimates were anywhere near the ballpark.

The integrity of the raft worries me increasingly with each passing day. The main air chamber tends to collapse in the middle, which causes the floor to bulge. Air leaks from the hole I patched increase, while both air valves refuse to seal and consequently leak. At least the many seams that keep the raft together are still intact; if they start to peel, we're in big trouble. The raft is constructed of several dozen plastic panels glued together, with each seam backed by a plastic tape. I still can't figure out how they glued the inside part of the last piece, but I damn sure hope they did a good job, used good glue, and that it wasn't raining the day they put the raft together.

The outside of the canopy has changed from bright orange to a pale, dirty white, which, in turn, has allowed the ultraviolet rays to eat away at the blue waterproofing on the canopy's interior surface. Why don't raft manufacturers use a bright reflecting surface instead of an orange that fades? Probably because of a Coast Guard requirement that's a hundred years old. A lookout on a ship is more likely to spot something bright—that is, if there's sunshine, something we've had little of so far. I dare not breathe a word to Sim that the raft has lived at least a week beyond its designed life. I'll keep that piece of news to myself, although I'm sure she's figured it out.

My engineer's mind churns. How much pounding can a seam withstand before it comes unglued and starts to leak? If we develop a leak in one seam, others will certainly fail—a domino effect. A hole caused by a fishhook or a fish or a piece of driftwood with a nail in it is a real possibility. It could happen anytime. With a hole of any size, even a pinhole, the raft will lose its buoyancy and begin to sink. We would have to pump continuously as the hole inevitably became larger. Sooner or later, water would surely seep in. The arches, hopefully still full of air, should keep the raft from sinking more than a foot or two. Maybe the four large and two small boat cushions would help keep us afloat. We would need to lie horizontally to maximize our buoyancy, and we would be constantly submerged. Sleep would be difficult, if not impossible. Fishing and making water would become real chores. We would be eyeball to eyeball with the sharks and triggerfish.

How long can we survive once we're in the water? The threat of hypothermia could be more real than the jaws of a shark. Immersed in the 80-degree water, the core temperature of our bodies would begin to drop after two or three days. We would put on our foul-weather gear and life jackets to keep warm. First we'd shiver, but as our internal temperature approached 90 degrees, our bodies would no longer regulate temperature. Shivering would stop, and we'd begin to get drowsy. Death from hypothermia, infection, fish bite, or drowning would be but a matter of time, a few days at the most. I pray for Sim's sake that I don't go first. We've talked at length about most of these possibilities, but our minds refuse to accept defeat and death.

If we must die, I hope that it will be fast. Once the raft disintegrates, I imagine us swimming for hours in panic and despair. Triggerfish take penny-sized bites from our bodies. As we bleed, sharks move in. At first, they brush by tentatively to test us. On their second or third pass, they bump us. Soon, they attack. It's over quickly after that. The raft sinks, and all trace of our earthly presence disappears forever. Only prayers, thoughts of our children, and our desire for life can chase these horrid images away.

Simonne reads my thoughts and says, "I pray for a dignified death. I'd like to glide down into the abyss slowly, like *Siboney*, accompanied by beautiful blue, gold, and yellow dorados and the singing of the whales and dolphins following me down. I remember the movie *The Big Blue*, and the attraction of the deep. What are we all searching for? Isn't it peace? Eternal peace. It may be not that far away."

ABOARD THE RAFT
LAST CHANCE
0020 THURSDAY • JULY 6, 1989 • DAY 22

A LOUD WHISTLE turns into a steady roar. Sim jumps up, absolutely convinced it's another ship about to run us down. She looks out and is faced by a dense black wall about to envelop us, much like an avalanche of mud. The sound increases and spreads, now deadened as we fall into a trough, then deafening as we rise to the crest of the next wave. Suddenly, it hits.

Thirty-knot winds gust to forty. Rain blasts the side of the raft. The canopy fills with air and forms a parachute-like dome above us. Great sheets of wind-driven spray shoot through the closed window. Massive waves approaching at more than thirty knots again threaten to swallow the raft. Water cascades through the canopy to bury us as we gasp for breath. Sim bails with a desperation brought on by memories of the sinking *Siboney*. The water gains. She prays aloud for mercy. "Bail!" I call out above the roar. "Bail, woman, we must beat the sea itself!"

I look at my watch and, with difficulty, find that it's one twenty in the morning. The storm rages on. Time stands still. We experience all the horror and terror of hell, a watery hell meant to last forever. Darkness is so complete I can see neither Sim nor the sides of the raft, but I can feel her desperation transmitted through the fingers that grip mine. I have always considered myself lucky. Good fortune has always followed me. I had wonderful parents, a great family, and a fun job. Right now, I can't shake the feeling that I've pushed my luck one notch too far.

Waves batter us at sea level. Sharks attack from below. Wind and rain pound us from above. We cry out to the highest. Lord, have mercy on us. If this punishment continues, we will not see another new day. This is surely the end. I cry out, tempted to give up, to curl up and let the sea take us. But the monster sea, so full of ogreish critters, will have to try harder if it really wants us. Rain continues to flood through the canopy. We take turns holding the fishing pole that makes the canopy more of a tent and slows the flood of water. Sharks attack without letting up, but the rain keeps me from counterattacking. Besides, there is no visibility. I can't even see Sim.

We can do nothing but pray. Lord, help us. Virgencita de la Caridad del Cobre, patron saint of Cuba, plead with God on our behalf. Help us. I close my eyes and see her. And below her is our raft, in her embrace, protected, cradled.

The sharks must have gone elsewhere, allowing us some respite, a meager sleep. Never has the gray dawn been so welcome. The wind drops as the day becomes lighter. We open the window to a pale gleam of light from a rising sun. We are battered, bruised, wet, cold, and hungry—but alive.

Siboney was an old boat. Granted, I rebuilt her completely, every frame and every plank, in 1968 in Manila after the typhoon. In 1984, I rebuilt her again, in Miami. We added a quarter-inch of epoxy resin and fiberglass to the hull, then fastened the glass to the frames with twelve hundred silicon-bronze wood screws. The boat was strong but, obviously, not strong enough. It should have withstood an attack by whales. As Alan Villiers has so aptly stated, "All loss of ship at sea is due to error." We made more than one error. We were in the wrong place at the wrong time in the wrong boat. Has my luck been replaced by stupidity?

The whales hit us below the waterline, amidships, to port, and to starboard. There we had laid up two layers of mat and two of thick fabmat fiberglass cloth. Under the keel and up past the garboard, we laid in an extra layer of mat. Before fiberglassing, we had cleaned out the seams and driven in and glued small wood wedges. The whales not only broke through the fiberglass but also cracked planks. Or possibly loosened a wedge, allowing water to flood in through a seam.

The opening could not have been gigantic. The boat did float for more than thirty minutes. I can visualize the sails, two miles down, still waving their sorrowful farewell to the skipper who took them across so many ocean miles.

Our eyes feast on the rising sun, one sunrise neither of us believed we would live to see. Each new ray helps our hearts grow stronger and our will to survive grow firmer. We breathe in this new day with its oranges, pinks, and reds, a display of colors to make van Gogh green with envy. Whitecaps dance over the deep-blue sea as we ride gigantic ocean swells. We are alive, delivered from a deadly dark catacomb where we were held captive through eleven evil hours.

The force of the wind no doubt pushed us to the northeast all night at close to a knot. When we surfed, propelled by a breaking wave, I am sure our speed was more than a knot. Anyway, we have passed the five-hundred-hour mark. Neither of us could have guessed on that first desperate dawn, with *Siboney* resting in her newfound cradle and we adrift no more than five hours, that we would continue to live as castaways for one hundred similar periods. We lived a full lifetime before that first dawn.

I have high hopes and a strange feeling that someone will soon find us. Twenty days have passed since we last saw a ship, twenty days drifting east toward the shipping lanes in and out of Panama. I row the raft in a circle whenever Sim kneels to look out. She always returns with the same report: no birds, no ships, no planes. We are alone and forgotten by all. We're forty-three days out of Panama, twenty-six since our last radio contact. WHAT IN THE HELL IS EVERYONE THINKING? WHERE DO THEY THINK WE ARE? WHAT IN THE DEVIL DO THEY THINK WE'RE DOING? Or does no one give a damn?

Around noon, I fish, but my luck in that department has run out. I get several strikes, but my hook is too big. Where in the hell were the bags of hooks when I needed them? Cast after cast bears no fish, and I begin to hoard my diminishing bait supply by baiting each successive toss with less and less bait. All fishermen have good days and bad days, and this one is terrible. I try one last cast. If it doesn't work, I'll save the remainder of the bait for tomorrow. I cast and lose the bait. It's half a cracker and a dab of peanut butter for the crew today.

I stow my fishing gear, which consists of turning the rod back to turtle-and-shark bonker. I coil the line and hang the hook safely in a hole in the seam of the arch. What can I do to put food on the table? Soon, we'll be out of crackers. We ate our last raisin, a mashed-up, sad-looking thing I found toward the bottom of Sim's toilet kit. I found two soggy cookie crumbs and ate those too, after offering them to Sim. Like every mother, she insists on feeding others first.

We are desperately short on food. The raft has gone weeks past its designed life. The closest land is seven or eight hundred miles away. And to top it all off, no one is looking for us. Even if there were a search party out, there is no way in the world we could be found. It would be like looking for a Volkswagen Beetle between Miami and Seattle in a six-hundred-mile-wide path. But then, I got us into this mess. It was all my idea. No one else can be blamed. If we die, I am the sole culprit. Yet dying isn't the whole of it. Not one person in the world will ever know how or where or when we died. We will have disappeared like so many other seafarers throughout the ages. Down to the sea in ships. Gone to sea never to return. To rest forever in unmarked graves in an unknown sea. How many wives and mothers and sons and daughters have waited fruitlessly for the return of a sailor from the deep and have gone to their own graves never knowing the fate of their loved ones? Every seafaring town I have visited has a monument in the town square with the names of those lost at sea.

Just as I'm sure Sally has received my mental messages, Sim knows that her mother is aware we are facing certain death. As time passes, her mother's suspicions will strengthen. When six months or a year goes by without word from us, her heart will break from despair and the loneliness and agony of not knowing what happened to her daughter.

When Sim suggests we send a message, I jump at the idea and right off have her dig under the covers for one of the empty Perrier bottles. On a sheet from the navigation workbook, I dictate as she writes a note in both English and Spanish that reads:

HELP JULY 6 1989

OUR SAILBOAT "SIBONEY" SANK ON JUNE
15. TODAY WE ARE 22 DAYS IN OUR LIFE RAFT.
PLEASE, WHOEVER FINDS THIS NOTE, CALL
COLLECT OUR SONS, CRISTOBAL AND ALEXAN-
DRO GOMEZ DE ORTEGA, IN MIAMI AND
INFORM THEM. TELEPHONE 305-667-7121

WE GUESS WE ARE BETWEEN COCOS ISLAND
AND LAND.

WE THANK YOU. GOD SAVE US.

BILL AND SIMONNE BUTLER.

Sim folds the note over and over until it fits through the neck of
the bottle with Help/Auxilio on the outside. Next, she folds several
dollar bills and pushes them alongside the note in hopes the sight of
money will cause a beachcomber to pick up and examine the bottle.
Sim screws the cap on tightly and tosses it over the side. The bottle
quickly falls behind, confirming that the wind and waves do push us
along in addition to the current.

Later in the afternoon, the wind picks up from the southwest,
which prompts us to try a trick we learned several days ago when drying the sailbag. When we tied the sailbag atop the canopy, it filled
with wind, acting much like a sail. I set the bag, it fills, and the raft
picks up speed right off. It stays up until past sunset, when the wind
begins to die. Besides, we can't risk losing it in the night, for it serves
many functions. When I clean fish, I put it under the camcorder case
to catch juices and blood that spill. At other times, we spread it over
the air chambers when hauling in fish to provide protection against
an accidental jab from a fish spine or a wayward hook. If Sim knew
how many close calls I've had with the hook, she'd hook me in one of
my dearest places.

On cool nights, we use the sailbag as a cover. Today it's delight-
fully dry after so many hours in the sun, and I throw it over me early
in the night. Sim lies, as usual, naked and soaked with perspiration.
The cotton cover, and source of her sanitary napkin supply, serves as
our pillow. The striped cover remains under us as a mattress and
wrap, but with each passing day, it becomes wetter and lumpier.

Unless the night is windy and rainy, the sailbag is all we need for comfort. On colder nights, I pull the wool blanket out of the bilge, wring it, and spread it over me.

Rain begins with isolated drops, then builds to a pounding downpour. The canopy no longer keeps rainwater out, and we struggle to stay dry for as long as we can. Over the sailbag, we spread the trash bag, which is not quite long or wide enough to cover us completely. The drips are continuous, but a lot fewer when I raise the canopy with the pole. I jam it against my leg, which works fine until I move or Sim moves or a heavy gust dislodges the pole and, at the same time, blows the trash bag off the sailbag. Then everything collapses. A bucket of water spills on us. I push my head farther under the arch to escape the worst of the drips or at least keep them out of my eyes and ears.

In the midst of this medieval torture, I manage to sleep. I can never tell if Sim sleeps, for she remains immobile, hair soaked, eyes tightly closed, hands on her chest clutching her rosary, the saddest-looking lips I've ever seen barely moving as she recites prayers so intense she remains oblivious to the many drops that drench her naked body. Her Mediterranean nose reaches out to heaven.

There is a positive side to the rain. There does have to be a connection between rain and sharks. Recently, sharks haven't battered the raft while it rains. I'll take rain over sharks anytime. Perhaps, in a heavy rain, the surface water loses its salinity, or does the pitter-patter unnerve them? When the rain stops, the sharks return. I dip the pole into the sea for the remainder of the night. When I stop, the sharks attack the raft within seconds. Sim prays constantly. I look at my watch at intervals of under ten minutes, expecting an hour to have passed. The night becomes an interminable struggle for survival, which cannot end too soon. If we are to die, may it be swift.

Ever so slowly, a faint lightening of the eastern sky announces that we have survived another night. The wind has died and the skies are clear. The sun, when it makes its appearance at eight in the bright-red eastern horizon, further confirms that we are moving east. Where *Siboney* sank, sunup was after eight thirty. Today the sun is up before eight. Forty-five minutes of sun time is 7.5 degrees, or four hundred and fifty miles. That coincides with my dead reckoning. But I don't like bright-red sunrises.

Sim lives her own red sunrise, as her body announces the start of a second menstrual period just three weeks since her last one. I was always under the impression that women tended to miss periods when scared to death. During her first period, not wanting to stir the attention of the shark population, we used one of our empty saltine tins to store her urine and soiled cloths. At the end, we capped the can and eased it away from the raft. Now we're much more blasé. Sharks pummel the raft whether we throw fish carcasses over or not. Blood and fish entrails appear not to make them any more aggressive. All the same, I remind Sim to always throw her soils to windward, for I don't want the raft to pick up a taint sharks will pursue.

Sharks and turtles pester us all morning. I land several good hits on fast-moving sharks, but there are so many of them that I miss half. When I look down, I see ten or more five-footers at the ten-foot level. To Sim's delight, several boobies perch on the raft this morning. The webbed feet of the mature birds are harmless. The younger ones have sharp nails, and we must shoo them off. My log entry for today, Friday, reads:

TGIF—EXCEPT HERE IT'S TSBF—TURTLES
SHARKS BIRDS FRIDAY.

It's lunchtime, and my stomach screams for something more than half a cracker. Our Fourth of July turtle banquet has awakened a gnawing hunger. I prepare the rod to fish and cut the smelly, three-day-old turtle meat into three small pieces. I cast and lose the first bait instantly. It's so rotten it barely stays on the hook. I cast again and lose that bait as well. Sim has closed her eyes and pleads aloud, "Give us this day our daily bread, have mercy, dear God."

I'm desperate. My last little piece of turtle meat is the most rotten piece in the can. I'd left it for last in hopes I wouldn't need it. If I lose it, the food chain will again be broken. We'll be back to where we were before we caught the turtle, unable to fish. The bait is so rotten it will not stay on the hook until I run the hook through it four times. I drop it gingerly in the water, and immediately I have a strike. The line becomes taut as the fish strains to escape. I give the line a hard tug, fully expecting to lose it, but to my great surprise, a fish flies on board. With a lightning-fast movement, Sim wraps it in the sailbag and bursts out laughing and crying. We hug and cry without shame. Prayer is power. We have just experienced a miracle, nothing less. Sim looks up and exclaims with a burst of faith, "God, we do not deserve your generosity, but we accept it. Thank you!"

I plunge the knife into the head of the rainbow runner to kill it and quickly slice out both fillets. In seconds, we dice them up and devour the tasty fish. The skin and inedible parts become bait. My next cast lands a five-pound tripletail. Minutes later, another tripletail is on board and in the bucket with the first. Sim cheers, her attitude much improved over minutes earlier. I clean and fillet what must total six pounds of fish. We eat until we are about to burst. We save what's left for supper and bait. From now on, I will keep a larger supply of bait on hand.

Food and water will keep us alive. I cut up the best parts of the fillets for Sim, as she has not fully taken to our raw fish fare and never eats enough to suit me. She's also a reluctant water drinker, so before I drink, I always pass the bottle to her and insist she take a second and third sip. Our water intake has settled down to a fairly standard two liters a day, with one full Evian bottle consumed throughout the day and another liter at night. Our bodies really call for no more.

The five spare liters of water fit under our feet while I keep the one in use between my hips and the air chamber. The empties create a storage problem, for when I turn, I usually squash one. The noise shatters Sim's nerves. I try all sorts of tricks to keep them out of the way, but nothing seems to work. There's still too much stuff aboard, and much of it is still soggy. We move the big black-and-white comforter, sopped and heavy, out from under us and drape an end on the canopy to dry. I dream of a dry bed, but I'm afraid that'll be a while in coming, if ever.

Where is everyone? I am sure the search has started. We are now forty-six days out of Panama and would be nearing Hilo in Hawaii if *Siboney* were still afloat. Our last radio contact was twenty-eight days ago. Is no one worried? What are they doing? Where in the hell are the planes? And ships? Anything. . . ?

Wind and current die in late afternoon. The raft swings wildly and spins when the smallest shark bumps it. A baby shark has been pestering us all day. They learn their nasty habits young. I'd rather be surrounded by tarantulas.

New seabirds join us. Our favorite is an all-white bird the size of a seagull with two long, feathered tails. It has round black eyes and hangs suspended above the raft, looking down at us. Frigate birds are our constant companions. A mother and its young hover above us all day and, no doubt, all night. At first light, they are always there, a hundred feet above the raft. They soar carelessly, their sharp eyes ever on the lookout for a meal.

The dry bedding improves the mood aboard. Sim's reading fills our hearts with hope. This truly gorgeous day closes with a spectacular sunset as the sun plunges into the ocean. I gaze west until night turns the clouds ever-darker shades of purple, then gray, and finally black. I give thanks for another day of life and pray for a quiet night. Stars appear, one or two at first, then hundreds. Both of us gaze out of our window, deep in thought. Sim breaks the spell. "Bill, will we make it?"

I have no answer, but try anyway. "Sure, sweetie. The children, your mother, our friends must all be worried. A month has passed since our last radio contact. Someone will come looking for us. Real soon."

Sim looks at me with her faraway look. "Do you remember the voice I heard when we first shipwrecked? It said, "Forty days, forty days," over and over. I really think our punishment will be forty days long. We do deserve forty days of punishment, for we have deserted God for so many years. If that's so, we have seventeen more days. I know that only then will rescue come. We have to accept it." I'm surprised and relieved that Sim has now relaxed from her daily bouts of anxiety. Seventeen days with less tension is what I need.

Sim's incessant harangues over our past relationship and our present situation have worn the hell out of me. She usually begins her barrage during the two hours prior to sunset, rehashing topics I considered long dormant. Like the blond hairs she found in her bedroom after returning home from a long trip twelve years ago. I swore then and over the past weeks have again insisted that I have never been unfaithful and have never ever taken and would never ever take another woman into her home. Ten days ago, with sudden death imminent, we played the entire scene over one more time. Her doubts will likely surface again, for she will carry them to her grave, or into the stomach of a predator.

The sharks arrive at ten and punish us nonstop until three in the morning. Tonight, for the first time in a week, my blows have no visible effect. I splash the paddle in the water until close to dawn, when I drop off to sleep.

A shark awakens us on this Saturday, July 8, when the sun is ten o'clock high. When I open my window, dozens of sharks mill under the raft. Never have we seen so many at one time. They are all four to six feet long and appear to be silky sharks. One after another takes turns slapping the raft. I repel them with pokes of the pole. After an hour, the entire mass of sharks moves on.

Sim sits up with a jerk and cries out, "Bill, listen, an airplane! A plane, a plane!"

"Hey, you sound like Tattoo. I don't hear it. Have you been nipping on the brandy behind my back?"

"It is an airplane! My God, an airplane! Listen!"

Now I hear it. The faintest of sounds, but it *is* an airplane, propeller driven. Sim searches the skies while I row the raft in circles. I take out the mirror. The sound of the engines becomes louder, then fades away. Sim searches the skies long minutes after.

Who were they? Where were they coming from? Are they searching for us? What else would bring a plane out this far? And where are they going? We must be getting closer to shore. That is the first sign of life, however remote, that we have had in more than three weeks. It's a good sign. We're not alone in the world. We have not been forgotten.

We spend the rest of the morning beating off turtles and sharks. What else is there to do? The turtle lovers are back under the raft and at it again. Sim is unmerciful; the lovers, totally carefree.

What do turtles eat out here? Carrion and the remains of dead fish are eaten by fish and sharks if underwater and by birds if on the surface. Turtles eat marine plants, but we haven't seen any plant life. They eat jellyfish, but so far we've seen none. What sustains them? Their giant shells must be huge warehouses for food and air. I read an article in *Smithsonian* magazine long ago that described an experiment with turtles. One continued to live normally for a month with its brain removed. I couldn't believe it then, but I believe it now. They probably needed a high-power microscope to find a brain in the first place.

Sim waits, fishing rod in her right hand. When the male turtle swims out for air, Sim shoots for its neck. The turtle paddles out a few feet, turns, and heads straight back to Sim. He must be in love with her. She deals out six more pokes. The turtle swims out and returns. The scene repeats itself every minute or two. I lie on my side with my back to Sim, intent on ignoring the proceedings. Sim prods me with the pole.

"Here, Bill, quick. It's on your side. I can hear it scratch the raft."

"I don't do turtles."

"You what? What does that mean? Hurry, take the pole. It's sinking the raft."

I remain inert and say, "I do not do turtles. Sharks, yes. Turtles, no."

"I can't believe what I hear. The man is crazy. He doesn't do turtles? We're attacked, and he doesn't move. Oh Lord, give me patience."

The turtle is back under the raft. Sim boils over. She screams some nasty words in French and Italian both at the turtle and at me. I refuse to get excited. It bumps the bottom of the raft and scratches along the side a bit, but I can't see that it's doing any damage. I am busy enough with sharks. The turtle will leave when it's ready.

When I decide to fish, I look down into our aquarium and into the noses of dozens of sharks that circle at different levels. I'll fish later. No use stirring things up.

Sim scrapes the toothbrush around the bottom of the peanut butter jar and spreads a thin layer on a cracker. We split the cracker two ways and wash it down with several gulps of water.

Sim turns white and clutches her chest. "My heart, my heart! Oh, Bill, I'm having a heart attack! Oh my God, I can't breathe. I'm dying! Oh my God!"

"You sound like Redd Foxx: 'This is the big one, this is the big one.' I'd have a heart attack if I carried on like you. Let the turtles be, and you won't have any heart attacks."

"This is real. I am having a heart attack! Pain runs all over my chest. I can't breathe! Oh Bill, help me, I can't breathe! Oh Lord, help me!"

"I think a little chest massage will help. Here, let me help alleviate the pain."

"Keep your hands off me. I'm serious. I'm having a heart attack and you're making fun."

"What do I tell your mother after I make it to shore? 'Mama, your daughter died of a heart attack. A couple of turtles doing it got her overexcited.' She won't believe it for a second. She'll figure I dumped you over the side for being a bitch. You get over your attitude toward turtles, and that's an order."

"I'm going to die. I know it. And you don't care. If I die, please, please don't throw my body over for three days."

"Three days! C'mon. You don't smell so great right now. Imagine after three days. You pop off, kid, over you go."

Sim is serious. "Don't ever do that. Let my spirit leave my body. It takes three days for it to leave the body and rise. Promise you won't throw me in right away."

"How about two days? If you die just like that and if I can't revive you, it would be a shame to let all that good meat go to waste. I could cut off my favorite parts."

"Butler, you are atrocious. How can you talk like that when I could be dying any minute? Oh, it hurts! Ay, ay, ayyy!"

"Perhaps if I could use a leetle tidbit for bait."

"Stop it, right there. Oh, I feel terrible!"

Breathing exercises finally relax her, allowing her to grab a short nap, which in my book is the best therapy.

Sometime after midnight, the wind increases, followed by lightning and thunder out of the west. Soon, rain pelts the raft until two or three, when I fall asleep. Sim shakes me out of my slumber.

"Bill, listen. What is it? It sounds like a freak wave."

I hear it, like a rumble. It does sound like a huge breaking wave bearing down on us. Sim looks out and screams, "Bill, a freighter! A freighter! Coming right down on us!"

I struggle up and lean over Sim, who has lowered her window despite the wind-driven rain. The bow of a large freighter looms high over the raft not two hundred yards away. Ahead of the bow, the now all-too-familiar bow wave builds and breaks with a roar. Navigation lights, like red and green eyes, look straight at us. My God, these people are going to run us down.

The rear of the stark white pilothouse stands lit like a ghost against the blackness of the night. The ocean transmits the roar of the machinery through the skin of the raft and into our souls. It's now evident the ship will not run us down but will pass close by. We're lucky. We never could have rowed out of its way.

"Help! Help!" we scream in unison.

"Sim, get the flashlight. Find the flares!"

"Here's the flashlight. It's too late for the flares. Besides, it's raining."

"Then the whistle, get the whistle!"

She finds the whistle and hands it to me. Sim yells as I blow the whistle and send SOSs with the flashlight, oblivious to the pouring rain. The ship's bow is alongside, and the rumble of the machinery vibrates the raft. Diesel smoke fills our lungs. We search for signs of life. Where is everyone?

The freshly painted side of the ship passes mere feet away. The decks are empty. We look straight up at the living quarters, not a hundred feet away. We see every detail clearly, even the doorknobs. There is no one on deck. The ship's stern comes into view, and on it, in large white letters, the home port of the ship, Liverpool. We can't make out the ship's name in the dark.

I continue to blow the whistle and flash the light. Sim yells and waves her shirt, which she has pulled off. The aft end of the ship is brightly lit. We watch in disbelief as the freighter speeds away into this dark and dismal night. We continue to yell as we hope against hope that we have been seen by someone in the pilothouse or that a crewman on deck may have heard our cries of distress.

The ship's stern becomes a pinpoint of light, then blends into the night and vanishes. Another ray of hope fades away, a fading star in this immense blackness, extinguished all too quickly by the drizzle. Once again we are alone. The ship passed by so fast, so cruelly indifferent to our plight.

I find the compass and ask Sim to check the ship's course. She holds the compass up as I shine the light. The freighter's heading is

150 degrees. It's probably steaming for the Panama Canal. That means we're closing in on land, although a course of 150 puts us way offshore. Where are they coming from? I generate a mental picture of the Pacific and come up with Honolulu. Shipping from the Far East will run closer to shore, on a great circle route. From now on, we should have the flares at the ready all the time. But shooting one this time would have been a waste. Once again I am certain there was no one on lookout. Not on a rainy night.

Sim collapses in my arms. Together, we cry out our frustration and our anger. What has the Lord planned for us? Is this punishment not enough? How long? How long? Soaked and depressed, I close the canopy and lie back down on our soggy bed. This event was like a bad dream. How many more frustrating events have we still ahead?

I look at my watch. It's four in the morning, July 9, Sunday, day twenty-five on the raft. We left Balboa forty-seven days ago. We have had no radio contact for twenty-nine days. I'm sure a search party will set out on the next clear day.

The rain has become a light drizzle, and the wind increases out of the southwest. A southwesterly tells us we are still far offshore. The closer we get to Central America, the more southerly the wind will become. I remember that much from the pilot chart. Besides, that's the way it was on our way out into the Pacific.

Rain continues through dawn. The wind increases to more than twenty knots to generate ever-stronger waves. The canopy lets both rainwater and seas in. The overcast is so heavy we cannot tell when sunrise is. It is now nine, so the sun is up somewhere behind the clouds. After midmorning, the skies clear and improve our outlook. Last night's ship hasn't been as hard on us as that first one, twenty-four days ago. We remain amazed that in an ocean this vast, two ships have practically run us down.

I fish early today and, with my second piece of bait, hook a three-foot shark. Sim holds the pole while I pull the line through the eye at the end of the pole. When the shark rises to the surface, I find that my only hook runs through the shark's lower jaw. Sim lifts the pole and the shark comes with it. I grab the leader and stick my hands inside its gills, where I hold it tightly. The shark flails its tail wildly as Sim hands me the knife. I slash the shark's lower lip, remove my hook, and drop the shark back into the water.

I no sooner let the shark go than I realize we haven't eaten in two days. We caught loads of sharks aboard *Siboney*, but I've never tried shark meat. I'm not quite hungry enough yet. Three small sharks chase my next piece of bait. I pull my line in and save my last pieces of bait for tomorrow.

The current stays strong all afternoon, the skies remain clear, and with three gulps of water, our stomachs are full. Strange how we can fool our brains—or are our brains fooling us?

At sunset, clouds increase in speed, indicating nasty weather ahead. Light, intermittent rain starts as soon as we button down the windows. Seas build again. Waves are nearly twenty feet and grow larger. Visibility is less than a mile.

Sim reads in the semidarkness, then grasps my hand and says with a faraway look, "Bill, I hope we make it, because I don't want to die before I confess my sins to a priest. Do you think God will forgive me if I don't make a true confession? I have a lot on my conscience, mostly things I should have done and didn't."

"Easy, baby. If you've confessed your sins out here before God, he has received your message. You've been forgiven even if you don't make it to a priest, but stop that talk. We're going to make it. Think positive."

"I try, but it's so hard. I do want to turn my life around so much. How is it possible we stayed away from God for so long? He could have helped both of us through our troubles. I don't understand how I could have been so blind. I was so close to God when I was a child, and suddenly it was as if I forgot who He is. What a fool I have been. I needed Him so much. . . ."

We have both missed enjoying the Lord's blessing for many years. When we return, we'll remedy that. What we need now is help. While Sim prays, I'll concentrate and send another message to Sally.

MOUNT VERNON, NEW YORK
0400 MONDAY • JULY 10, 1989

Sally Smith tosses fitfully next to her husband, Brian. Their shaggy-haired dog Charm lies curled at the foot of their bed. The dog grunts whenever Sally thrashes.

Her eyes open wide. Her heart beats wildly. Something is wrong. The feeling of terror is inescapable. She sees a pitch-black ocean. Dad and Simonne are in a raft. There is deathly danger. "We've got to do something," she thinks.

She jumps out of bed. Charm follows Sally to the darkened kitchen of their small fourth-floor apartment. She looks up to God. "I need help. What should I do?"

Calls to the New York Coast Guard yesterday were fruitless. The Miami Coast Guard, on the other hand, was very helpful. They contacted the San Francisco office, which said they would check around to determine if anyone had come across Siboney.

She pours a glass of milk and returns to bed. Charm follows. Sally lies awake. There is something deadly wrong. "I know Dad is in trouble. I really know it. What can I do? What should I do? I'll give the Coast Guard another call first thing in the morning."

ABOARD THE RAFT
LAST CHANCE
0900 MONDAY • JULY 10, 1989 • DAY 26

HEAVY RAIN eased us into our first deep sleep in two weeks. We awaken to an empty air chamber and a raft that barely resembles the customary oval. The floor sags deep into the water. Our battered bodies float on a bed shaped by the sea. What happened to our timer, the sharks? Have we grown accustomed to their incessant pounding, or have we worked our way out of shark country? That would be fantastic news. Perhaps the salinity in the water has changed, or they have tired of harassing their plastic toy.

Today is Monday and the beginning of our fifth week adrift on this great Pacific Ocean. Our children are at this moment either in school or at work. Are they not worried? Is help on the way, or have we been forgotten? Never in my wildest dreams could I have imagined that we'd be out here this long. Where is everybody? I've sent mental signals to Sally every night, sometimes in the wee hours of the morning. Am I getting through, or am I fantasizing? I feel contact, but is she getting the message? When I open my eyes, Sim gazes out the window.

"Good morning, sleeping beauty. Are you interested in the morning news? Fidel sentenced Ochoa and three others to death in Cuba. Menem took over in Argentina. Arabs attacked an Israeli bus. Fourteen dead. Bush is in Poland. And the big fires are still going strong out West." Sim continues. "I suppose that, with all that going on, everyone is too busy to hunt for two lost sailors. I really cannot believe that no one is searching for us. It's not possible that two people can go off the scope for thirty days and nothing, absolutely nothing, happens."

"Speaking of nothing happening," I say, "I've got something happening, and we'd better plan on how to do it quick."

"Use the bucket. Don't put it off. Go on."

"I need music and *Playboy*. If you hum, that'll do it. I've got my own little centerfold, a bit bedraggled, but still *bellísima*."

"Stop your baloney and get it over with. When you're finished, I want you to cut the matted hair on the back of my head. Now, do your thing and be discreet, will you? My gosh, I haven't seen anybody do it in their pants since my kids were babies."

"Slow down, kiddo. There's no chance I'll do it in my pants. Voilà, madame, you see, no pants. Besides, do you think it's that easy after weeks of not pooping? Give nature a break. OK, here I go. Hold the bucket." I struggle onto my knees and sit on the wobbly bucket as Sim holds me with one hand and steadies the bucket with the other. I strain. The cramps are terribly painful, but nothing happens. A long time later, I give up and crawl back into my bunk exhausted. Sim fills the bucket with the dozen things it normally holds: knife, fishing reel, gloves, cord, and the gun case with the scissors, nail file, and can opener.

Sim berates me. "I cannot believe it. All that fuss for nothing. You are a catastrophe."

"You didn't hum. C'mon, I tried hard enough. I almost fainted, you yo-yo. What should I have done? I'm so full of it, it hurts. That was a bad drill."

"Do something useful like cut my hair. Cut it short, here, like this, inside the matted parts." I chop off big mats of Sim's hair, which I pile on her lap. I think I've overdone it, but then, I'm no Vidal Sassoon.

I fish early. We are both starving, for our increased ingestion throughout the last week has reawakened our appetites. The bait, in a tin can next to my feet during the past three days, is so incredibly smelly that I gag with the first whiff. I dump the entire rotting glob onto the filleting board, evil juices and all, and pick out the best pieces as the nauseating stink fills the raft.

With my second cast, I land the same shark I caught yesterday, sliced lower jaw and all. What a dumb, persistent little rascal. I jerk it out of the water and hold the violently writhing beast by the gills until I cut off its head. Once I remove my hook, I throw the head out as far as I can, which brings on a wild fight among the triggerfish until the inevitable long, black shape bullies its way through the morass and gulps down all that's left.

With the head of the shark removed, Sim relaxes but still keeps an eye on me. I throw the old bait away, clean the board of the dark, smelly juices, and gut the shark. Whenever we caught one back in the Bahamas, we removed the jaws and dropped the body over the side, for we always had better fish to eat. The meat runs along the length of the body and is divided into four sections, each separated by a membrane. I cut a bite-sized chunk and try a piece. It's chewy, with a vinegary taste. Though I'm hungry, it's not really that appetizing.

I cast with my fresh bait and instantly hook a rainbow runner. I quickly fillet it and feed it to Sim. Pieces of meat around the head become fresh bait. In no time, I have a two-pound tripletail on board.

"We're back in business," I proudly exclaim to Sim.

"You're terrific. I love you. Thank you, Lord, for your bounty and generosity," Sim says with traces of fish on her lips. A tear runs down her cheek, generated by genuine awe at the series of miracles that continue to keep us alive.

Instead of waiting for the tripletail to die, as I've done in the past, I place it on the filleting board and hold it firmly with my left hand. With the knife, I cut along its dorsal fin, then run the knife along the central spine until the fillet is loose. After the other fillet is removed, I toss the carcass into the mass of triggers and sharks and watch the ensuing battle with sadistic joy. At sea, the big guy always wins, not unlike things ashore. I wash the scales and blood off the filleting board and stack the fresh fillets on the paddle. With the paddle on my chest, I stretch out alongside Sim, feel for the meat with my fingers, and then cut little pieces, smaller than half-inch cubes. Simonne gets most of the tripletail, and I eat the shark. Sim is as tough to feed as a finicky child and refuses to eat all that she needs to survive. And I treat her as I would a child. I look her right in her eyes, knife in my right hand, and tell her that if she refuses to eat, I'll force-feed her. And I will. There's no way I'm going to explain to her mother that her baby died of hunger in my care. I gorge myself yet leave plenty for tomorrow's bait.

The wind picks up, and seas build to fifteen feet even before we finish lunch. Low, fast-moving, dark clouds quickly bring rain as visibility drops to less than a mile. What continues to bother me is the absence of larger sharks. I keep my concerns from Sim, but I keep wondering why. Did the shark I hooked send out vibes to his brothers to watch out for the bad guy on the raft? A shark hasn't touched the raft since late morning. To the patter of rain, we nap and awaken at last light.

On our customary evening look around before sunset, we see a heavy black cloudbank rolling in from the southwest with the portent of nasty weather on the way. No sooner do we button down the windows than heavy drops begin to fall. Seas quickly build to twenty feet, and breaking waves again begin their repetitious collisions with our fragile craft. Is there a wave out there that will overwhelm us? A huge vertical wall of water that will, for an instant, mark our burial place with a mighty swath of white foam? Or will we be allowed to live?

Sim reads at last light. I have her read the parable about the lost sheep twice.

> *What man of you, having a hundred sheep, if he has lost one of them, does not leave the ninety and nine in the wilderness, and go after the one which is lost, until he finds it?*
>
> *And when he comes home, he calls together his friends and his neighbors, saying to them, 'Rejoice with me, for I have found my sheep which was lost.' Just so, I tell you, there will be more joy in heaven over one sinner who repents than over ninety and nine righteous persons who need no repentance.*

We are so lost! Sinners of the worst sort who now repent. Will no one venture out into the wilderness to look for us?

Rain falls all night as the seas subside. The night is terribly quiet. Almost too quiet. Where in the devil are the sharks? And there are no turtles either. Something strange is going on, but what is it? We pump air every two to three hours and pee about as often. Sim, bundled in her corner of our miniature home, listens intently to the radio for a long while. We're both awake long before dawn.

After first light and with the sun about to emerge, I lean over and ask, "You were on the radio last night. Any headlines?"

"Ochoa is in deep trouble in Cuba. They ratified his death sentence. I wonder what's the real story there. Big sex scandal in Japan. Prime minister and a geisha. Big fires out West still raging. Why don't they come and get some water from out here?" We both feel so much less lost as we stay in touch with world events. How would it be if we had no contact at all with the outside world? We'd be totally isolated. The escape and solace Sim receives through her little radio have helped keep her going, but the big question is, how much longer will the batteries hold out? When will we pick up a news item about a search for two sinners from Miami who have disappeared in the Pacific? Or is no one worried?

Today is our twenty-seventh day on the raft. Tomorrow we reach the four-week mark. Someone has to be searching. Not today though, for with weather like this, planes will not be flying. A passing ship wouldn't see us even if it ran us down like the last two nearly did. We spend most of our time deep within the troughs. If a ship that passed a few feet from us couldn't see the raft and the raft was bright orange back then, what chance do we have with a vessel a half-mile distant? Besides, we're convinced that today's ships post no lookouts, since they run so shorthanded.

When dawn arrives, it finds two sopped souls lying on soaked bedding in a soggy raft. Rain has poured through the canopy all night, and it seems as if Sim bailed continuously. Most of the water runs to the lowest part of the raft, which is under my rear end. For it to flow toward Sim, I have to lift my bottom and arch my back to concentrate my weight on my head and feet, both perched on the sides of the raft. I hold up my cushion to expose the bottom of the raft as Sim pushes on the floor and soaks the rotting sponge, then squeezes the water into the can. She then patiently waits for more water to trickle down from the cushions, the foul-weather gear, and the covers, and repeats the process. A fussy homemaker, she keeps going, trying to get the last drop, which is, of course, impossible. I grumble from my awkward position for her to hurry, which, of course, does no good.

What would our lives be like up in the northern latitudes? If the boat had gone down off Japan, we would not have survived, and we shiver at the thought. On the other hand, we might have been found sooner by one of the many Japanese fishing boats. Where in the hell are all the fishing boats? The seas around us teem with life. Perhaps when the weather calms and clears, the boats will be out.

We saw the ship that passed several nights ago much too late. By a horrible chance of fate, Sim had taken a good look thirty minutes earlier and had seen nothing. That's the price we pay for the comfort and safety of an enclosed raft. With the front and back of the raft permanently closed, we can only see out the sides. But I had rowed the raft around and given Sim time to get a good look from the top of a swell in every direction. If we had looked in time, we could now be steaming toward Panama in a warm, clean bed. As I reflect on our bad timing, Sim looks out, jumps, and calls out:

"Bill! A ship! A ship! Coming to us! There, can you see it? Oh Lord, be merciful, help us! Let them see us this time!"

Sure enough, a small white freighter heads our way. It's still a mile away, but on a heading that will take it right by us. Sim quickly grabs the three flares from her toilet kit and hands me one. I remove the outer layer of protective paraffin as Sim unzips the canopy and brushes it aside.

The morning is hazy, but the ship is so close that there is a good chance the watch will see one of our flares. The approach angle is perfect, and I wait for them to get closer. Once the wind angle is right, I strike the cap igniter against the head of the flare. Nothing happens. I try again. Then again. On the third try, the flare bursts into life. Hot blue-red flames shoot out one end as pieces of slag spurt into the sea. I hold the end of the wooden handle far out over the water, for a single drop of molten slag on the air chamber would sink the raft and spell our end. Hot flames burn my fingers, but I refuse to let go.

A dense cloud of smoke from our flare billows toward the sparkling white ship as it approaches at more than fifteen knots, perhaps twenty. We search the decks for signs of life, but we see no one.

But then, who would be out strolling on a dark, drizzly morning like this? My flare sputters and dies. In seconds, the ship will be at its closest.

"Sim, quick, give me another flare!" I cry out. "He's still heading our way." Sim has waved a shirt and shouted for help all the while. With nervous agitation, I prepare the second flare. It ignites as the white ship speeds closer. The cloud of gray smoke from the first flare crosses the bow of the ship as the second flare begins to burn brightly. Dense smoke carries amidships and across the bridge as the white ship passes alongside. If they don't see it, they will surely smell it. Sim sees the door to the bridge open, and someone steps out. Sim waves the white T-shirt tied to the end of the fishing rod ever more desperately. The door closes, and the small white freighter flies by. Minutes later, it is but a blur in the southern haze.

I kneel, stunned. I have just burned two flares out of our total of three. Now we have only one flare left. Why did I shoot the second one?

Sim is adamant. "He saw us, Bill. Someone on the bridge saw us but decided not to stop. Oh Lord, help us. Why did you shoot two flares? No one will ever see us now!"

"Hand me the compass," I command.

The white ship's course is 120 degrees. Unquestionably, it's heading for the canal. But from where? Hawaii again? We must be in the shipping lanes. We have gone twenty-four days without sighting a ship, and now we've seen two ships in two days.

I wasted two flares. Visibility was bad, and at the speed they were moving, it was obvious the ship was racing somewhere. They probably saw us but couldn't stop. Their schedule for transiting the Panama Canal would not allow time for a stop. They might radio rescue units on shore . . . but they might not, since they could be reprimanded for not stopping. When I voice my thoughts, Sim cries out and calls them criminals. In the old times, she says, laws were stricter. The International Court in The Hague would have hung them high and dry. I don't know about that, but why argue a moot point?

Regulations at the Panama Canal are so strict that, even in our case, had we missed our scheduled transit, our fine would have been three hundred dollars compared with the hundred dollars it cost us to pass through. The white ship no doubt had a set transit time, perhaps was running a little late, and was racing to Panama. To hell with the son of a bitch.

I try to hide my distress and frustration from Sim, who is upset enough as it is. Every ship that passes without sighting us further confirms my feeling that we are invisible. Our best chance is at night, when we can fire a flare, except that now we have just one. To hell with ships. On top of it all, we have again lost the current and the wind has died. Waves continue from the south. The raft swings aimlessly.

It's time I fished. With my first cast, I catch a blue runner. On my next cast, I accidentally snag a huge sea turtle. I reel it in slowly so as not to excite it. I turn the turtle with the pole to put its menacing beak far from the raft. I hand the pole to Sim and grab hold of its left front flipper. The hook is somewhere underneath. With one eye on its beak and the other on my hook, I follow the line to the hook, twist it, and pull it loose. The turtle jerks up, snaps at me, then swims off. Whoa, that was close.

Now that we are in the shipping lanes, we have to increase our vigilance. To do the job right, we should take a look every half hour, and even then we'll miss some ships. A ship goes from horizon to horizon in less than half an hour, more like twenty minutes, but will spot us only on the approach. Our best chance is still at night. Damn. We are down to one flare. Damn me for missing that bag of flares. Damn!

This fact suddenly dawns on Sim. "I can't believe you wasted two flares on that ship, and not only two flares but two out of a total of three flares. Now we have one left. One. Do you know what that means?"

She takes a short breath and continues. "We're not going to make it. I know it. We should prepare ourselves for the worst. No one will look for us. Those stupid ships that pass cannot see us. We don't know where we are or where we are going or where land is. God has given up on us. It's all over, Butler."

"That was dumb," I admit. There was too much daylight for the flare to be seen properly. The light rain had cut visibility even further. We could see the ship clearly because it was large, but the crew couldn't see us. How could they? The raft is smaller than most waves, and we vanish within the swells for long periods of time. And no one uses lookouts on oceangoing ships any longer. Far from land, even we have left *Siboney* unattended many a time. I would set a ten-mile intruder zone on the radar and go to sleep. How many stranded sailors did we pass as we slept?

Sim is right. I should never have shot off that second flare. Even the first flare was a mistake. These flares work best in the dark.

Sim squares off. "You're not going to touch that last flare, Butler, not without talking to me first," she thunders. "Do you understand the significance of being down to one flare? How in the world did you miss that bag of flares on the bunk? It was right there. I saw it. It must still be floating around somewhere."

"I really don't know. It was dumb of me."

"Too many more dumb moves will get us killed. Oh Lord, have mercy. Help us. Do something. Send us a ship or a plane. Push us to land."

The raft swings as the drizzle becomes a downpour. Sim removes the psalms from the ziplock bag she carefully stows under her headrest and reads before darkness encloses our little world.

Several bumps and a scratch announce the arrival of one of our flippered foes. It's foolish to go after them in the rain. Even heavier rain begins at two in the morning. We lie on our backs, sailbag over us and the plastic trash bag again covering the sailbag. A dozen drips fall simultaneously from the canopy while we struggle to keep the trash bag in place. I push my head farther up under the arch where I can keep the drips from dropping into my nose and ears. I can't see Sim but can hear her sputter. Soaked before the rain started, we're now thoroughly sopped. Sim bails.

This is the second day with no shark activity. It's not normal. After more than three weeks with sharks battering the raft all day long, suddenly the sharks are gone. What's going on? The sea isn't like that. There must be a reason, but I can't imagine what it is.

I pray the sharks have all left for good. Don't hurry back. They probably left Mr. Turtle behind to make sure we don't get bored. A turtle has been with us for hours, bumping and scratching. Sim tried a couple of shots an hour ago but missed and ended up drenched.

Dawn welcomes us with more rain. I peek under the canopy and find a string of low, black clouds again approaching from the west. Great. A good storm will push us to shore. Everything aboard is soaked, so what's a little more water? The logbook, our writing tablets, and the camera are the only dry items on the raft at the moment. Through most of last night, I kept the log dry on my chest, under the plastic trash bag.

The constant rain has caused the warts on my leg to grow large and black. My back is a mass of open sores brought about by lying for days on a T-shirt soaked in salt water. Sim says my back looks terrible and spreads lotion on the worst of the sores whenever I sit up to fish. When I turn on my side to give them a chance to dry, Sim complains I take up too much space. Damn it all and damn her too. She's a great companion, but her incessant negative attitude wears thin. Why can't she be a bit more positive? We're going to make it. I don't know how, cramped and uncomfortable as we are, but we're going to make it.

We've tried every combination of positions, but none works for long. On our sides, I fold my knees into Sim's. While it feels great to get off my back, I can't hold the position for more than twenty minutes without getting a cramp. This is about the time it takes for Sim to fall asleep. When I must finally turn, I awaken Sim, who gets completely out of joint. So much for four-man rafts. Next time we'll get a ten-man raft . . . NEXT TIME???

I can hold back my stomach cramps no longer. Since my last try, I have never been without pain, and I announce, "I've got bad news again. I've got to go."

"Bad news? That's terrible news. Why don't you jump in the water and do it? It's raining, Butler. Your timing is bad. Can you hold it?"

"I can't. I've had terrible cramps all morning. The moment has come."

"OK, get it over with." Sim empties the bucket and sets it on one of the small cockpit cushions. She holds it while I climb to my knees on the wobbly floor. I live the most horrible hour of my life. Several times, I come close to a dead faint. Sim supports me throughout the ordeal. Never, ever, have I felt such excruciating pain. Tears roll down my cheeks. I collapse on my cushion thoroughly exhausted yet relieved. I hope I never have to go through that again. Totally drained and dizzy, and feeling five pounds lighter, I quickly fall asleep.

When I awaken, the weather has cleared. Sim must have pumped, as the raft is solid. In the middle of the afternoon, feeling much better, I fish and quickly catch our limit. I clean the first fish and throw the carcass as far as I can. The usual horde of triggerfish head for it, but they suddenly scramble and swim in the opposite direction. Then I see why. A great white shark with a head two feet in diameter swims casually up to the fish and gulps it in a flash.

I freeze. No wonder sharks haven't attacked the raft for two days. That great white has been under us all that time. I dare not mention a word to Sim and continue to clean the fish while I look over the side for any motion. The great white is nowhere in sight, but what do I do with the blood and fish juice? That great white has been casually munching on all those carcasses I've thrown over the last couple of days. I now don't dare throw any others over the side. Or will it get stirred up if I cut off his snacks? Will it then snack on us? This is without a doubt our most dangerous moment so far. This unpredictable killer could turn on us at any moment. Our last breath may be but moments away.

I empty the bucket and dump in the two fish carcasses and all the juices. Sim wonders why I'm messing up the bucket, and I tell her it's because I plan to use the whole fish for bait. She looks at me skeptically, yet doesn't argue. I get the impression she'd rather not know the real reason.

I feed a rainbow runner to Sim, then divide the three tripletails. We end up stuffed with what may well be our last meal. While I fished and filleted, Sim dried the bedding and put order into our makeshift home. The foul-weather gear came out from deep beneath us soaked with water. Each piece must weigh close to twenty pounds. Also out and drying is her life jacket, which has been out of sight for the past several weeks, buried under the cushions.

From one of its pockets, she removes the ziplock bag with our passports, cash, traveler's checks, and credit cards. We normally travel light on cash and heavier on traveler's checks, but the political upheaval in Panama prompted us to go a little heavier on cash. On arrival in Panama, we found there was little to buy except for the basics, which were fairly inexpensive. In the Free Trade Zone, we did find excellent French wine, which now rests in fourteen thousand feet of water.

In the ziplock bag, we find that the two thousand dollars in cash and three thousand in traveler's checks are clean and dry. They all get a bit of sunshine before going back in the pocket of the life jacket together with a set of family snapshots, our passports, and our American Express card. You should never get shipwrecked without one.

As night falls, the weather clears, seas abate, and the current increases. The wind blows gently from the southwest. I like the combination. This has all the portents of a fine evening, except for the company of that great white. What does it have on its primitive mind? Is it waiting for some signal, a faint vibration, a sound, an odor, what? But then, it's been with us for two days and has only come close to feed. Let's hope it doesn't touch the raft. Otherwise, it will be the big casino. I dare not muse on that any further.

WHAM! The raft spins.

The second violent whack spins the raft another 180 degrees. I bounce up like a coiled spring. Is it the great white? When I look out, I'm met with one of the happiest sights I have ever seen. The regular sharks are back. I would scream with joy except Sim would be further convinced I am crazy. How does she say it . . . craaayzeeee!!! What's going on? Pole in hand, I wait for the next pass. I can't see the shark, but I see its trail of phosphorescence as it swims by. I stab at it as it slides alongside the raft along with four or five similar shapes. The pack is back. I relax with a sense of immense relief. I know how to deal with this bunch. The great white must have moved on.

Sharks batter the raft all night. A large turtle swims under the raft and stays with us. Neither of us sleeps. Sim prays. During the more violent of the attacks, she holds her St. Michael's medal between her fingers and asks him to protect us, to free us from danger. At two in the morning, things quiet down, and she listens to the radio while I try to snooze.

We pump air more often. Intervals are down to an hour and a half. Where is the air leak? Could a seam be opening? That would be the definite beginning of the end. Once one seam goes, the others will soon fail too.

God have mercy. Please save us. I splash with my paddle. Sharks hit us whenever I stop. I splash endlessly all night. At five, I give up, roll over, and sleep. Sim takes over.

When I open my eyes, daylight greets me. Sim's awake. I throw her a kiss. "*Bonjour.* Any news this morning, madame? What's for breakfast? Is the coffee ready?"

"Just a few headlines. Laurence Olivier died. China says it will not have mercy for the ringleaders of the riots. The new president in Argentina says he's going to squeeze the Argentineans and their economy. Good luck to him. Bush is in Hungary. He gets around. That's it from the newsroom. And as for the coffee, sailors who sleep late in this pension miss breakfast."

At nine, the sharks begin their customary assault on our nervous systems. Later, a turtle swims by to check out Sim's attitude. Sim reacts as usual. She becomes frantic and strikes at it with all her energy, ignoring my pleas to relax. She genuinely hates turtles and pokes at them whenever they're within range. The turtle swims out ten feet, turns around, looks up with those crude, black-ringed eyes, takes a breath, throws Sim a kiss, and heads back straight toward her.

The scene repeats itself again and again. I'm afraid Sim will have a real heart attack if she continues. Her honest aversion to turtles and her conviction that they will tear the raft apart are beyond reason. This same turtle has been pestering us for almost two weeks and has done no damage. "Sim, I'm going to fix the turtle so it'll go do something else."

Sim looks at me with a quizzical look. "What are you going to do?"

"Pass me your scissors. The big ones."

Sim has two pairs of large scissors and hands me the pair with a long, sharp blade. I wait for the turtle to swim to my side of the raft, then nudge it closer with the pole as I gently turn the shell toward the raft so that its head, with the dreaded beak, faces away from us. That beak could easily cut the raft in two.

With its left front flipper in my left hand, I gently lift it up out of the water and away from the beak. I plunge the five-inch-long scissors deep into the turtle's neck with a twisting, turning motion. The turtle reels and lunges at my hand with its ugly beak. I quickly release the flipper and pull out the scissors. With a violent splash, it swims away. Adios, you devil. We won't see you again.

Sim couldn't see what I was up to. "What did you do?"

"I gave it a scissors job. It won't be back."

"Poor thing. That's not fair. I don't want to hurt them, just scare them away." Maybe so, but this devil has left us forever. So I hope.

We put our sodden bedding out early today to take full advantage of the rare sunny weather. A day this clear is perfect for an air search. The planes should be out today, and we must keep an extra-sharp lookout. If we see a plane, should we use the last flare or save it? Save it for what? If the great white returns, it may be too late. If the Coast Guard won't help, why don't the children hire an airplane? The bank will provide the money. My friend Gus can be the captain. But then, where should they look? We've been adrift four weeks. We're seven weeks out of Panama, forty-nine days, and if we hadn't sunk, we should be approaching Hawaii. That's where they will search. They have a tough equation to solve before even getting airborne. We did talk to hams in California a few hours before we sank, but how would our rescuers locate them? Meanwhile, we have been on the move. At three-quarters of a knot, we've drifted nearly five hundred miles.

A waft from the bucket reminds me that it's time to deal with that stinking mess. I save several pieces of bait, then dump the rotting lot over the side and wash the bucket. Triggers and sharks scramble for the scraps. The great white is nowhere in sight. My noontime fishing expedition is a bust, for I use up all my bait and catch nothing. The fishing cycle has again been broken. That was dumb of me. Why didn't I postpone fishing until the fish were biting? Or save more of the carcasses?

Sharks and turtles return. We recognize individual turtles by their color, size, and markings. One with a red splotch on its shell, probably from a collision with a freighter, has been with us for two weeks. Another has a broken shell. One of today's turtles is new, caught in the same strong current that pushes us east.

Each nudge takes us closer to a landfall still too far off to calculate. The light breeze from the south and a bright sun dry the bedding. As night sets in following a brilliant sunset, we catch sight of a waxing moon, a sight that provides us with hope and dreams. Our family could be looking at this same moon at this same moment. If it were only possible to bounce a rescue signal off it to one of them and get some action.

The whack of a shark jolts me out of my musings. I grab the pole and look into uncountable tiny mirrors, each ripple reflecting moonlight like a giant fireworks display, ever changing but constant in its brilliance. I can see nothing beyond the surface of the ocean. The raft receives two more jolts. I paddle and turn the raft away from the moon, but I still can't see a thing. Four hard whacks follow. Moon, why are you doing this to us? You have always been good to us. How we've yearned to see you, and now we must pray clouds cover you. Otherwise, the sharks will have the upper hand.

The sharks leave us around two, and we're allowed a short nap. When I turn, Sim is listening to the radio. She calls to me, "Bill, radio reception is good. Shall we do it?" I had asked Sim to call when she picked up two or more strong stations that didn't fade out right away. We hope we can locate the source of a radio signal by rotating the radio until the signal disappears.

I tell Sim, "OK. You tune to the station and I'll do the fix."

She passes over the radio and earphones. "Here's Radio Sandina in Managua, Nicaragua."

I put on the earphones and turn the Walkman until I can no longer hear the broadcast. Sim, with the compass in one hand and the flashlight in the other, awaits my signal. I rotate the radio until the station disappears and then place it over the compass.

"Thirty degrees," I call out. "OK, Sim, get another station."

We repeat the process with a station in Costa Rica, which bears 60 degrees. Thirty degrees to Nicaragua and 60 to Costa Rica puts us many hundreds of miles offshore. We have probably traveled almost five hundred miles and have five or six hundred more to go. But at least we are moving toward shore. First the sun and now the radio have confirmed it. We'll check these two stations again in a week.

The current holds steady all night. A brilliant day greets us when we awaken. It's Bastille Day, July 14. The sharks gave us a break last night, and we fell asleep seconds after their last whack. *Vive la France!* I call out when I first notice Sim's eyes open.

"Thank you, dear," Sim says with a faraway smile. "Wouldn't it be wonderful to be in Paris today? We could have stayed with my relatives. It's nine here, so in Paris it's three in the afternoon. The parade must have ended. I heard Bush and Gorbachev and dozens of other fat bananas are there for the bicentennial."

"Wow, we could have been on the Champs-Elysées with the bands and all the people. This is the party of the century."

"Yes, and here I am, stuck with you in the middle of nowhere. Not really that bad a place were it not for all those sharks and turtles, and the fish meat in your beard. It's good that I love you; otherwise, I would have only two choices: kill you or kill myself."

"It's good that I love you, or you would be out there swimming, after all the nasty things you've said. Hey, *vive la France*. Look what I have for the party."

"A Heineken. Where did you find it?" Sim is semishocked. As stow master, how did she let this item slip past her inquisitive eyes?

"Zee skeeper has zee private stock. Except that's it for this jaunt." I have kept it hidden under my head inside an old stinky sweatshirt bought in Balboa. The can has started to corrode and will not last much longer. I offer Sim the first sip. Two sips later, we're both high. Tipsy, we delve into the events that led up to the storming of the Bastille and all the momentous events that soon followed. Simonne sings the "La Marseillaise" twice, and amid shouts of *"Vive la France!"* and not a few tears, our celebration ends.

The beer can quickly empties, and we break out a saltine each for lunch. I drink my usual large glass of salt water, then wash the nasty taste out with a gulp of fresh water and a cracker crumb. This is our second day without fish. I will snag the next bird that comes close whether Sim squawks or not. Two days ago, when a small booby perched on the canopy, I moved my hand slowly toward it until I touched the web of its feet. I will first grab the feet of the next bird that comes along, then quickly put a hand around its neck to keep the long, hooked beak from cutting into me.

Then I'll either stretch its neck or twirl it. Our Spanish cook at our home in Cuba twirled them over her head. Seconds later, the chicken was dead and simmering in boiling water to loosen its feathers. I will twirl the bird I catch, then cut off its head with my knife. I can already hear Simonne's horrified protests. Am I up to it? We can afford to wait a couple of days, but no longer. Besides, Sim will let out a double squawk if I eat one of her bird buddies on Bastille Day.

At noon, we enter a trash line, usually a sign that land is not far off. Could there be a river nearby that empties into the ocean? The line runs north and south, and we traverse it on our easterly drift, once again confirming that the wind does push us along. We cross pieces of colored plastic, leaves, and small pieces of wood. When Sim spots a larger object ten feet from the raft, we row toward it and find that it's a pumice stone, three inches long by two wide and one inch thick. It has little stones embedded all through it and is so strange that we keep it. If this is truly a trash line that started onshore, then we're a lot closer to land than the radio signals indicate. On the other hand, it could be munched-up ship trash. But the pumice stone? Where did it come from?

Simonne picks up faint radio signals in the late afternoon. Though she can't make out words—it's more like a rumble—she has no doubt it is a shore station. When she first listened four weeks ago, she heard absolutely nothing until midnight. AM radio waves have a range of a hundred to two hundred miles, depending on the power of the station. When we cruised the Bahamas, we lost all the Florida stations when we were a hundred miles out. As we get closer to shore, she should pick up stations earlier in the day. If she doesn't, we'll know we've drifted into the westerly flowing current and are on our way to the exotic islands of the South Seas.

We make two liters of water, skip supper entirely, and await nightfall and the arrival of sharks. Whoever the timekeeper is in shark country never fails to signal. At ten P.M. sharp, the attacks begin. A light cloud cover helps block the moon, but there is still enough light coming through to keep me from seeing our nemeses. The sharks are particularly vicious tonight and strike the raft with machine-gun precision.

I plunge the fishing rod into the water while lying on my back. As a precaution against losing it, I've tied a six-foot length of cord from the pole to my wrist. I hear the midnight chirp on my watch as I fight off an urgent urge to sleep. I never stop moving the pole in and out of the water, for I've found that the splashes do keep away all sharks except the mean ones. Sim prays all the while.

Days ago, before I started to tie the pole to my wrist, I had fallen asleep with the barrel end on my chest. Apparently, I moved in my sleep, and the pole slipped off and started to go over the side. Sim caught it at the last moment. Now I keep the pole tied at all times, which creates a problem when Sim needs it in a rush to beat off a turtle. What would we do if we lost our first line of defense against sharks and turtles? Besides, the pole is part of my fishing gear. We could not survive for long on drinking water alone.

Sim prays, rosary in her hand, her eyes fixed on the canopy, her face worn and forlorn. Our hands still joined, I pull her toward me to give her a kiss. We stay together for the longest time. Today is day thirty-one aboard *Last Chance*, day fifty-three out of Balboa, and day thirty-four since our last radio contact with land. Is no one searching for us? Does no one care? On the other hand, we alone got ourselves into this mess, and alone we must find a way out. I am now convinced that no one will come looking for us. If they do, they'll never find us. We're invisible, a six-foot bump in a million-square-mile ocean. The odds are a hundred times better to win the lottery than to be found at sea.

We share a cracker for breakfast. Then, while it's still cool, we make two liters of water. Sim has the morning report: "Bush and Gorby enjoyed the party in Paris. There's a Soviet sub on fire off Norway. Do you think the kids will make a connection? Probably not. Leona Helmsley is in deep trouble with the tax people. Her trial's going on in New York. The world goes on without the least concern over our fate. We are so insignificant. Why should anyone worry? Of course, if Trump or Michael Jackson had vanished, it would be another story."

"Forty days," continues Sim. "Our punishment is forty days. At that time, God will send someone to save us. Moses went up the mountain for forty days, and Jesus stayed forty days in the desert. We have forty days of Lent and the Muslims have Ramadan. Yes," she says with a distant look, "we must wait for the fortieth day to pass. You'll see. Help will come!"

"Sim, I think you're right. C'mon, cheer up. Let's celebrate our anniversary. Can you believe you've been in this waterbed with your lover for an entire month? Isn't that the greatest? You always wanted a long honeymoon."

"What honeymoon are you talking about? With sharks and turtles and a shaggy, fish-smelling raft mate? It's been a little crowded. But really, one month? How much longer will the raft hold together?"

"The raft will last until we reach shore or someone finds us. If no one saves us, we'll save ourselves. We've traveled at least five hundred miles so far. Another few more, and we're home. Let's eat a can today," I continue. "It's almost Sunday and an important milestone. Not too many people drift around the Pacific Ocean or, for that matter, any ocean for a month."

Sim digs under the bunched comforter that makes up her headrest and comes up with a small can. She hands me the bent can opener, which I force back into shape. It doesn't quite remove the lid, and I need to use the knife to pry it off. Simonne takes the handle of the toothbrush and ladles a white paste into my mouth. It turns out to be cream of mushroom soup. We savor each tiny morsel until we finish half the can. It takes all our self-control to stop and leave half for supper.

With our hunger partially satisfied, we play a game of dominoes. I win. When we tire of that, we play twenty questions while the afternoon slowly dwindles away. I stump Sim with the castle in Disney World, and she gets me with the Miraflores Locks of the Panama Canal. We stop playing when rainwater leaks through the canopy and the wind increases to more than twenty knots. Thirty-foot swells roll under us like express trains. Six-foot breakers ride their tops and wash completely over the raft. We hang on for dear life in our seaworthy little craft. Before night sets in, we finish the mushroom soup. Sim reads and prays, and I prepare for the long night ahead, so full of unknowns.

By the time midnight comes around, we have seen everything. Sharks, turtles, rain, wind, and huge breaking waves. On the plus side, we have a strong current. The weather is out of the southwest and isn't improving or changing. Sim now prays for high wind and waves like I do, as she realizes we need speed to reach land and safety.

Time is our enemy. Every day that passes increases the chances of disaster. And our raft, all considered, has stayed together marvelously. It wasn't designed by a long shot for this kind of duty, but it has taken incredible punishment and is still pretty much in one piece.

I hear Sim scream, "Bill! What was that? Quick! Look!"

I try to open my eyes, but they're glued shut. I pick at the hardened ooze and work them open. I'm in a daze. In fact, I have been dreaming, unusual for me. "What's going on, Sim?"

"Something is in the raft. It flew in the window. Here, it's over here. Take the flashlight."

I switch on the flashlight and feel around. My hands tighten around something slippery and long. "It's a flying fish, Sim. Wow! We've got bait for tomorrow. We're back in business!" It could also make delicious ceviche. On *Siboney*, sailing with my sons, we always had three or four flying fish on deck in the morning. We scaled and cleaned them and marinated them in lime juice. "You've never tasted anything as good as flying-fish ceviche," I tell Sim. "Pass the lime juice; I'll show you."

"I hope a dorado doesn't decide to jump in," she exclaims. "It would tear the raft apart." Dorados spring ten feet into the air and, when they land, give the ocean a mighty slap in an obvious show of ecstasy.

I put the flying fish into the bait can and turn back to Sim. "Do you want to hear my dream?" Sim nods, and I recount my dream.

"We are on a raft much like this one. It's a clear, blue day. When I look out, I notice we're in Biscayne Bay. It's Sunday morning, and the bay is full of boats of all sizes. Sailboats and powerboats pass close by. People on board wave at us but keep going. I can't imagine why none of them stop. We wave and yell, but it doesn't do any good. They can't hear us.

"Several boats from Matheson Hammock Marina motor up and stop. Our friends say hello. We chat for a while and they drive off. I don't know what to think. They act as if our floating around the bay in a worn-out raft is normal. Shortly after, all the boats leave, and we are again alone. That's the dream."

Sim nods. "I had a Biscayne Bay dream myself several nights ago. It took me hours to fall asleep that night. It always does. I couldn't find a comfortable position. While I tried to sleep, I prayed to God to save us. I thought of my babies. I cried and drove myself into a complete mental mess. All the while, you were snoring. After a long time, I got so tired that I fell asleep and dreamed. I still don't know what to make of it. It was so vivid and in full color."

She has me curious. "So tell me."

"We were on a boat. *Siboney?* No. It was, but it wasn't. We were on Biscayne Bay, in Miami, near the Rusty Pelican restaurant. I can see land. Then, suddenly, it's not the bay anymore. We're on the high seas. Where? I don't know. The water is dark green.

"A strange-looking boat comes our way. It looks like a square houseboat. As it passes, I notice it's black and has large windows, like a house. I can see furniture inside. On the roof of the houseboat sits a man. A large man, like a Viking. He has a red beard and a wide fur hat. He looks wild. I hear a voice say, 'This is *der Schwarze* Ole.'

"The man sits with his booted legs over the side, his right elbow touching his right knee. He looks down at us but does nothing. The boat passes. We scream and call. The boat doesn't stop.

"We see several other houseboats coming, like a procession. The first is English; I can see inside. There is a fireplace and flowered sofas. A white-haired mother and an older son are having tea. They chat with each other, oblivious of us. There is no time to call. They continue on their way and disappear.

"Another houseboat approaches. This one is French. I hear voices; I see people. Children are laughing. A piano plays and food is on a table. It too vanishes.

"Then comes the last houseboat. It has a German flag. This time, I can see inside a large rustic room. Five little girls are there, sisters, all dressed in pretty flowered dresses. Blond tresses hang from their heads. The father sits on stairs that come from above. He has a little nursery rhyme written on a banner in German. It says something about his five little daughters and how proud he is of them. There is much joy and happiness. This houseboat also leaves, and again everything is quiet and empty. I am alone and I wake up."

I shake my head. "That's a first-class dream. It's strange that we both had dreams involving Biscayne Bay. Will we ever see it again?"

Sim is earnest. "There's a message there. In my dream, four boats passed us. The first was Scandinavian, the next English, then a French, and the last German. They all flew flags, but none of them saw us. On the raft, a Norwegian ship passed us on the second day. An English ship passed us a week ago. Two more ships, a French and a German, will pass by, but they won't see us."

She continues dreamily. "The last houseboat had the man singing a nursery rhyme in German. I'll hum it for you. I used to sing it to my Cris when we lived in Germany. It's so soothing, optimistic, loving, so consoling. God sent me this dream to lift up my heart, to give me hope." Tears stream down Sim's cheeks while she hums the tune.

A thundering wave drowns out her last few notes. Another great mass of black water capped by deep froth collides with our fragile vessel. The windward side of the raft collapses from the weight of the water.

ABOARD THE RAFT
LAST CHANCE
0130 MONDAY • JULY 17, 1989 • DAY 33

THE STORM RAGES throughout the night. Bolts of lightning highlight towering breakers that attempt to overwhelm our battered raft. In the midst of the maelstrom, sharks and turtles locate the raft and attack without letup. Our black, water-filled world is a scene from hell. Salt water and rainwater mingle to find and soak our last shred of dryness. Air loss increases under the harsh punishment. We pump and bail in a mad struggle to keep the raft afloat, ever ready for the expected, the unexpected, or sudden death from a bolt of fire, a rogue wave, or a predator.

A hellish roar and a rending smash carry the raft into the chasm of a trough. *Last Chance*, on its beam ends, shoved off a towering precipice, threatens to flip. Instinctively, I lean heavily to the high side and pull Simonne over with me. The sea passes over us while bucketfuls of seawater burst into the raft. We hang on as the wave spends its energy and speeds on, oblivious to the bobbing bit of battered plastic in its wake. The raft slides down into the abyss made by the retreating wave, then rises to face the next onslaught. That would have been a wet wave even for *Siboney*. My dear *Siboney*, you now rest forever in a cold, black, wet grave. We sailed together through rough weather and calm seas. My sons even sank you three times, but you popped back up, stronger than before. You have a long history, but now you are gone forever.

Dawn catches me by surprise. The raft is soft, which means Sim has also slept, a most unusual phenomenon, and the sharks have left, also unusual. When she dozes, I do my best to stay awake to keep sharks and turtles away, but she's had terrible luck with that. No sooner does Sim drop into a deep sleep than a shark slaps the raft with the force of a freight train. Instantly, she's up, terrified and unable to snooze for another half day.

The morning, though heavy with rain, is more welcome than a bright, sunny day back home. We open the leeward window to escape in some small way the confinement of our minuscule habitat. Dull-gray seas sweep underneath and speed away. We follow each wave as it rolls downwind, longing to speed with it to its inevitable collision with land.

Today, Monday, July 17, is our thirty-third day on the raft, near the end of our fifth week. That we are still alive and healthy is a constant source of amazement to both of us. Sim appears to have lost about thirty pounds, most of it excess fat. We've talked about dieting for years, but not this way. I wrap my hands around my upper leg. My thumbs completely overlap. Weeks ago, they barely touched. Most surprising, we haven't had a cold or an infection of any kind. Where are the customary boils of the castaway? And I've grown accustomed to the sores on my back, which Sim douses with fresh water whenever they itch.

We have a dozen and a half crackers left and one rusty can with who knows what in it. If it's more of that diet Veg-All, over it goes. Today the flying fish will be converted into bait.

Noon brings calmer weather as seas subside and skies clear. In the distance a school of fish jumps out of the water, leaving a wide froth on the sea. I put out my line with a piece of the flying fish on the hook but get no takers. There are no fish anywhere near the raft, so I stow the fishing gear. Together, Sim and I make two liters of water, eat a cracker each, and then start to nap. A loud splash and the sound of heavy breathing startle us.

Sim jumps up and calls out, "Dolphins!" Several circle as one of them slides under the raft. They're three times as big as the "Flipper" variety common in the Caribbean, and they're gray with light spots all over. Let's hope they chase the sharks away, as legend claims. Dozens of small fish leap out of the water to escape their hungry jaws. Frenzied triggerfish jump wildly while the dolphins plunge from school to school to feed. I continue to watch the activity out of my window as Sim struggles to sleep.

School fish dart desperately over the ocean in search of safety. They dive under our raft with the dolphins in hot pursuit. The water surrounding the raft boils as the dolphins come up for a brief breath and dive again with a violent kick of their four-foot tails. Hundreds of fish bump the raft as they try to escape their predators. A white froth surrounds us as triggerfish leap out of the water. They're so close and so many. Would it be possible to snatch one with my hand? I decide to try.

I put on my gloves and empty the contents from the pail. Sim has her back to me and appears to be asleep. One fish almost jumps into the raft. I lean over to grab at one of the black shapes. I touch it, but it shoots away, too slippery to hold. On my second try, I wrap my hand firmly around a fish and lift it into the raft. It's black with a tiny mouth. I drop it into the pail. In seconds, I catch and drop three more fish in the bucket. The fourth one jumps out and onto Sim's feet, who jumps up with a "What's that?"

"A fish. I've been fishing. I caught four fish."

"You used the flying fish?"

"Madame, watch my hands. Faster than the eye." In minutes I plop three more fish into the pail, now almost full.

"You're fabulous. Oh, I love you. I'm so happy." Tears stream down her cheeks. "What are they?"

"Triggerfish. Not the best eating, although they are a delicacy in the Bahamas and in some of the Caribbean islands." From the looks of it, we have an unlimited supply. They are like piranhas and will bite anything, including cloth and, of course, human flesh. Their skin is as tough as leather. "I hope this dull knife will cut through their hides," I say to Sim. "Dig out your nail file, and I'll sharpen the knife before I begin."

I set up the lid to the camcorder case on the paddle as my filleting board and press hard to saw through the hide of the first fish. I open it all the way around and remove the fillet, complete with hide. I do the same with the second fillet and toss the carcass far from the raft. Dozens of its school buddies quickly remove all the remaining flesh. As it drops deeper, the dull-gray shape of a shark moves in and gulps what's left. I remove the fillets from the hides and toss the skins over the side. Fish again scramble. I cut the fillets into half-inch cubes and offer Sim the first bite. She savors it and declares it not too bad. We finish seven fillets and leave the rest for bait. Stuffed for the first time in days, I pass Sim the water bottle and then retire, my day's work done.

Rain starts before midnight with a violent squall from the east. It kills the last of the west wind and pushes us away from land at an alarming rate. The current is light, the raft swings, and not far away, Sim hears a whale blow. This thirty-third day has been full of surprises. On to day thirty-four. Oh dear Lord, be kind; have mercy.

When morning dawns, we find the boobies have left us, seemingly for good this time. Storm petrels weave their nervous way inches over the waves in search of an unwary baby flying fish. Above, two frigate birds soar, observing, waiting, hoping. Today is Alex's eighteenth birthday. Simonne has been on a guilt trip for days and expresses her inner sorrow. "I shouldn't have left him alone to face the rigors of the world. I'm missing this most important of birthdays. What is my poor baby doing? I hope he's not alone. I'm a terrible mother."

"Happy birthday to Alex, Sim. Let's celebrate." We sing "Happy Birthday" while tears roll down Simonne's cheeks. We top off our party with a drop of brandy each. There is still a half inch left in the bottle, and we've been nipping on it for a month.

Sim saddens. "My poor baby, I wonder what he's doing all alone. I hope some of our friends invite him over. He's probably lonely and worried to death over the fate of his mother. I hope his father called from Spain and his brother invited him out to dinner or something. Poor baby, how could I have abandoned him? I am the cruelest of mothers, leaving a young baby alone like that."

"Baby, he's bigger than I am, and better able to handle himself than most twenty-five-year-olds. This is doing him a lot of good. Away from you, he'll learn fast how to solve his own problems. You mother him too much. When you see him next, he's going to be responsible and mature."

"When I see him next? Will I ever see him again? Don't you understand we're not going to make it?"

"You're dead wrong. We've been adrift thirty-four days. If that voice you heard is right, we have just six days to go. Our test is about to end. God isn't keeping us alive only to let us die. He teaches and waits for us to learn how to best live the rest of our lives."

Sim nods. "You're right. I should have more faith."

I try for a change of mood. "Let's have a little game of dominoes to celebrate the first day of our sixth week adrift."

I find it easier to sit up now that I've lost my paunch. Before we start, Sim washes my back with fresh water and spreads a tad of her hand lotion on the worst of the open sores.

After midmorning, a heavy black cloud out of the east develops into a full-fledged squall. This new dimension further confuses the waves and kills what little wind was starting to build from the south. With no current and an easterly wind, we'll soon be back where we sank. Oh dear Lord, have mercy on us.

The squall lasts less than an hour, and as the sun struggles to reappear, I hand-catch two triggerfish for bait. Next, I land a large tripletail, then stop, not wishing to load the raft with fish we can't eat. I put it directly onto my filleting board and quickly remove both fillets. The top of the camcorder case, full of blood and insides, spills over onto my crotch before I can empty it over the side. There's everything in it now. Blood, scales, pieces of fish. Sim picks scales off my belly, legs, and bottom. How I dream of a dip in the ocean, but the triggerfish would skin me within seconds.

A light southwest wind starts to build in the middle of the afternoon. The current returns, skies clear, and the sun shines. That it shines as well on two infatuated turtles makes the day less than perfect. Under, around, out, and back again, the male chases the female. The female tries by every means to remain chaste; he does his best to keep the ocean full of baby turtles. Sim gets terribly worked up. She says words in Italian that sound highly improper. I lie back and hope I'm not next on her hit list.

The day is bright and clear. As I scan the horizon, I study the makeup of a string of white clouds to the east.

"Sim, look, there to the east," I point. "See those clouds, the ones that go straight up? Those are land clouds. Heat generated on land funnels moisture up and forms that type of cumulus. A cloud that hovers and does not move downwind is indicative of land. Often, it hangs downwind from the center of the island. Keep your eyes open."

The cloud does not move. We watch it with hope in our hearts and a prayer on our lips. Land. Never have I yearned for land more than I do now. Land, with people and green trees and birds singing and gardens with flowers. Sim's thoughts run along the same track as mine. "I can see our garden at home, our empty house, the palm tree growing by the canal, the cardinals at the feeder, and my young Alex, just turned eighteen, alone in the world."

MIAMI, FLORIDA
2315 TUESDAY • JULY 18, 1989

The Butler residence, empty of all furniture, rocks to the sound of a live band and over a hundred screaming teenagers. Alex is celebrating his eighteenth birthday. Mom and Bill are far away on their dream trip, sailing around the world.

Alex invited forty of his close friends to a full-blown birthday bash. These friends in turn invited their friends. Each paid three dollars to get in. Alex planned to have a good time and end up with money in his pocket to finance the balance of his summer vacation.

Haphazardly parked cars line the streets leading to the Butler home for two blocks in every direction. The quiet residential neighborhood has never seen so much activity. One of the boys parks his car in a neighbor's driveway. The neighbor threatens him with a shotgun. Another neighbor notices the scene and calls the police. Minutes later, several cars full of skinheads pull up and crash the party.

The Dade County SWAT Team sends in their full resources in reply to the phone alarm. They surround the house while a police helicopter hovers overhead, its searchlight lighting up the scene. The police enter the house but find nothing out of order. Outside, the crazies have other ideas. The police decide to stop the party, and the teenagers quickly disperse. Alex's eighteenth birthday party is over.

ABOARD THE RAFT
LAST CHANCE
0800 WEDNESDAY • JULY 19, 1989 • DAY 35

W E AWAKEN ABRUPTLY at eight in the morning to a dozen quick whacks. A large pack of greenish-gray sharks attacks the raft from all directions, their big bulging eyes full of mischief. I land my first hit on a five-footer, then bonk three more in a row. Left behind is their unmistakable oily wake.

"Sim, I can't believe what I'm seeing. Look. Two of the sharks have tags. One has a round white tag, and the other tag is long and red."

Sim's reaction is immediate. "I'd like to meet the son of a bitch who tagged them instead of blasting them to pieces. That's criminal. To be eaten by a tagged shark. Who would ever believe it?"

"The sadists probably recapture them to check their stomachs. Oh, look here, this one has a French passport and blond hair!"

"Stop your dumb joking and beat them off. They're going to destroy the raft before too long. How many in the pack?"

"They're hard to count, but there are at least twenty, and they are all about the same size. Did you know that from birth, sharks pack together in groups according to age? Otherwise, the bigger ones end up eating the little ones."

"Butler, you are the great living encyclopedia. Anything else, Cousteau? Answer the big question. Why do they continue to attack the raft? You say to spray, but why? I'm not sure I buy that."

"There's not much floating in this part of the ocean. These sharks must be males intent on leaving their mark. Many animals do the same. Even humans mark, although we are a bit more subtle." Sim sneers and sticks out her tongue at me.

Their attack pattern is always the same. They turn belly up as they come abreast of the raft, then run their belly along the side and spray. At the last moment, they instinctively whip their tail, possibly to spread their oil. I stab at every shark that approaches within reach. If I hit one behind the eyes, it flips its tail with a splash, then circles five to ten feet below the raft. Sometimes it comes up for another poke, but usually it stays deep only to be replaced by a more adventurous brother. After an hour, the pack leaves as quickly as it arrived. I don't get a chance to settle back down before the sound of a gurgle announces the arrival of a turtle.

As it heads straight in, I pass the pole to Sim. "Your turn, sweetie. Turtle ahoy on the starboard bow."

The sea boils with triggerfish as I prepare to fish. They await my next cast, their toothy mouths spitting water, their black beady eyes on my every move. As soon as my bait just touches the water, dozens leap for it. Before they grab the bait, I jerk it up and drop it ten feet away. The triggers rush to the new spot. Before they arrive, I jerk up my hook and drop it in the original place. Much of the time, I lose my bait to a triggerfish that leaps out of the water and sucks the bait right off the hook. The triggerfish mouth is solid teeth. Wide open, the mouth of an average trigger is no more than the size of a penny. When it strikes a bait, it either sucks it in fast or grabs a piece of the bait with its teeth and pulls it off the hook. When a tripletail is in range, I drop the bait right on its nose. More often than not, the tripletail spooks and a trigger steals the bait in a second or less.

Before I lose all my day-old, mushy bait, I put on my gloves and quickly catch three triggers. With fresh bait, I cast back and forth again to lure the shy tripletails closer. One swims in. When I drop the bait on top of it, it strikes and, with a hard jerk, runs off with my line. I pull the line taut and in seconds board a two-pound tripletail. Two more tripletails quickly follow, one a monster of five pounds that barely fits in the bucket.

I drop the next bait over the side and, without noticing, let out too much line. The bait sinks out of my sight. I feel a tug and tug back. The line tightens. Sim grabs the pole and pulls the extra line up to the eye of the pole. She holds the pole out from the side and takes line in as I haul. I look down and freeze. It's a big bull dorado, at least a forty-pounder. I've yearned to catch a dorado from day one, but a more manageable one. This one could rip the raft to pieces were it to thrash. Sim holds the pole far away from the raft while I arrange the sailbag to cover the air chamber and my lap. I prepare for the inevitable fight for which the so-called dolphin fish are known.

I pull on the line and Sim takes it up. Surprisingly, the dorado isn't putting up a fight. We really don't need this fish, since we've landed more fish than we can possibly eat. Perhaps I can get my hook back and release it. I ease the line in hopes it'll jump and spit out the hook. My ploy fails. I pull on the line until the fish is inches below the surface. I can see it clearly now. It's big, bright blue with silvery yellow streaks. Why doesn't it battle for its life? My mouth waters. Since we left Panama, I've hungered for dorado.

"OK, Sim. Here it comes. I'll lift it onto my lap. You drop the pole and cover it with the sailbag. We've got to keep it from the side of the raft at all costs. Ready? Now!"

The sailbag, doubled up, covers the air chamber over which I will pull the fish. I heave, and the dorado is on my lap and covered by the sailbag in less than a second. We put our weight on it and look at each other with amazement. It can't escape now. We laugh and shout. Sim passes me the knife, and I stab the beautiful animal a dozen times about the head. It quivers and dies seconds later. Its shimmering colors turn a dull blue at the instant of death.

We look at each other speechless, unable to believe what we have done. This bull dorado weighs forty-five if not fifty pounds. Two castaways landed it on a flimsy raft in the middle of the Pacific Ocean. This has to be a record of some kind. And it'll stand forever because no one else will ever do anything this crazy again. With three tripletails and now this dorado, we have far more than fifty pounds of fish on board.

"I'm starving for dorado so I'll fillet it first," I announce. "First, get the camera and take a picture of the big fisherman." I push up against one end of the raft with the dorado lengthwise in one hand and the five-pound tripletail in the other. Sim pushes herself up against the other end of the raft and snaps. Wow, that's a shot for the record books.

I slice a fillet from the tail, cut it into small chunks, and promptly pop a chunk into my mouth. The meat is mushy, not like the usual dorado, and the taste is strange. I hand a piece to Sim, who gags.

I ask, "What's wrong?"

"That fish is bad. Feel the texture; it's not firm like dorado meat. And it tastes funny. Bill, that fish is bad. It's sick."

I cut a piece toward the head, and the meat there is also bad. It appears to be old and tastes rotten. This dorado had to be on the verge of dying when I caught it. It was unable to compete for food and hit my tiny piece of bait. I recover my hook from deep inside its stomach, which means I would have had to kill it anyway. I drop the dorado over the side, where it sinks like a fifty-pound brick.

I prepare the big tripletail and make Sim eat a few bites, but the rotten dolphin meat has killed her appetite. When we're finished, over half of our food remains. Why did I ever go for that last cast? Must be the unquenchable lust of the fisherman.

Evening is upon us. Sim reads as wind and waves again pick up, and by the time night falls, a good breeze blows out of the southwest. Waves build. Great. Let it blow.

I look over at Sim. "Are you awake?"

"Awake? You're a real comedian, or do you think my name is Bill Butler? I pray this terrible wind and big waves stop. I can't take it any longer. Some of those waves bash the raft harder than a shark. How much more punishment can this raft take?"

"Only five days to forty," I remind her. "I hope that little voice called it right. I'm ready to bail out."

"Speaking of bailing, give me a hand. Move your behind and hold this cushion up so I can get to the water." Sim bails strenuously. When I push down on the floor to make a sump, triggerfish bite my fingers through the fabric. Water drains from the bedding and foul-weather gear to fill the sump.

When the new day dawns there is no wind and no current. We have seen no planes, no ships, no birds, and no land. Sharks batter us, and turtles try their best to mate with the raft. The raft has lost much of its integrity. We pump air every forty-five minutes to keep the air chambers from bending in half.

"Bill. A terrible thing happened last night. A United jet crashed in Sioux City, and there are a lot of dead. That's terrible. Think of all the poor people who died. Horrible, horrible. Just before the plane crashed, they were all praying in the cabin, no doubt like us, pleading with God to be saved.

"And we're still alive. I can remember back to our first day or two on the raft when you worried about staying afloat for a week. Here we are, after five full weeks, doing not all that badly.

"You are a zombie. We're drenched to our bones in a rotten, leaky raft lost in the Pacific, battered constantly by wind, waves, and sharks. Butler, wake up. Our situation is critical."

Sim's negative attitude depresses her and bothers me. "We're alive, kid," I say. "There are a lot of good people in Sioux City who aren't. Let's thank God for taking care of us as well as He has. Think positive. We're going to live; we're going to make it. Perhaps not in the next few days, but we'll make it. God will help us if we help ourselves and maintain our faith in Him." Sim, rosary clutched, prays. Her focus is far off. Tears stream from her tired eyes. Thoughts of her mother and children plague her, since she is so sure she won't see them again. I find nothing of comfort to say. Sometimes silence works best with Sim.

Late in the morning when the rain stops, we put the bedding out to dry. The sea continues to flatten, and the sun makes an earnest try to shine through several layers of clouds. Our spirits improve. At one o'clock, I catch two triggerfish. With fresh bait, I quickly land two tripletails. The second tripletail pulls loose from the line and flops around inside the raft until Sim pins it with a cushion. The hook isn't on the line and has to be lost. Later, when I fillet the tripletail and cut its stomach open, I find our only hook deep inside, surrounded by a gullet full of small fish. What luck. What would I have done if I lost my only hook? I can't count on catching many fish by hand.

We eat until we're stuffed, pump up the raft, and snooze. Later, after Sim reads, we finish the tripletail and fall into Sim's favorite subject and one I try to avoid: our excellent chance of dying. I can't argue with her, for most of Sim's points are valid. We've defied the odds thus far. Will our luck continue?

It's better than for many in the Sioux City crash. Many good, God-loving people aboard that airplane died while we continue to live in an environment thousands of times more perilous than the one they lived in until those last few seconds. Like an air crash, when we go, will it be all over in seconds? We are being allowed to live but for how long? Another week? Another month? We must continue to pray to the Lord for help and His mercy. I see no other way out.

The current picks up speed during the night and pushes us to the southeast. When the current is strong, the raft defies the wind and waves and lines up with the current. The long side of the raft points in the direction we move. When the current lessens, the raft will swing through 20, 30, and up to 90 degrees either side of our course. With no current, the raft drifts perpendicular to the wind. With these daily observations, I plot our daily dead-reckoning position. But really, how close am I?

"Preparing for night" is part of our established evening routine. Sim puts the flashlight, flare, compass, and radio next to her head. I tie the air pump next to the valve. Our eyeglasses and watches dangle from pieces of fishing line above us. The pole rests lengthwise next to me, ready for instant use. We each have a paddle close at hand. A bottle full of water lies next to my hip, ready for the night's consumption. Sim reads just before last light.

ABOARD THE RAFT
LAST CHANCE
0700 SUNDAY • JULY 23, 1989 • DAY 39

I AM GLAD THE TRAUMA of Alex's eighteenth birthday is far behind us. Sim had been next to impossible to live with for a week. What the kid needs is a chance to fly on his own, away from his mommy.

The past several days have been relatively easy—not too many sharks, no major storms, and good fishing. Now we greet a beautiful day, our thirty-ninth adrift. Tomorrow is day forty. I hope the voice Sim heard was the real thing.

This is perfect weather for drying. We drape our bedding over the canopy, one corner at a time. We dry each edge, careful it doesn't fly into the briny deep. By midafternoon, all the bedding is back in place and enjoyably dry. Sim rearranges our stores, and we lie back to enjoy the fine weather, the peace, and our dry bed.

It's peaceful except for a nagging whistling sound. Air is escaping from the patch I fitted on our first day on the raft. Whenever a wave washes over it, water covers the leak and makes it whistle. Air leaks faster than a week ago. Sim's remark earlier today of "I don't like the sound of that leak" started me thinking.

In fact, I've wanted to check the patch for several days. Sooner or later, I will have to adjust the two patches to reduce air loss. The repair will have to be done on a calm day, such as this. Why not try to fix it now? We have an hour or two of light remaining. Sim will not want me to touch the patches. I'll have to convince her a step at a time.

"Sim, I think I'll take a look at the patches."

"What do you plan to do?"

"Just look at them."

She looks into my eyes. "You're not going to take them apart?"

"No, never. I just want see if there is anything loose."

"You shouldn't do it."

"I'm only going to make sure everything is OK."

"I am not sure."

"Look, it's losing more and more air, and unless we do something, we are going to end up pumping air every few minutes."

"See, I knew it. You want to fix it. Bill, you're not going to take the patch apart. That's final."

"I wouldn't do anything without telling you. I'll just check to see if they're loose, that's all."

"I don't know. Let's think about it."

"It'll be days before we get another calm day like this again. I should take a look at it now."

"Let me think about it."

"Holy mackerel, think about it. It'll be dark, the weather will pick up, and we'll be pumping every ten minutes. OK, think about it. But get ready to pump."

"Do you promise not to take anything apart?"

"I said I am only going to take a look at the patch to see how it's holding. If the wing nuts are loose, I'll tighten them. If we wait any longer, it'll be dark, and we may as well forget it."

"How are you going to do it?"

"First, we have to let the air out of the arch facing the patch."

"Let the air out of the arch? No, no. I don't like that at all."

"Don't worry. I'll let out only enough so I can lean over and reach the patch. It'll just take a minute."

"OK, but be careful. And no crazy things."

"Relax, baby. In a few minutes, I'll have it fixed."

We haven't taken air out of the arch or, for that matter, put any in since we first filled it after we sank. It has held air perfectly, a constant reminder how easy our life would be had we not torn the raft when leaving *Siboney*.

"Sim, let's go. Let some air out of the arch."

Sim unscrews the air valve and air slowly whistles out. She closes the valve, then reopens it to allow more air to escape. I can tell she is worried.

"OK, Sim, that's good. Let me see if I can get to it."

I turn on my knees and lean over the arch and canopy. I reach the patches easily. Each patch is an oval disk, about an inch and a half by three inches, made up of two parts. The part that goes inside the tube has a rubber gasket and a screw stem. The other half fits outside the tube and fits against the rubber gasket. A wing nut runs down on the screw stem and, when tightened, seals the patch.

Both wing nuts are tight.

"Bill, what are you doing?"

"Checking the wing nuts."

"You promised not to do anything!"

"Don't worry. I'm just looking at it to make sure it's tight."

As the original hole was too large for one patch, I aligned the two side by side. Air escapes from the space between the two. Three weeks ago, I dismantled the inboard patch and moved it closer to the other patch. While the patch was off, the emergency internal sleeve kept us buoyant. The adjustment worked.

Sim is anxious. "Bill, what are you doing?"

"I'm making sure the patch is tight. They are slightly apart. The plastic I put in last time isn't doing the job. That's where the leak is."

"Bill, don't take it apart!"

"Hey, don't worry, have patience."

I jostle the inboard patch. It would leak less if both patches were closer. I need to loosen it.

"Bill, how is it?"

"Fine. Just a few more seconds."

I loosen the wing nut one turn, but the patch is still too tight to move. I turn the nut another half turn. It's still too tight. I ease it again. Then a bit more.

"What are you doing?"

"Relax. I'm just checking the patch."

"What do you mean? Don't you dare take the patches apart. Promise."

"No problem. I'll be finished in a minute."

I loosen the wing nut another partial turn. Without warning, the wing nut flies off with the top of the patch right behind it. There's a sudden outrush of air and the raft collapses. Instantly, the air chamber becomes limp and the raft begins to sink. I stare momentarily at the gaping hole and the three pieces of the patch in my hand.

Sim screams. "What's happening? My God! My God! We're sinking! What have you done?"

"The patch came apart. Pump! Fast!"

Sim had plugged the pump in as a precaution and dives for it as she prays loudly, "Holy Mary, Mother of God. Save us!"

My knees push the floor of the raft even deeper, but I have nowhere to move. The air chamber is now an empty piece of limp plastic. Half the patch is inside the air chamber, but the rubber gasket has slipped off. My knees push the floor deeper, and water pours over the side.

Sim, under the collapsed arch, pumps furiously and prays aloud in French. I take the patch out of the hole and reseat the gasket. Water rises over my feet. The hole starts to go under. I pull the tube up and insert the patch with my left hand. Water fills the raft. Within seconds, the raft will sink from under us, the air tube full of water.

I fit the inside half against the other patch and put the top half on. Luckily, the parts are on a wire welded to the end of the screw. I can't lose them. Water reaches my waist. Sim treads water, still pumping. I hoist the corner with the patch to keep the air chamber from filling with water.

Sim cries aloud, "My God. We're sinking! Oh Lord, save us."

"Sim, relax. Pump! Don't stop! Don't harass me."

"Are you crazy? We're sinking. What have you done? Oh Lord, have mercy on us!" She begins to scream in either French or Italian. It drives me crazy and I scream back at her.

"Sim, quit screaming, for God's sake! Pump!"

Sim hasn't stopped pumping. More water pours over both sides of the raft. Empty water bottles float away.

"Have you fixed it? Bill, we're sinking. Fast, fast, be fast. Our Father, who art in Heaven . . ."

My nervous fingers struggle to complete the job in time. The top half must go on exactly in line with the bottom half or it will not hold air. My waist is underwater now. I shift my weight. The patch is going under again, but this time I can lift it no farther. The air tubes are entirely empty. Seconds remain before the raft sinks all the way.

I fit the top of the patch in place, spin the wing nut, and tighten the assembly. I drop quickly to a horizontal position and spread my weight over the entire bottom. The sides of the raft rise just several inches above the water.

"Sim, I'll take over pumping. Bail! For goodness' sake, bail!"

Water floods the raft. Everything is underwater. I pump frantically, but the air chamber doesn't fill.

"Sim, how does it feel? Is it getting tighter?"

"I can't tell."

Sim bails while I pump air. Ever so slowly, the air chambers expand, and the raft regains a little of its buoyancy. The bedding and clothing, so carefully dried earlier today, are all soaked. Night closes in on us. Sharks batter the sides of the raft. We could have been in the water right now.

Sim can hold her anger back no longer. "You bastard! You tried to kill us. I told you not to touch it! You're a murderer. A terrorist."

"I thought the emergency air chamber was full."

"You're stupid. You almost sank us. Another second and the raft would have sunk."

I can find no good excuse for my blunder. Seconds separated us from death. If the raft had filled with water, the tube with the open hole would have sucked in water. There would have been no way to empty it.

The single inflated arch would not have kept us afloat. It was an almost fatal, inexcusable mistake. I feel like an idiot. Sim lashes at me with all her fury. I take it because I know I was wrong. Otherwise, I'd choke her and throw her to the sharks.

Once the main air chamber is rigid, we inflate the arch and close the canopy. Will my hurried patch job hold? Soggy bedding lies in lumps under us. It had been so dry, drier than it had been it weeks. Now, it will never dry. The salt water will rot it like our T-shirts.

Sim fumes silently, her pressure valve about to blow. I came within seconds of sealing our fate. I honestly saw the raft plunge toward the deep. The patch came together with no more than a second to spare. At the last moment, when our fate hung in the balance, I felt the hand of the Lord guide mine. I could never have done the job alone. Thank you, dear Lord. You have helped us at our time of greatest need. Don't leave me now, ever.

Simonne hasn't stopped bailing. On her knees, she searches out water in the bilge. Together we wring out the bedding, which Sim then piles on top of me to continue to sponge the remaining water.

Sim rages silently as she spreads the wet bedding underneath our trembling bodies. She arranges the comforter over the cushions, then bunches up a corner as a pillow. We lie on the cold, soggy comforter, exhausted and shaken by our brush with a slow, painful death.

Our body heat slowly warms the comforter, and we manage to snooze until heavy rain awakens us. Water pours through the canopy. Seawater continues to drain to the sump created by our behinds. Sim bails while I pump air. The air chamber has held for an hour, which is surprising considering how fast I put the patch back together. I may have to adjust it again. But fat chance Sim will let me.

Simonne bails through the night. She uses a sponge when there isn't enough for the can. Bailing is an escape valve for her ire. Dawn is upon us before we know it, and her bombardment starts again. I've been readying myself all night. She organizes her thoughts, prepares her missiles, and lets fly.

"Why did you do it? Why? Can you just answer that single, simple question? Why?"

"I thought I could improve our lifestyle, keep from pumping so much."

"You've improved our lifestyle all right! That is, if you enjoy living in a soaking bilge. Butler, you've done a great job improving our lifestyle. Now we are pumping more often than before. You've soaked everything on board in salt water. We have lost our toothbrushes and toothpaste, and God knows what else floated away. Improve our lifestyle. Bah!"

Sim barely breathes before she continues. "You are a criminal, Butler. You tried to kill me yesterday. How anyone can be so stupid is beyond imagination. Why couldn't you leave the patch alone?

From now on, you touch nothing, not one thing. Do you hear me?"

"Hear you? You're yelling so loud they can hear you back in Miami. I thought the inner tube had air in it like it had when I fixed the patch the first time."

"You thought. Your sick thinking almost got the two of us killed. I thought this raft was tough after it got us through all those storms and shark attacks. You have now proven it's just a piece of junk. A small hole in the air chambers and it's over. That's all I needed. I couldn't sleep before; imagine now!"

I can't argue. It was stupid of me. I should have first made sure the inner tube had air. Or better yet, I should've left the patch alone. Now I've killed what little confidence Sim had in the raft.

Meanwhile, I pump air and Sim bails. I make two liters of water. When the sun shines through, I try to dry our bedding, but it's an exercise in futility. Then I wring water out of the foul-weather gear. Not much success there either.

Sim lashes at me. "Toss that overboard. I have never seen foul-weather gear that absorbs more water. If I fell overboard with it, I'd go straight to the bottom."

"We've got to keep it. We might need it to keep warm."

"Butler, you are sick. Don't even bother to explain how that soggy, heavy jacket is going to keep me warm. I worry about you. Your brain is no longer functional. Maybe it's from eating too much triggerfish. Helllpppp!" she screams. "Get me out of here!"

I look for a hole to hide in. I refuse to argue, and honestly, I have no argument. Somehow the logbook and workbook stayed dry. They were on top of the camcorder case at the opposite end of the raft, which floated higher because of a trapped air pocket. At least we saved something. I enter my debacle into the log.

Life must go on. I fish. I first hand-grab three triggers for bait. I cast for a tripletail. I use every trick I know to bring them in. Hundreds of triggerfish follow my every move. I tie a triggerfish carcass by the tail and hang it under the raft as a diversion. I cast out quickly as the triggers busy themselves with the carcass. They catch onto this ploy and cover both spots. When sharks move in on the dead trigger, I pull it out quickly. Another bad idea. I had better watch myself.

Today, trigger is the only thing on the menu. I had so hoped to improve Sim's disposition with a better meal. Simonne tries to dry the covers all afternoon. As evening approaches, our gear is a bit less soggy. Her readings have an increased meaning today. We thank God for saving us. Another second and the raft would have sunk. Thank you, Lord, thank you. I pray myself to sleep.

Simonne only interrupts her prayers to bail and help me pump air. I awaken to pump the air chambers full, then continue to doze. Sim can't get to sleep, her blood still pure adrenaline. The night is endless. Sharks arrive at two and batter the raft for an hour. A turtle and more sharks bother us until the wind shifts to the south.

Sim screams into the night. She howls like a wolf in a pathetic plea for help, for reassurance. I listen to her cry long into the night. By the time the skies lighten, the wind has built to a good blow. *Last Chance* scuds along. Both current and wind propel it eastward. An occasional wave showers water under the canopy to soak us. Low, fast-moving clouds sweep past on a collision course with land, now possibly no more than two hundred miles to the east. This is day forty-one on the raft for us, July 25. At nine o'clock tomorrow night, we will have been adrift one thousand hours. Sixty thousand minutes!

I keep my calculations in my navigation workbook. I keep both in a plastic bag next to my head. I have been doing some mental navigation. One thousand hours at one knot yields a thousand miles. That would put us closer to the coast than our radio signals indicate. One thousand hours at three-quarters of a knot totals seven hundred and fifty miles. That would put us three hundred and fifty miles off the coast, a very plausible result. One thousand hours at half a knot would have us six hundred miles off the coast. Radio fixes and the strength of radio reception tell us we're closer than that.

An average speed of three-quarters of a knot over the past forty-one days, when considering both current set and the effects of wind and waves, should be close to actual. That means we have three hundred and fifty miles to go. At a speed of three-quarters of a knot, we will need five hundred hours to reach shore. Five hundred hours equals twenty days. Lord, have mercy on us. Can we survive? Can the raft make it?

How can this flimsy raft hold together that long? Closer to shore, we will again be in the shipping lanes. Sooner or later, some alert crewman will surely see us. Also, we should spot the commercial fishing fleet. Why haven't we seen a single fisherman? Are there too many sharks to make commercial fishing interesting?

Sim sits up and looks out. Her face lights up. She calls:

"Bill, a ship! Up there! About a half mile. It's big!"

The ship steams at high speed a quarter mile to the north. It's heading west. They have transited the Panama Canal and are on a great circle route to the Far East. High waves and lack of sun kill any hope of being seen. I still haven't had a chance to use the mirror that came with the raft for signaling.

Sim turns away from the ship. "How many ships does this one make?"

"There's the *Ter Eriksen* and the one twenty-four days later, then the white one, and now this one. Four. We're going to see more ships from now on. We must keep watches. The one on watch must paddle around every fifteen minutes to scan the entire horizon."

"Aye, aye, captain. What do we do when it rains? Or at night with only one flare?"

"We pray and hope." I can't get Sim to focus on the upside of our future.

In minutes, the ship is but a dot on the fading horizon. It came to save us, and we did not grasp the opportunity. We didn't signal; we didn't wave. There's no doubt about it. God will not save us unless we meet Him halfway.

Sim's dejection shows on her face. "I wasn't looking. God did mean to save us in forty days. Oh, Bill, why didn't I look out in time?"

"Sweetie, He will save us; there's no question about that. He sent that ship as a signal, but we are not yet ready. He meant to show us He could save us at any time. We need more time."

"More time? Oh Lord, how long? How long? Have mercy on us. We have begged for forgiveness; our reconciliation is complete. Why continue to test us? There are so many bad people in the world that really deserve punishment. Why us? Why have you singled us out for this terrible punishment? Save us, Lord! Save us soon! Don't wait until it's too late. Do it now."

"Easy, baby, remember who you're talking to. He will save us in His own time and in His manner. Your frustration every night with

God is not helping. He's up there waiting for you to come around to Him. He's not going to save you until you place yourself in His hands and quit your complaining."

"Forty days is enough. I can't take it any longer. It's too much, too too much! I know that we both went our own ways without thinking of God. I know my shortcomings, my sins, and my lack of gratitude. Oh God, don't be cruel and vengeful. God, have mercy on us, take us back, please! Please, please let it be over soon, soon." Tears flood down her cheeks.

She's gone too far. "Stop that!" I bellow. "He will not save you with talk like that. God waits for you to put yourself 100 percent in His care. The way you're acting, there's little hope He will save you. And He won't save me either since I'm stuck alongside you."

"Enough of you, Butler, playing the saint. You are a bigger sinner than I am, so be quiet. You of little faith and much less devotion. Where do you suddenly get all your faith? It's weird. It's inconceivable that you should preach to me. You. All your life you've been known as Bad Billy Butler."

"Bad or not is not the point. I believe 100 percent that God will save us. I will wait until He is ready to get us out of here. You want everything to happen now, now, now! Your way and on your schedule. Life doesn't happen that way."

"Well, I feel good when I complain and cry out to heaven. At least there is a dialogue. And God, being God, understands. Job also complained. I know I'm impatient. I'll try to improve."

I put my arm around Sim as we lie naked on our sodden bedding. Soon we sleep.

The southwest wind blows steadily. Ten-foot waves mounted on twenty-foot swells wash under and over us. Mountains of water hurry by to some shore far away. Take us with you, oh wave, I cry out. A wave passing under us now will reach shore before nightfall. We, on the other hand, will have drifted a mere fifteen miles by nightfall. I'm becoming almost as impatient as Sim.

If we only had a vessel that could sail. Or a raft that could skim the waves or one we could row or steer. If we had the dinghy, we could jump in and sail away. We'd be onshore in three days or four. Yet, in the dinghy, we could sink and never reach a safe haven. The raft is slow but steady and more or less safe—that is, if I stop screwing with it.

The two A.M. express arrives on schedule. The shark batters not only the raft but the core of our nervous systems. I poke the six-foot silky shark twice with the pole and never faze it. I pray to the Virgen de la Caridad del Cobre, the patron saint of my native Cuba, asking her to help take this demon away. Seconds later, the shark departs. Thank heaven for prayer, and thank you, Virgencita.

At four in the morning and then minutes before dawn, other sharks attack. They hammer the raft and threaten to split it open. I row for hours with a steady splash. The ploy works at times, but often it makes no difference. When things quiet down, I fall into a deep sleep.

I awake to the presence of a third person at the far end of the raft, near my feet. It's so dark I can't see my toes. I sit up, eyes now open wide, heart pumping madly, and grope for our visitor. But where is he? There is no one. We're alone. It's just Sim and me. I lie back down, now convinced the entire scene was just a dream.

I snooze for I know not how long, then wake again with the same feeling. This time, however, it's no dream. Someone is in the raft. Our visitor is near my feet. My heart beats like a bongo drum. We are not alone, of that I am sure. I lie, eyes wide open, and search the darkness. What is it? Who is it?

I'm unable to sleep after that, and listen to the rain as it pounds the canopy. The wind continues to pick up as we remain on our easterly course. Breaking waves roar in from the south and toss us about without mercy, making sleep impossible.

God wants to save us and has helped us every day. The voice Simonne heard so many weeks ago was right. "Forty days," it said. We had to spend forty days on the raft. Help would come on day forty-one. The ship passed minutes after four in the afternoon on day forty-one, caught us asleep, and as the saying goes, we missed the boat. We didn't trust our inner feelings that told us to keep an extra-keen lookout throughout day forty-one. We dismissed that inner voice. Another error.

We weren't keeping a strict lookout because our near-sinking was still on our minds. And what about my vision? Was it a warning to stay awake and look out? Or did the Lord join us aboard to comfort us? I lie open-eyed, awed by the scene.

The sun slowly makes its appearance. Clear skies promise a dry day. Simonne, listening to the radio, is far away in her own world.

She takes the earphones off. "Every day I can hear stations later in the day. A week ago, I received only static starting at six in the morning. Now the sun is up, and I still hear Costa Rican stations clearly. Here, listen."

I put the earphones on. The signal isn't perfect but it's not bad. I hear music. We can't be much more than two hundred miles away, possibly less. When we hear a station right through the day, even at high noon, we'll be within a hundred miles. Today's signal lingers until ten, then fades away. Land remains hundreds of miles to the east.

"I heard a couple of news items. Fidel says he is going to stick to the hard line. Khashoggi, the big Saudi millionaire, is in deep trouble with the President Marcos–Philippine theft case. He's out on a ten-million-dollar bail. Chicken feed for him. There was a plane crash in Libya, all dead."

"Whatever happened with that Sioux City crash? Did anyone survive?"

"Yes, but over a hundred died. They still don't know what caused it."

At noon I catch six triggerfish with my hands but zero out with the hook. There are hundreds of triggerfish under the raft. All wait inches below the surface for anything that moves. One bit me yesterday when I got my fingers too close to the water. They bite Sim when she dips a cloth in the water to wash herself. Her daily rubdown with salt water is followed with a few drops of fresh water.

A triggerfish bites through my glove as I cut it open. Several of the tenacious little devils have nipped me after both fillets are out. Yesterday, I caught one trigger too many, and when I threw it back in, the waiting triggers thought it had been filleted and attacked it fiercely. They killed and devoured it in less than a minute.

Triggerfish meat is firm yet not tough. Sim now says she prefers it to the other fish I catch. With lunch over, we move our bedding around to dry. My shirt airs on the canopy, stiff with salt.

We must pump air every forty minutes, so my "repair" didn't help. The empty peanut butter jar contains forty or more strips of paper, which Sim uses to wrap the plug. Sim remains in charge of raft air chamber tightness. After two hundred strokes, the raft feels hard as a rock to me. I call over to Sim with a "Check it," and she comes back with her usual "Not yet." I've failed to convince Sim that higher pressure will make the air leak out faster.

Since we must pump air every forty minutes, deep sleep is a long-forgotten luxury. I sleep longer than Sim, and often she pumps alone. Even back on land, I seldom have trouble falling asleep or staying asleep. Sim is like a watchdog; a mere whisper has her awake and alert. She says she sleeps like a mother does, antennae out, ready to jump at the smallest cry.

Another ship passes close by at four in the morning, this one heading east, toward the coast. It must be bound for Puntarenas. Sim sees it when it's abreast, too late for a flare. We're beyond disappointment at these near misses. Sim, an hour later, picks up a Puntarenas radio station. These are two positive signs that we are closer to shore.

The next day seas ease, though the current and long, high swells continue strong out of the west. Not a single ship passes all day long. Simonne keeps a tireless vigil that, I happen to notice, is concentrated on a single part of the ocean. Night comes upon us quietly. Simonne reads, then continues to murmur her nightly prayers.

A calm, clear morning greets us as we rise and fall to the rhythm of twenty-foot swells. Simonne has been looking out the window intently since dawn. Has she seen something? For days, I've watched dark shapes on the horizon that look like long hills, and when I'm at last convinced they could be land, they disappear. Sim continues to look in the same general direction. I keep my eye on Sim for any change in expression.

Sim is the official lookout. I am more awkward, heavier, and can't see well without my glasses. Two or three times each day, she turns on her knees, pushes away the canopy, and scans the horizon. I grab a thigh to steady her and, jokingly, give her a little push toward the side.

"Bill Butler," she declares, "don't you dare!" I retort with a "How could you think such a thing?" and give her a second nudge. My hand reaches all the way around her leg now. She has lost a lot of weight. Gone are her mighty thighs and her big bosom.

The morning passes quietly. Together we produce the usual two liters of water. I stretch out again while Sim returns to the window. She has been staring for an hour now, always in the same direction. I see her lips curve, and with a triumphant look in her eyes, she turns toward me.

"Land!" she calls out.

"Are you sure?" I don't really take her seriously.

"Land. Land! I'm sure of it!"

"What kind of land? What do you see?"

"It's far away. Like a small hill. There are two hills. But far away."

"Where? Let me see it."

I struggle up and follow Sim's pointing finger. The swells are more than fifteen feet high and the waves two or three, a calm day for the Pacific Ocean. To see it, I have to wait until we are on top of a swell and then look in the right direction.

I see nothing. I wait for the top of another swell and give up. "I can't see it," I say and lie back down.

"It's hard to see."

"What does it look like, exactly? Here, draw a picture of it in the workbook. Hold the page at arm's length and trace the land to the exact size."

Sim, sitting now, keeps one eye on the island. She holds the log workbook up and draws the contour of what she sees. Her sketch is about three-quarters of an inch high and one inch long. She draws one hill to the left, which is north, a quarter inch higher than a hill to the south. I get up a couple of more times but fail to see it.

"Sim, check the bearing of the mountain with the compass. That'll make it easier for me to spot."

The compass is always hard to find. I can never fully understand how, in such a confined space, something as large as the compass can vanish. I find it under the life preserver and hand it to Sim. She trains her eyes on our tiny speck of hope.

She calls out. "It's 120 degrees. Let me see. Yes, 120."

"OK, now let me take a look."

Sim paddles the raft around so my side faces east. I hold the compass up and find 120. I wait for the raft to climb to the top of a swell and see it. A single mountain with two uneven bluish peaks. It *is* land, it's beautiful, and it's about thirty miles away.

We take turns looking at the island throughout the afternoon, because an island it must be. It's larger than when we first saw it. Our hopes run high. The sun sets on two happy castaways. Sim is ecstatic. This is her happiest moment since Panama. As darkness falls and she reads, we dream of a sandy beach on a faraway isle.

I cannot recall what islands lie off the Central American coast except for Isla de Cocos. I know there are several small ones, but they are all close to shore. But this can't be Isla de Cocos. Isla de Cocos is to the north and behind us. This island bears south of east. Besides, how can we be in sight of it when all the boobies left us weeks ago? Where else could they have flown? I fall asleep with this quandary on my mind.

We have a day or two before a landfall. How exciting, castaways on a deserted island. Or is it the mainland? Two high hills on a lowland. That would be better yet.

Wind and waves ease during the night, but both are still from the south. If we are to reach the hills, we need wind out of the west. Thanks to the strong current, our course has been east all night.

The sharks are particularly nasty tonight. Our faithful two A.M. visitor bashes the raft with a vengeance. This shark alone is intent on destroying us. Since it first appeared three weeks ago, we have traveled more than two hundred miles. How does it find us, night after night? I'm 100 percent sure it is the same animal.

Nevertheless, our night is full of hope. Land is at hand at last. We are traveling toward the east. A ray of promise shines over us for the first time since being cast away forty-five days ago. Even the sharks that batter our raft bother us less tonight. The weather is calm and clear. Stars are out. When dawn comes, the land should be closer. Our hopes and spirits soar. I fall asleep with Sim's prayers in my ears.

Saturday, July 29, dawns clear and bright. We have been awake for hours, desperate to catch a glimpse of land, land that offers us our first real hope in seven weeks. When it dawns, will it be closer? Are we heading for it? First light holds off for an eternity. Finally, darkness yields to true dawn. The eastern horizon erupts bright red. We look. The island is there, and it's closer than yesterday.

Sim's excitement equals mine. "Let's row," she calls over to me. "Let's row, come on."

We jump at the thought and deflate both arches, which leaves the raft "topless," a floating inner tube. We pass a line under the raft and tie the ballast bags against the bottom of the raft, which hopefully should make it easier to row. I tie the pole to one of the paddles, converting it into an oar, and hand it to Sim. My paddle is a flat piece of plastic six inches wide and twenty inches long.

"Sim, you set the pace, and I will follow to keep the raft headed toward land."

We row surrounded by a flat, calm ocean and a crimson sky. We float easily on the long swells. Today's sun is about to emerge. We're alive. Dear God, thank you for everything. We don't deserve your mercy.

We pull on the oars with unknown strength. Sim leans into her paddle without stopping. I push water to keep up with Sim. The open raft gives us an exuberant sense of freedom. We are one with the world. Visibility is perfect. After fifteen minutes, we rest and take in our vista. Life is so great. Our world is so beautiful. The sun emerges from behind orange clouds. Light fills our eyes and hope overflows from our bodies. Excitement saturates our spirits. We are alive after six weeks adrift, and land is at hand.

If we were to drift with the canopy down, we would not miss a single passing ship. We have so longed to take in the true beauty of our surroundings. We row, our eyes attached to the two hills ahead that loom large and inviting. Twenty minutes later, we take another break. We row, but the raft makes no headway. The island, outlined against the bright eastern horizon, stands out clearly, still far away. I wonder how high the peak is. Is it a hill or a mountain? Is it an island or mainland Central America?

After another thirty minutes, we give up. The island is more than fifteen miles away, and it's obvious we'll never reach it by rowing, at least not from this distance. We must conserve our energy, save it for whatever unknowns arise from the deep or on high. If the wind and current push us closer—to within a mile or less—then we'll row. But it's hopeless to try from this distance. The wind picks up from the southwest.

"I've got a great idea," I exclaim. "Let's sail."

"You've tried that before and it didn't work. What makes you think it'll work now? How do you plan to do it?"

"We'll inflate the bow arch and let the wind blow into the canopy. I'll row to keep the raft stern to the wind. Simple. It should work."

"It's not going to work. Besides, I get scared when the canopy is down. Suppose we tip over?"

"Simonne, look, there is no wind. The sea is calm. What's going to tip us over? What do we have to lose? Let's try it for a while. Come on, Sim, how else will we ever know if it'll work? What do you want to do? Stay out here for the rest of your life?"

"OK, go ahead. But it won't work."

I completely deflate one of the arches and row the raft around so the breeze blows into the inflated arch. I steer toward the sun and the island. An hour passes. We haven't moved.

"I told you so," Sim says, but I can tell she was hoping it would work.

"OK. It didn't work."

"Besides, I don't like the ballast bags tied. The wind is picking up. Look at those waves. Come on, Bill, quit playing around."

"All right, all right." With my near-zero credibility, it's useless to argue for more time. We reinflate the arch, rerig the canopy, and untie the ballast bags. The raft catches the current, and we lie back down, more frustrated and exhausted than ever.

Simonne draws the contour of the island to scale as she did yesterday. The contour hasn't changed, but it's almost twice as high.

The exercise has made us hungry. We will open our last rusty can at lunch. I jiggled the can yesterday to determine its contents. It sounded like it was part liquid and part solid.

Looking back, it's probably just as well we didn't bring more cans. We would have eaten better up to now, but all the remaining cans would be nearly terminal. In Miami, we meant to remove the labels, mark each can, and then dip them in varnish or paraffin. Who would've guessed then we were destined to drift in a small raft across the Pacific. Besides, most cans sank with the boat.

At one in the afternoon, Sim fishes the can opener out of the gun case. When I pick up the can, I find it's leaking. The can was fine yesterday.

Sim looks it over and says, "Last night, when I told you I heard a swish of air, I was so afraid it was coming from the raft near the window. Well, it was the can when it popped. I felt something sticky on my hand when I poked around early this morning. What a pity, we might have eaten it yesterday before it popped. No, it was already bad then."

I open it anyway. It's a can of pears. The pears smell and look good. A light layer of foam covers the syrup. Sim, official sniffer onshore and at sea, sniffs. The pears smell fine. I dip a finger into the juice and put it in my mouth. It tastes fine. On closer inspection, Sim cocks her head, shakes it, and points over the side. I shake my head. No, no, it looks good to me, and I plead, "I'll just eat one or two."

"Baby," says Simonne, "I know it hurts, but we cannot take any chances. Right now, we are healthy. We haven't been sick. It's a miracle. If we eat this, we take risks that could be fatal. Suppose we get botulism? I don't even want to think about it. Let's not take a chance."

Over it goes. Our last can of food.

I slip on my gloves, and in minutes, six triggerfish fill the bucket. I remove the twelve fillets and pile them on the paddle. I cut them into small pieces and pass the choicest chunks to Sim.

I've become a triggerfish connoisseur. The biggest ones are the tastiest. The bad part is that I lose most of the big ones because I can't get my hand around them. I always taste a small piece of the fillet before passing it on to Sim. Seemingly identical triggerfish taste different, and some parts of the fillet are better than others. The part of the fillet closest to the head is the best. I cut the tip of the fillet for Sim, then separate a piece with bones and toss it into the bait can. I eat the rest. Sim will eat the tips from four or five fillets. I eat until I can eat no more.

While I fished, the raft leaked air faster than before, though it always has lost more air when I fish. After lunch, we pump air every twenty minutes. I tighten the string around one of the valves, but that doesn't help. Sim checks for anything that may be rubbing against an air tube and finds nothing. We listen for the hiss of escaping air. We hear nothing. What can it be?

Before sunset, we take a bearing on the island. It's now 105 degrees compared with yesterday's 120 degrees. We are drifting down on it from the north. If we stay on this track, we'll pass south of it. The current pushes us east and the wind swings from the south all the way to the west. Tomorrow, we will be closer and better able to estimate our approach.

As the sun falls toward the western horizon, it takes with it a cornucopia of reds and purples. The sunset reminds us of heaven and hell as depicted in old religious paintings. Our hell is about to end, and soon we'll be on an island in heaven. We witness the most spectacular sunset so far. We enjoy every ray, every changing cloud, every reflection from every wave, our hearts full of hope and expectation. Tomorrow should bring us closer to land and safety.

Sim sits while I prop my head up with an extra boat cushion. We watch in silence as day evolves into night.

Land. Land is a double-edged sword. Land is safety, a beginning, and an escape from our predators. To reach shore will be to live again. Through the past forty days, death awaited each day as the sun set. True odds have been against our living to see each new day. We must reach this shore. When we get closer, we'll row until we collapse.

Once onshore, we will find a way to live. We'll wait for a boat. If it's a large island, it may have stands of bamboo. I could make a boat, a catamaran or a cross between *Kon-Tiki* and a Polynesian outrigger. We have a knife to cut the parts and rope aboard to lash it all together. We can do it. If by chance it's Isla de Cocos, there will be people onshore. They will help us.

On the other hand, arrival on a windward shore at night could be tricky. I dream of gently gliding toward a soft sandy beach, the moon full, a gentle breeze edging us on. I'll jump over first, lead the raft in, and then hold Simonne's hand as she joins me in our newfound haven.

But what would happen if we arrive on a dark, stormy night? Rough-breaking seas could push the raft toward rocks, a half mile from solid footing. If the raft tears and sinks under us, we'll swim in heavy current, predators circling ever closer. We search desperately for a handhold on the jagged coral as it tears our flesh. Blood gushes as we climb higher, toward a minute rocky outcrop far from the island. Our raft lies on the bottom.

I awaken from my wild imaginary wanderings with a shudder. It's so very dark. I hear Simonne pray, and I follow with my now revitalized Lord's Prayer. I pray more intently tonight than I have in forty years. Bring us, Lord, to a safe haven tomorrow.

ABOARD THE RAFT
LAST CHANCE

0830 SUNDAY • JULY 30, 1989 • DAY 46

AYLIGHT ON this Sunday dawn finds two wide-awake castaways. Sim, on her knees, scans the horizon. The forlorn yet expectant look on her face is that of a human in dire need. She clasps the compass in her right hand as she waits for our treasure island to emerge from the shadows of this new day. She, as well as I, is sure it will be there—large, verdant, and close at hand. Though seas are calm, the ever-present twenty-foot swells hide the horizon from view 80 percent of the time.

She sweeps the eastern horizon in the few seconds we ride atop a crest. Yesterday, the island was twice as large as when we first saw it. Today it should be as high or higher. Yet current and wind have not been that strong.

Sim's voice falters. "Bill, I can't see it. It's not there." She turns, glances at the compass, gets her bearings, and then concentrates on a small piece of horizon during the few seconds we hang on the crest of the wave. Solemnly, she surveys the rolling seas for some sign of land. Suddenly, she calls out:

"There it is! Oh, Bill, it's the same size as the first day. We're farther away. The current has pushed us backward, the wrong way. How can this happen? How can we go backward?" Tears run down her face as she collapses in my arms, shaking with grief.

I was afraid this would happen. The sea is punishing, ever full of surprises. Days ago, becalmed, I had a feeling we were not going east. Without a landmark, I couldn't really tell. Sim's heart is broken. She had built up so much hope on reaching our island. I had as well, but dare not show my disappointment.

"I knew it. We are not to be saved. How can this happen?" Sim's profound distress is contagious. "How many other days have we traveled in the wrong direction? What's going to happen to us?"

"I really don't know." It's no use making up stories or playing the macho. "We lost the current. Pray it returns."

It cannot be Isla de Cocos. I'm sure we passed it two weeks ago, the day when all the birds flew off. If the two hills are part of the Central American landmass, it will not matter much where we head. If it's an offshore island, we will drift past it and to the mainland. That is, if the current returns, or if the storms out of the west return. Too damn many ifs.

This could be one of the islands off Panama. If I remember correctly, the coastline swings east after Punta Mala. Noriega uses one of the islands as a prison where he tortures political enemies. We heard all about it when in Panama. I shudder. What will happen to us if we drift toward it?

I study my raft-made chart of the Pacific. My dead reckoning tells me mainland Central America could be less than two hundred miles to the east. Isla de Cocos is behind us, unless we have been drifting backward. How many other days have we not drifted east?

I draw a picture of the pilot chart to recall how the current runs in this part of ocean. From way out west up to a hundred miles off the coast, I am sure the current runs east, toward the coast. After that, I can't remember what happens to it. It must go either north or south. My guess is that it runs south, toward the Panama Canal.

Visible proof that we have gone ten miles or more in the wrong direction sets the mood for the day. We have had no propulsion of any kind for two days. No wind and no waves. And worse yet, I sense there is no current. I make an entry in the log:

DISTANCE TRAVELED IN THE LAST 24 HOURS:
7 MILES WEST

I hide it from Sim.

When seas are high and the wind blows more than fifteen knots, breaking waves propel us downwind. Often, a single wave pushes us six feet in two seconds. Days ago, as we sat becalmed, Sim had prayed and prayed for wind. A monster of a storm materialized out of the west. We hung on for dear life through the night. In the morning, while it was still rough, I pleaded, "Sim, baby, next time, don't pray so hard for a storm," which provoked a nasty French sneer.

I toss out a piece of paper. It stays inches away from the raft for several minutes until it sinks out of sight. There is no wind and there are no waves. There is no current, or if there is, it doesn't flow to the east. We remain becalmed all morning.

"Hey, Sim, go ahead and pray for a storm. You and all our good friends in Miami who prayed for fair winds have overdone it. We'll never get out of this predicament stuck in a dead calm."

Not all the news is bad. We have a miracle from an entirely unexpected quarter. The leak in the air chamber has been increasing daily. Yesterday, toward evening, we had to pump every half hour. Around midnight, we fell into a deep sleep. When we awakened three hours later, we found the raft had hardly lost any air. Today we have been pumping every hour. We have no explanation for what happened except that someone up above is looking out for us.

I cannot find a comfortable position. When I lie on my side, my legs or elbows always bump one part or another of Sim's anatomy. She complains loudly, mostly concerned with her internal organs.

"Bill, get your elbow out of my liver."

"Move your leever."

I get punched. And I move my elbow. I'll never figure out why the French are so concerned with their "leevers." Most probably it's because of all the red wine they have to process.

During the afternoon, the wind picks up from the southwest. We are on the move again.

I catch ten triggers. I gorge on twelve fillets while Sim eats three. We make two liters of water. Three other liters are stored under the cushions.

Sharks batter the raft. I beat them off until rain starts. Heavy drips soon soak our bedding and us. But who cares?

I take a bearing on the island: 120 degrees. This means we are drifting north of it instead of south as yesterday's bearing indicated. Heavy black clouds hasten nightfall. When the rain stops for a few minutes, I take a look around. My God. A shark three times longer than the raft circles ten feet away. I don't say a word to Sim. I curl up next to her and hold her tightly. As total darkness sets in, I look out again. The big shark and all the small sharks have disappeared. What surprises does the sea have in store for us tonight?

Rain pours through the canopy and onto us until dawn. We cover ourselves with the wet sailbag and the trash bag and huddle to stay warm. As this forty-seventh morning aboard the raft dawns, we know not what to expect. Will we be closer to the island? Will we even see it? Or will heavy overcast cut visibility?

A light breeze from the southwest greets us Monday, July 31. What was not soaked yesterday got it last night. I keep the logbook near my head in our driest place. I don't know how much longer the pages will remain dry enough to write on. Sharks were not a problem last night. That big shark may still be around.

The skies slowly lighten. Soon we'll know. Did we again drift backward? Sim has been at the window since first light. She calls out with a happy ring to her voice, "There it is! Bill, it's much closer!" I peer out. Sure enough. The island is there, large, looming blue in the hazy morning light.

"Get a bearing."

"It's . . . it's . . . 160 degrees. Let me check. Yes, 160."

"That's not good at all. That means we are passing it to the north. If the current runs south, we could reach it. This wind from the southwest pushes us away."

"What do you think?"

"It's too early to tell. Can you see any features, rocks, beaches?"

Sim reports, "The contour has changed. There's only one hill, but I see nothing onshore."

I shudder at the thought of an approach on a coral-laden rocky outcrop. If there is light, we could row around the reefs. The ballast bags would surely catch on the rocks or coral. If the approach is in the dead of night—and these Pacific nights seem the blackest any-where—what could we do? We'd try to row steadily offshore to await daylight—that is, if we could. We'd be safe on land, our odyssey over. It appears to be a large island, five or ten miles long. The peaks are high, perhaps a thousand feet. People certainly live there. Fishing boats must visit regularly. We'll wait for a boat to take us to the mainland. Or I'll make a boat, a sailboat. The striped comforter would become a sail. Butler, you are a dreamer!

We could live on the island for months as we built up our strength. We can make water. There's bound to be food. Simonne is a wizard at spotting edible tubers and fruit. Taught the old ways by her Italian grandfather, she could certainly keep us fed. There are bound to be bananas. We still have a few matches—soggy, but we can surely find a way to make them work. Bill Robinson and Simonne Crusoe. On our Treasure Island. What fun. Come on, wind. C'mon, current. Take us to our new home.

There is no other land in sight. Sim is right. It is an island, and an island far away from the mainland at that. Near the northwestern tip, Sim spots a fishing boat. It's too far away to signal. What island is it? Isla de Cocos? Never. We passed it weeks ago. We are much, much closer to the mainland. Sim holds the workbook at arm's length. The island is now more than four inches high compared to a half inch when we first saw it three days ago. If we hadn't drifted west, we would almost be there. With luck, in a day or two, we'll make it, God willing.

I hurry my fishing expedition before rain begins again. After lunch, when Sim sits up to look for the island, she sees something else: a twelve-foot hammerhead shark. We embrace tightly and stay out of sight. Hammerheads eat everything: plastic rafts, watermakers, and dirty castaways. I don't dare play poke-the-shark with him, and remain motionless for hours.

Wind and waves increase. Water splashes through the canopy. Sim bails. Looks like another wet, rough night ahead. The wind picks up out of the southwest by west at fifteen knots. If it doesn't shift, it will push us north of the island.

Sharks attack fiercely all night. On the one hand, it's good news. The monster must have left. I try to repel them, but poor visibility keeps me from scoring any solid hits. I splash the pole in the water. This keeps the sharks circling several feet under the raft with only the most intrepid rising closer to the surface with mischief in mind.

Dawn is slow to arrive. I look at my watch constantly, only to find that mere minutes have passed instead of the hoped-for hours. Sim has been at the window for the past hour in search of ships and for a telltale light on the island. We have to reach shore soon. The raft has lost its integrity. As waves pass under us, it folds in half. We've lost a lot of weight even with our heavy fish diet. Neither of us has had a bowel movement in the past few weeks. It's most probably nothing but a case of "nothing in, nothing out." Anyway, it's surely good for a notation in the *Guinness Book of World Records*.

"I see it," she calls suddenly. "Pass me the compass."

"Are we closer?"

"Yes! Yes! It's big. And we are very close. It's at 220 degrees. Yes, 220."

I get up to look. Rain clouds shroud the top half of the island. It's not more than four or five miles away, six at the most. Trees line the hill. What can we do to reach it?

"Sim, let's row."

She is ready at once. Once again, we tie the ballast bags up against the floor of the raft to reduce drag. We row furiously for over an hour, but the current is too strong. It's like trying to row a grand piano upriver. We make no progress, and give up. We must save our strength for a possible catastrophe.

The island grows smaller as all three forces—wind, waves, and current—push us away. It's definite now; we've missed it. Safety was so close at hand yet unattainable. Neither of us can speak. Our thoughts follow a variety of paths, but they all end up at the same bottom line. Will we ever be found? Will we ever make a landfall, or are we to roam the seas forever? A mythical, ghostly raft to be found years from now with nothing but bones bleached white by the sun.

We return to our everyday chores. We make water, and fish for triggers. Sharks attack the raft all through lunch. They don't attack while I fish. I wonder why.

Later in the afternoon, I snooze and Sim is the lookout. I hear her gasp. I open my eyes and feel the raft rise. It goes up for a few moments, then drops back.

"Sim, what was that?"

"A whale shark."

"A what?"

"I'm sure it was a whale shark. It was huge. It's head was ten feet wide or more! Its mouth was as wide as its head and could have easily swallowed the entire raft just like Jonah! It was brown and had white spots all over its body. My God, it was more than fifty feet in length!"

Fortunately, whale sharks are not carnivorous. They feed on plankton and other microorganisms. What next? How we do we get out of this aquarium full of monster sea creatures? Today it's only a gentle giant but tomorrow, what?

The slack current allows the raft to swing to the whims of wind and wave. It reminds me of my life. I also have drifted aimlessly in a life without direction. On the raft as we have drifted, a strong new current has begun to reshape my life. At first, the current was weak and I swung with indecision. As time has passed, however, a strong spiritual stream has taken hold of me. Every day brings me closer to God. A new strength grows inside my heart.

Sim reads my thoughts. "Do you think we'll reach the island? What can we do? This raft isn't going to make it much longer." She looks up. "Oh Lord, why are you testing us in this way? Isn't forty-eight days enough punishment? How much longer must we suffer?"

"Simmer down, baby. God will save us in His time and in His manner. We are in His hands. He will save us."

"Save us when? Why doesn't He save us now? Perhaps we have been so bad that He doesn't plan to save us at all. He's torturing us, and in due time, we will die. I'm sure of it."

She calms, and I reflect. This island can't be far off the coast. If we miss the island, in three or four days we will be on the mainland. Besides, the closer we get to land, the better chance we have of seeing a fishing boat. They can spot us much easier than a freighter. They're closer to the water and go slower, and they have lookouts watching for fish.

Frigate birds follow our every move. Fishing boats normally head for birds. New varieties of shorebirds have joined us. The coloring of the boobies has changed from the ones that slept around the raft five weeks ago. Where the earlier ones were white, these are dark brown. The black portions of the first group are now white in the newcomers. Interesting. I suppose Darwin or Audubon has covered the subject. As night approaches, all the seabirds leave to roost on land. If we could only fly away with them. A hundred conflicting hopes and fears race through our heads. I fall asleep as Simonne prays.

Sharks attack the raft all night. I fight them off until rain starts around seven in the morning. I open the window, pump up the raft, and fall asleep in seconds.

Sim shakes me awake. I open my eyes to bright daylight, instantly on alert to face this new emergency. Still in a daze, I cry out, "What happened? What's wrong?"

"What's wrong? You spend all night sleeping while I have to bear all the attacks from sharks and turtles, pump air, bail, and listen to it rain. All you do is snore. It's not fair. I need company."

"What? Am I hearing correctly? You have shaken me awake to inform me that I am sleeping too much. Is that what you are saying?"

"It's not right that you sleep and I can't. And when you're sleeping, I feel so lonely. I can't stand to be by myself. I can't bear it," she whines, tears streaking her cheeks.

"I should toss you over the side. After I make most of the water and put all the food on the table and pump most of the air and spend the night fighting off sharks, I get harassed when I finally grab a little sleep. I cannot believe what I'm hearing. Get me the logbook; I want to make an entry."

Her face falls. "Forgive me, baby. I felt so depressed and lonely. I know we're going to miss that island. I so hoped to reach it. I was so sure we were going to be safe onshore. When it became obvious we would get no closer, I just got crazy. Will you forgive me?"

"Never, unless you give me a big kiss and then put some of your lotion on my back. It stings all over. How is it?" I roll over on my side.

"Terrible. You have ugly open sores from your shoulders to your waist. I'll clean them." She sprinkles several drops of fresh water to wash the salt out of my wounds, then spreads the last drops from a nearly empty bottle of hand lotion. My back feels much better right away.

"Did you see the island? Where is it?"

Sim has taken a bearing. "It's way behind us, fifteen or more miles, and bears 240. It's gone."

"Your news isn't all bad. Now we know we are back in the current, and we are making time to the east. We know that we will hit the coast of Central America. Let us now forget the island and keep our sights to the east, where our new hope lies."

I pull out the logbook and review our entries since we first saw the island. We spotted it first on July 28, day forty-four, at a range of twenty-five miles. This is day forty-nine, and the island is fifteen miles astern. We've drifted forty miles to the east in five days, and that includes a day or more of drift to the west.

The day is dark and dismal, and heavy black clouds shroud the island in a veil of rain. Rainsqualls again soak us. I take advantage of the cool, rainy day to make two liters of water.

When the rain lets up, I pluck eleven triggerfish out of the ocean and into the bucket. Sim insists I fish only for triggerfish. When I cast for tripletails, I may get nothing in an hour, and all that time she has to pump air into the leaking air chambers. The truth is, I enjoy my fishing interludes.

The triggerfish have destroyed my hands with their tiny, painful barbs. I've counted more than thirty trigger sting marks on my right hand alone. On my little finger, near the first joint, I have a dozen barbs. This is the finger that wraps around under the fish when I grab it. My thumb and index finger are also full of the telltale red stings.

Night arrives early, and we settle down to another interminable nightmare. I flick the flashlight on for a second whenever my watch chirps and a dozen times in between. The striped comforter under us is so lumpy and wet and stiff that I can lie in one position for no more than a few minutes. To turn is agony, for the sores on my back scream. I move the bedding aside and rest on the bare plastic cushion for an hour, but it turns out to be less comfortable. My watch chirps. At long last, it's six A.M. Two more hours to dawn.

When I awaken next, Sim has the window partly open and is peering out. I keep quiet. If there is any news, good or bad, it will come soon enough. The outside corners of Sim's lips point down in her typical look of despondency. The news will not be good. She turns and notices I am awake.

"The island is nowhere in sight, but visibility is only three or four miles. I'll check again in a couple of hours, after the rain lifts. The weather will clear soon, and the southwest wind is picking up. The current is also strong."

"You're a great first mate. Skipper sleeps in, and mate has the morning report on the bridge. At least you didn't shake me awake again."

"I should have, the way you were snoring, except I know the racket you make keeps the sharks away. It did attract a turtle, who probably thought it some kind of mating call."

"Turtle? Where is she? Was she good-looking? I'll take anything now that my raft mate has sworn celibacy. I'm going deaf and blind, and I get no pity. Say, I had a super dream. Do you want to hear it?" Sim nods.

"We're on this raft in the Pacific, and it's a clear, sunny day with medium-sized waves. A big sportfisherman, like a fifty-foot Hatteras or Bertram, heads for us. The captain is big and fat, and there are several tourists on board. I wave like mad. They see us and stop next to the raft. The fat man calls out and asks what's the matter. I tell him our boat sank, that we've been at sea for weeks. He guns the engines in neutral.

"I plead with him to save us. He yells down to hurry up and jump in if we want to, but to leave the raft. He's in a fishing tournament and can't wait. I argue that it'll only take a second to pull the raft aboard. He says no, there is no room and to hurry up, or he'll pull away.

"We jump on board and go with him to Isla de Cocos. We swim on a sandy beach, eat well, and party with a group of people. Then he leaves in a hurry and says he will be back for us later. And I wake up."

"Sounds like one of my dreams with the unhappy endings. Now that we've missed the island, what happens?"

"We head for shore. The weekend is coming up. People come to these waters from all over to fish for big blue marlins, sailfish, and tuna. The sportfishing gang should be out Saturday and Sunday. The commercial fleet probably heads for shore on Friday and heads back out Sunday night. We must keep a sharp lookout."

Sim nods. "I've been dreaming of food," she says. "Do you remember that little restaurant on Madison Avenue where we had the blinis after visiting the Metropolitan Museum? I dreamed we were there, sipping that delicious, cold white wine and eating blinis. Oh, I'm so hungry for real food."

"I told you never to talk about food. Blinis. I'd give anything for a blini. I never ate one before that day. When we get back, I'll take you to New York for a blini bust."

The morning passes with light banter, watermaking, and a nap. I catch my usual dozen triggerfish, serve up lunch, and nap again. When I awaken, Sim looks out and the rain is over.

"I see the island. It's the same size as when we saw it on that first day a week ago, and it bears 260 degrees, almost due west."

"More proof that we are moving in the right direction. There is land to the north and east, and the current and wind push us in that general direction. All we have to do is keep the raft afloat until we reach shore. We have food and water and nothing else to do but husband the raft. We'll make it, sweetie, we'll make it." Poor Sim, hair matted, gaunt and pale, looks away to the east. She tries so hard to believe what I'm saying.

Our small feathered visitor is back. The same small black seabird has slept aboard every night for a week. It alights for a rest and flies off when I fish or if Sim chases a turtle. As night begins to fall, it lands on the canopy. It leaves before first light.

The bird is all black and about the size of a seagull. Its webbed feet are pink and delicate. We see its little feet through the canopy. This one has been good company. When we open the canopy, the bird gets uptight and stares down, watching our every move.

This morning, I watch our little dark seabird preen. It pushes its beak into its preen gland, picks up oil, spreads it first into wing feathers, then works toward its tail. I sit up. The bird takes no notice of my motion. Can I catch it? Its feet are no more than two feet from my head. If I could move my hand under it, then come up quickly, I could grab it. Lying here, more dead than alive, it's time I check out my reflexes . . . and stir Sim up a tad.

Sim eyes are closed. She's probably praying, thinking of her children. This will liven up my day. I decide to go for it. Carefully, I study the angle of attack and wait until the bird is busiest. With a thrust, I grab its feet. Surprised, it struggles and squawks as it desperately flaps its wings. Sim sits up with disbelief. I grab the bird around the neck with the other hand.

"Do you like my birdie? It's going to be lunch today. How would you like me to prepare it?" I tease.

"Bill Butler, don't you dare! He's one of my friends. He's been with us for a long time, and he trusts us. You're not going to harm him."

"No? Watch. I can't decide whether to wring its neck or stretch it. Which is better? We can sure use a change in diet." I run my fingers under its neck, and all I feel are bones and feathers. This creature does not have a single ounce of meat.

The bird's squawks can surely be heard back onshore. Its wings flap wildly, and just when Sim is absolutely convinced I'm ready to wring its neck, I release the bird. It flies away at top speed. Sim hits me with the ultimate nasty look, but things soon settle down to our usual boring routine of inching along at a rate that's impossible to perceive.

Evening comes quickly. Sim reads six psalms, which increase in meaning as we move closer to the realization that God's help is our only hope. He has performed so many miracles for us already. He has decided we are worth saving but that the cementing of our faith in Him needs more time. Sim has come a long way from the time a few weeks ago when the sighting of a ship and its disappearance beyond the horizon would cast her into a long period of dismal despair. Then she questioned the heavens and argued with God over the why of our punishment. "Why is He doing this to us?" she had asked. "Why not to Noriega? Why not to all the crooks and war-mongers, killers, and monsters? There are so many nasty people in this world. What have we done, oh Lord?" she had cried over and over. "Have I killed? Robbed? Have I hurt someone on purpose?" She tormented herself terribly and searched her soul for sins, plead-ing out loud for forgiveness.

It is now totally dark. The raft rocks gently in a rolling sea. We feel the current push us ever eastward. We pray, then lapse into a light sleep, our hearts full of hope. Later, the two A.M. shark awakens us right on schedule. I no longer try to hit it with the pole. My prayers get better results.

The dawn of a new day is at long last upon us, though a high cloud cover hides the rising sun. Sim is up and scans the western hori-zon for the island, fearing it may turn up closer. She sees no land. Its bearing yesterday, August 3, was 260 degrees, nearly west.

With all the excitement created by the island, the increased air loss problem has been put on the back burner. We pump every hour if we are quiet and every half hour when I fish or move around to poke at sharks. Sim has checked her side of the raft and as far around the canopy as she can reach but has found no air leak. I've run my wet hand over the outside of the air chamber, particularly where I jabbed it with a fishhook several days ago. I'd hooked a tripletail, which suddenly got away, and the hook embedded itself in the air chamber. My heart skipped about six beats. At first, I didn't dare remove it, but when I did, luckily the hook hadn't gone all the way through. And lucky for me, Sim had been looking the other way or I'd have been flogged yet again.

Up on my knees, I hang over the side. I follow a line of bubbles near the waterline to a thin sliver of a break in the fabric behind the air cylinder support. Sharks slapped the cylinder around until it broke loose, but not before it wore through the fabric. I tie together the two flaps that held the cylinder in place and stuff rags over the hole, which seems to slow the leak.

The shark pack is back, and they attack for most of an hour. One of the first hard whacks loosens the rags around the hole, and I can hear the whistle made by the bubbles. Now that I know where it comes from, it's suddenly louder, like a ticking bomb. I hang over the side and rearrange my rags. One rag has fallen away, and the others are thoroughly rotten. I tie odd pieces of string around the other rags. As I work, Sim pumps air nonstop.

We need a patch, and we've used up our only two. Besides, those patches are almost two inches wide, so I would have to open a two-inch hole in the air chamber to insert the inside half. We'd be heading for the deep again before I got it all put together. And Sim would have a heart attack if I so much as suggested such a move.

To plug the tiny hole, I need a screw, and I ask Sim if she's seen one around. Sim quickly pulls the fishing reel out from under her head. It has two long screws that at one time held it to the rod. The line on the reel keeps me from removing the long screws. I must empty the reel. I loosen the drag and pull on the line, but the reel has corroded and the drag does not release. I pull harder, and a few inches of line ease out. Fifteen minutes later, I have taken no more than ten feet. With three hundred yards on the reel, this little job could take days.

I cut away at the line on the reel with the knife, and in no time I've got a major snarl. Impatient now, I hack away at it and snarl it even worse. I use the knife as a saw and throw over the side all the strands that come loose. I try to remove the screw by slanting it to one side, but there is still too much line on the reel. I cut more line off and try again. The screw still will not come out. I give it a tap with the knife handle and force it out. To my dismay, the screw isn't stainless steel as it appeared, but chrome-plated brass. When I forced it, several threads were damaged. It's now useless.

To get the second screw off the reel, I cut away another large wad of nylon line. Once the screw is safely out, I put both wing nuts on the good screw. I prepare two gaskets from a pair of leather gloves and cut two washers from the camcorder case. I plan to push the head of the screw into the hole, followed by a washer, and then a gasket. On the outside of the hole, another gasket and washer will be followed by the wing nut.

I make an oval washer half an inch wide and one inch long, which will have to slip into the hole in the raft, which is, as best I can tell, the size of a pinhead. I cut the top washer about one inch in diameter and make a hole in the middle with the scissors. I assemble it all on the screw: oval washer, smaller gasket, gasket, round washer, and wing nut.

I work all day on my project. Sim has helped me cut the leather gaskets but has said nothing. Night is upon us as I finish. I'll make the repair in the morning, when I'm rested. The night is typical; we bash sharks, pump air every forty minutes, and turn over and around dozens of times in search of a comfortable resting spot. However I lie, my bed is rock hard, freezing cold, and sopping wet. Miraculously, I sleep.

Saturday, August 5, day fifty-two of our voyage in *Last Chance*, dawns quietly. Except for our two A.M. visitor, we have had a relatively quiet night. Seas roll gently under the raft, and a light southerly breeze keeps the temperature in the raft near perfect, at least for me. Sim and I have two different body thermostats. She heats up faster than I do and strips down to bare skin while I'm still wrapped under a cover.

The day is perfect to fix the air leak. The patch is ready to go. Sim begins to pump as I turn onto my knees and lean over the side. I unlace the flaps that hold the compressed air cylinder, untie the maze of string that holds the rags, and feel for the hole.

Sim worries. "Bill, be careful. Don't make the hole any bigger. Don't do any damage. Do you hear me?"

"Yes, dear." If I listened to Sim, we'd never try anything.

"Don't 'yes, dear' me at a time like this. We could die."

"*Sí, mi amor.* Hand me the patch, pump, pray, and be quiet."

"You're impossible!"

As I push the head of the screw into the hole, a loud hiss makes my heart skip. I hesitate. Sim had said not to make it worse, but worse it will have to be to allow the screw and washer in. I push a little harder, and the air hiss is again magnified. What have I done? Is this the right way to do it? Suppose I open the hole, and the fix doesn't work? I give it another shove, and the head of the screw slips in. Now it's the washer's turn. The head of the screw is a quarter-inch wide. The washer is a half inch. Oh my God, will it work?

Sim gasps loudly as air gushes out and creates a noisy sea of bubbles. I can't get the washer in without first cutting open the hole. I draw back and look down at the bubbles and think. What do I do now? Whatever I do, it must be fast and it must be sure.

Sim, busy pumping, can't help hearing the escaping air. "What's happening? Can you fix it?"

"I'm almost finished," I lie.

"How much more?"

"I'm almost through."

In reality, I'm in a dilemma. I don't dare open the tear any more. If the fix doesn't work, what will I do then? I try to relax and think.

"Bill, I'm getting tired. Have you fixed it? I hear a loud noise. What have you done?" Sim pumps faster to stay ahead of the escaping air.

"I'm almost finished." Damn. I don't dare open a bigger hole. I better leave it alone. I pull out the screw head. A loud hiss confirms the hole is larger than it was before. I hand the assembly to Sim.

"Hold it."

"What happened? I thought you had it fixed. My God. Listen to that air coming out. Bill, what have you done? Lord, have mercy on us. He's done it again!"

"Everything is OK."

"What do you mean, 'OK'? I can hear the air coming out. It's worse!"

"I'll have it fixed in a jiffy."

"HELP!" she screams.

I work feverishly. I lace the flaps back up and stuff all my rags between the hole and the flap. The leak is definitely a lot worse than before. I rearrange the rags a dozen times. Nothing helps.

"So, what happened?"

"I couldn't get the patch inside."

"I knew it. You made the hole bigger. You did it again. You really want us dead. Not even God can save us if you keep hindering His efforts."

"The hole is the same size. Listen. It's the same as before. No problem."

" 'No problem,' he says. No problem. My God. Here we are, surrounded by hordes of sharks, lost in the Pacific, in a raft with a new, man-made, monstrous air leak, and the man says no problem. You're a horrible menace, Butler."

"What do you suggest? Are you planning to swim for it? Go. So long. Can I help you over the side?"

"You're detestable."

"It's probably genetic. Perhaps brain surgery can help when I get back."

"Get back! The captain says 'get back' in one breath, and in another he does his best to kill us. Bill Butler, you're not going to touch another thing on this raft. Nothing. Are you listening to me?"

"Am I listening? They can probably hear you back on the island. OK, that's it. No more repairs. You do it."

We settle back down. I should have thought the problem out in more detail. At the moment of truth, I failed to follow through with my plan. If I had opened a slight slit in the tube, the patch would now be in place, the air loss contained, and Sim calm and quiet.

I make two liters of water while Sim keeps pumping every fifteen minutes. This cannot go on. I have to do something, but right now I am shaken and scared. Every time Sim looks at me, I recoil. But she is right. I need to be extra careful. A false move now and nothing can save us. I know she would like me to fix the leak, but at the same time, she fears the outcome.

I prepare to fish against Sim's protests. Not a triggerfish is in sight. I chum and the bait remains untouched. We've never had that happen before. Other fish race around, nervous. Earlier this morning, in the distance, we noticed a school of fish breaking water. They jumped as if they were either feeding or trying to avoid being part of someone's breakfast. I throw out a few more pieces of bait, and a few triggers come in. In twenty minutes, I catch ten. As we lunch, we find out why all the fish are so nervous. A pod of large Pacific dolphins feed nearby.

We count five large dolphins, three times heavier than our Florida "Flipper" variety. These are ten feet long and are dark gray with small darker spots. With powerful thrusts, they zoom around, feeding busily. The shark pack circles at the ten-foot level, never far from the raft but careful to remain out of the way of the dolphins.

At three in the afternoon, all hell breaks loose. The dolphins start to feed in a wild frenzy. They go crazy and drive their thousand-pound bodies at high speeds in search of the two hundred pounds of fish they need every day to survive. It appears they are intent on getting today's ration from under our raft. As the afternoon progresses, the dolphins feed more aggressively. The sharks join the fray and also zoom inches from the raft in their quest to swallow whatever is in their path.

Their prey, mostly triggerfish, badly in need of shelter, head for the raft. We become the center of activity. Sharks and dolphins bump the raft without stopping. A foaming sea of fish surrounds us. What should we do? What can we do? The situation has quickly turned deadly. We continue to pump air every fifteen minutes.

The animals become wilder. Incredibly, the sharks and dolphins work as a team, each exciting the other into more savage bursts of speed. We, in turn, become tenser, for instead of dispersing, the battlefield centers around our raft as the afternoon progresses. We pray for darkness in hopes the sharks and dolphins will take their fill and leave. They seldom feed at night, but when night falls, the frenzy continues at full tilt. Large masses of phosphorescence speed under us. The raft is battered and made to spin. I yell and splash the pole, but nothing works.

We lie down and try not to panic. There is nothing we can do but pray. The dolphins are tireless and have turned the sharks into wild feeders. Small fish leap out of the water to escape frenzied jaws. The fight drags on late into the night. My mind races to come up with a way out. I sense none. My watch chimes. It is now midnight.

Suddenly, the raft shoots straight up out of the water. It feels like we're on a bucking bronco. The raft shakes fiercely from side to side, tossed up, down, right, left, and forward in violent jerks. I hold Sim tightly as I try to fathom this new crisis. What has us in its grip? I fully expect to see a set of gigantic bloodthirsty teeth emerge through the floor of the raft. Sim prays aloud and beseeches her favorite saints for help as never before. We're thrown a foot up with each savage thrust. This is surely the end. Time stands still. Whatever it is, it does not release its hold. This poor raft is doomed. We hug each other tightly, convinced our end is close at hand.

The raft explodes from a violent convulsion, then becomes quiet. I brace for the sudden rush of water. It's over, and we're still afloat. It had to be a shark caught in one of the ballast bags. A dolphin would have torn the entire raft to shreds.

Moments later, we're thrown into the air by another savage thrust. Sim screams. I hold her tightly in one arm and grab the pole in the other. We're pushed around furiously, propelled through the water by an invisible turbulent force. Time comes to a stop. Then, all movement stops as quickly as it started. We're still alive. Oh Lord, what test do you have for us next? We believe. We believe!

ABOARD THE RAFT
LAST CHANCE
0200 SUNDAY • AUGUST 6, 1989 • DAY 53

THE CIRCUS around us continues to unfold. The wild ride two hours ago still has us badly shaken. Those two episodes could not have lasted more than a minute or two each, but each seemed like an hour. How the raft holds together has me in awe, as sharks and dolphins continue to jostle us. By the smaller size of some of the phosphorescent tracks, we can tell that even the dorados have joined in the bash-the-raft game. We hang on and pray as never before. Will this eternal night be our voyage to eternity?

Why are we still alive? Why didn't the shark caught in the ballast bag destroy the raft? I still do not know what damage the monster did, but it had to have broken the bag to pieces to escape. What happened two hours ago is nothing but another miracle. I squint into the darkness. Breathing and splashing confirm that the melee remains at a peak. Two more strong bumps shake the raft. The raft rises. A hard, rasping thump along the floor of the raft throws us off balance.

Sim cries out, "Bill, they did it! They holed the raft!"

"What do you mean?"

"There's water coming in. We're sinking!"

I am about to tell her she's wrong when I feel the rush of cold water. Water quickly rises over the cushions. Sim pulls up a cushion, and I hold it as she bails frantically. The night is too black to search for the leak. We must wait until dawn. Sim bails without letup while I pump air. Now we have two serious problems. I turn on the flashlight and find an empty Evian bottle, which I cut in half. With the larger container, Sim can keep up with the leak if she doesn't stop.

The scrape we heard had to be a dolphin. Its dorsal fin sliced a hole in the bottom. What luck it didn't tear the air chamber. Or is the floor of the raft coming apart at the seams? I dare not speculate further. We must await morning. Exhausted, I fall asleep at once.

Sim bails nonstop for three hours. At five, I take over. She curls up and falls into a deep sleep. I dip the bottom half of the Evian bottle into the bilge and toss the water over the side. I bail a full container every three or four seconds. It's hopeless to look for the damage. It could be anywhere. Outside, there is no activity. Damage done, the monsters have all left, like the whales that sank *Siboney*. Damn them all! Damn every single beast in this ocean.

I bail right through sunup. Sim awakens, the epitome of a castaway—disheveled, wrinkled, and naked. Now we must look for the tear. She separates the cushions in the middle of the raft and finds that the leak is coming from the bow. She moves the gear piled on the port cushion onto the starboard side, lifts the cushion, and finds no damage under it. She then moves all the gear to the port cushion, lifts the cushion, and exclaims, "Here it is. My God! The tear's three inches long and the water pours in. How can we fix it?" With the cushion removed, water gushes in faster, bubbling inside the raft. I bail furiously.

The gash is a foot or so from the bow and near the center of the floor. A dolphin in a high-speed pass surely cut a corner a bit close. Sim presses the two sides together to slow the flow but cannot keep it together. I let air out of the air chamber to make the bottom of the raft less taut.

"Let's try to sew it closed, Sim. Do you still have that needle and thread? I'll hold it while you look."

Sim digs into her toilet kit and pulls out a shiny darning needle and a package of thread. I thread the needle with six strands, then push the blunt needle through the fabric while Sim bunches both sides of the tear together. The can opener is my pusher. I get the first stitch through and tie it off.

Two stitches later, two strands tangle and break. On the next pass, all the threads tangle. I cut the thread and leave one stitch in.

Sim bails while I cut a two-foot length of the parachute cord supplied with the raft and unravel it until I have a single strand. When I have the needle ready, Sim drops the bailing can, pulls up both sides of the tear, and holds them together to slow the flow. I push the needle through the holes I had opened, and the tear comes together as I work my way down to the aft end of the raft. Eleven stitches close the hole, though a trickle of water continues to flow into the raft. At least we will not have to bail nonstop.

The raft is a total mess. Cushions, bedding, gear, all of it sopping wet, is spread in every direction. Worst of all, the logbook got wet.

"Sim, let's reorganize the cushions."

"What do you mean? What crazy idea do you have now?"

"Water will continue to leak into the raft. If we leave the cushions as they are, we'll be swimming in water all the time. Besides, there will not be enough room to bail."

"And how do you want them now?"

"We'll put one on top of the other on the long side of the raft. That way, we'll stay drier, and we'll have a groove in the middle to scoop up the water."

"I don't like the idea."

"Why?"

"We'll fall off. It'll be uncomfortable. I don't like it."

"OK. Then get ready to swim all the time. And how do you plan to bail? The cushions cover the entire bottom. One on top of the other is the best solution. There will be a space between your cushions and mine."

"Bah! Let me think about it."

"Think about it? Until when? Until after we're neck-deep in water for a week? What in the hell is there to think about?"

Somehow we find a way to lean back and rest a bit. Sim bails every fifteen minutes. I hold up a cushion as she dips under it. If she waits twenty minutes, water rises over the cushions and soaks my shirt. On the other hand, it's been soaked for weeks, alternating between salt water and rainwater.

I insist, "Come on, let's do it."

"OK. But I don't like it."

On our first day in the raft, we placed our four cockpit seat cushions crosswise atop the floor. The seats on *Siboney* were wider toward the bow and narrower toward the stern, thus we have two cushions that are about four inches wider than the other two. Instead of four cushions crosswise on the floor of the raft as we have had them until now, we place one atop the other next to the air cylinders. This leaves an eight-inch gap in the middle of the raft. Two smaller cushions, each a foot square, support our heads. Our feet rest on life preservers, jackets, and wet bedding.

Our gear now sits directly on the raft floor, and the space between the cushions is perfect for bailing. I take advantage of the cool weather to make two liters of drinking water. Sim offers to help, but she's busy enough bailing four times an hour and pumping. I soon have the water made, and fish caught, filleted, and served. We settle down for a quick lunch.

Both of us find it hard to adjust to the new cushion arrangement. I put the wider of the cushions on top to provide more surface to lie on. But the top cushion slides off every time we move. Our situation gets worse by the hour. We can no longer huddle to keep warm. Bilge water rises over the cushion several times each hour and resoaks my shirt. My back sores sting as though I am on a bed of a thousand needles. And to make matters worse, it's raining.

Sim stays awake and bails every fifteen minutes all night, so afraid is she that we will sink. I am unable to convince her that cold water lapping our bare behinds is a fail-safe, early-warning system. The seas are so calm and quiet I can clearly hear the hiss of air escaping from the hole behind the rags. I've got to do something about it.

"You're not going to touch any part of this raft again. Ever again. Are you listening?"

"Yes, dear." Damn it. How can she read my mind in the dark?

"Don't 'yes, dear' me, you ugly monster. Have a little respect. If it wasn't for me, you'd be dead."

"Yes, dear. Hey, listen," I say. "What's that?"

Sim looks out the window. "Dolphins. They're back. Oh Lord. How long? How long will this continue? There are two, no three, four, five. Oh no, they are the same ones! Not another day like yesterday." A dolphin the size of a pilot whale blows a mixture of water and air inches away from the raft.

Sim is nearing the end of her rope. Tired and totally distraught, she bellows, "They really want to destroy us and the raft. I know they will not leave until the raft is in pieces. And you didn't cut loose the broken pieces of the ballast bags. I told you they were hanging down all torn and could entangle a shark or dolphin. But no, you ignore my suggestions. It's OK to tinker with the patch and almost kill us, but when real maintenance needs to be done, you do nothing. You are a pain, Butler."

"Sweetie, you know what they say. For pain, take an aspirin. Either that or just pray, will you?"

"Pray, ha! I'll probably pray that the dolphins swim away with you and leave me in peace and quiet."

"You'd be bored in no time. Give me a kiss."

"Give you a kiss? You have thirty days of rotten fish hanging on your beard. I'd probably get salmonella. I'd rather kiss a jellyfish. Besides, we have work to do. Let's try to fix the air leak. It's too dangerous to have all those problems together. We must resolve them one by one, or we won't make it. Why can't you arrange the rags like you did on the first day?"

She is right, but I don't need her prodding. I know we have to repair the air leak, but I need to relax before I try. I nod off. When I awaken, Sim snoozes.

At noon, I fish, but our usually teeming aquarium is void of life. The dolphins surely have scared them all away. The triggerfish remain calm when dozens of sharks swim within their schools, but when dolphins appear, they panic and vanish.

An hour later I try again, but the ocean is still empty of fish. Not another super-shark, I hope. The sea is glassy. There's a light wind out of the southwest. A current out of the west pushes us east. I make two liters of water. Will I be strong enough in a week or two to continue making water?

The logbook is sopped and now weighs several pounds. It contains a record of our voyage until day fifty-two. Today is August 7, day fifty-four on the raft. We're seventy-five days out of Balboa. The trip to Honolulu from Panama should have taken no more than sixty days. We're fifteen days overdue. Is no one worried? If they are, why isn't anyone looking for us?

"Sim, where's my camera?"

"You must be kidding. Your camera went under days ago."

"Where is it?"

"Under your feet."

I dig my Minolta out from under a pile of foul-weather jackets. It's exactly as Sim said, soaked inside the protective ziplock bag. I should have removed the film with the shots of the big dorado and the snapshot on the Fourth of July. Over the side and into the depths it goes after I remove the film. The film is soaked, and when I rewind it, the emulsion peels off. So much for that illusion.

The triggerfish return late in the afternoon, and soon after, dinner is on the paddle. Sim eats better now than she did weeks ago. While we eat, the continuous gurgle from the air leak reminds me that soon I must do something about it. Sim bails every fifteen minutes. She manages to get the water to drain to a spot in the raft where she can bail easily by shifting her body around. When I bail, the water is everywhere except where I want it. When I sit up to bail, the water collects under me, where I can't get to it. So I let Sim be in charge of bailing. The bilge rat, though I keep that name to myself.

A red sky lingers at sunset. I'm up, watching the ever-changing cumulus on the western horizon. I call out, "Sim, look. There's Alf."

"And over there, there's Mara." Mara was our schnauzer. Cloud watching has always been one of our favorite pastimes while at sea. Layers of orange and red clouds rising above the calm sea leads to sunset. Sim reads from her now very damp assortment of cards. We watch as the last remaining light plays with the clouds overhead. My prayers are more intense tonight as our little vessel, no longer stout and sturdy, floats gently toward the east.

"Bill, are you awake?"

"Yes."

"I just heard the news from the Voice of America. The tax people got Leona. There's a big protest in Hiroshima on the forty-fourth anniversary of the bomb. I'm glad we're not there. They haven't found the ten people on the oil rig that fell into the water off Texas. Big summit in Honduras of Central American leaders. That's it."

"Better than the *Miami Herald*. Is there any mention of two ding-dongs missing in the Pacific Ocean? Isn't anyone worried? We go off the scope for two months, and the world goes on. Is no one looking for us? What must one do to get attention?"

I can't believe no one has notified ships in this area to be on the lookout for us. So many ships have passed within a mile or less. How many others passed while we weren't looking?

Sim turns onto her knees and looks out the window. I wrap my hand easily around her upper thighs.

"I see a ship. It's far away. No running lights, only two white masthead lights. The lower light is in front. It's coming this way."

Sim has learned how to read ships like a pro. Large oceangoing ships have two bright lights visible when the ship is heading in our direction. The lower of the two lights is near the bow of the ship. The angle between the two lights tells us whether the ship is coming directly our way or not. In this case, the lower light facing us confirms it is heading in our direction. If the two white lights don't line up, Sim can tell it is not going to pass close by. I dig the compass out from under the covers.

"Sim, where is it?"

"Let's see. Look, it's there."

I follow Sim's hand and flash the light at the compass for a brief second. The ship's course is 340 degrees. That means he's heading away from the canal. The ships we have seen in the last two days have passed to the east or inshore. This ship is inshore but not as far as the others. Soon one must come close, heading our way.

I take another look. "He's still heading for us but far away."

"Shall we use the lantern? Shine an SOS?"

"Not yet. Still too far away."

Sim lies down, worn out after her fifteen-minute spell as lookout. In a few minutes, I row the raft around to face the ship. Swells are ten feet, and the ship is out of sight most of the time. It will pass about a mile and a half toward shore.

A mile and a half. We drift at a rate of ten to fifteen miles a day. Let's call it twelve miles a day, or half a knot. In three or four hours, we will be in that ship's line of travel. Perhaps the next ship that comes by . . .

"That ship is gone. What time is it?"

"Two twenty."

"Over five hours to dawn. I have to bail."

Every time I sit up, my cushions slide toward the middle of the raft. I must move them back, then arch my body with my head on the air tube and put my feet on the end of the raft before Sim can bail. Sim shoves my cushions back up against the side of the raft. She fills the bailing cup, and I throw it over the side. Six or seven dips and the bilge is dry. I plug in the air pump and start to fill the chamber with air.

WHACK.

The sound of the air pump must excite the sharks. We never fail to be punched. I've tried to pump air quietly, but the sharks still hear the noise and attack. Luckily, there is no moon tonight, and when I sit up, I can see several large shapes under the raft. I remain ready. Sim's side receives several bumps. More hits on Sim's side. Then a hard whack spins the raft around. I thrust the pole in the water and use it as an oar. We come back on course, and I wait.

"Bill, you have to pump. The raft is limp."

I still haven't seen the shark. This one is smart. It hasn't hit my side of the raft yet. I lie down and resort to splashing. It's quiet. The shark has left. I pump the raft up and nap. When I awaken, dawn is approaching. Sim still dozes. I turn on my side and begin to bail. I can't get much at a time but at least enough to keep it from soaking Sim.

That's a laugh. Soaking Sim. She's so saturated I could wring a quart of salt water out of her. She sleeps, hair in a tangle, blue flakes from the canopy spotting her face. I look her over. She has lost a lot of weight. Her thighs were the last to slim down. She's lost her bottom and belly and, sadly, her pretty bosom. Three weeks ago she was at her perfect weight. Now her body consumes what little fat remains. When I wrap both hands around my thighs, I now have a six-inch overlap, though I eat more than a pound of fish a day. Sim stirs.

We kiss and hug without a word. Nights take their toll on us. The invisible, lurking death that surrounds us is so oppressive that, even if we do nap, we awaken exhausted. The gurgle from the escaping bubbles constantly reminds us of the raft's air leak. Yesterday I lost another of my precious rotten rags. I have tied each of the remaining rags with several strings. We pump air every twenty minutes, and the raft is always limp. The floor collapses under our weight and doubles in two whenever a wave rolls by. Two or three times a day, I rearrange the rags. Nothing stops the leaks.

Over the past week, I have gone over why I failed to fix the leak. I simply lost my nerve. I hesitated to open a quarter-inch hole in the fabric for my backing plate to enter. I should have forced the entire assembly through the hole and let the air leak out for a few seconds. That's what I'll do next time. No, not next time. Now. Right now.

It will take every trick I learned in forty years as a salesman to get Sim to go along with the new patch project. I have the new parts ready. I assemble them, test them, and then take them apart. Sim has been watching me out of the corner of her eye.

"What are you doing?"

"What?"

"Don't try to fool me. You're making another patch."

"I'm just keeping busy. Using my hands. I'm the nervous type."

"You, nervous? You don't have a nerve in your body or a brain in your head. Bill Butler, I know you. You can't leave anything alone. You're going to screw things up again. Last time you fooled with the leak, you made it worse."

"You always exaggerate."

"Butler, the Lord is watching everything you do. And so am I."

"Sim, I am only trying to make the raft safer. That hole is leaking more and more."

"That's because a fool fooled with it instead of leaving it alone."

"This time, I know I can do it. Look at this patch. Mod II. So much better than the original model. It's going to work. Our pumping days will be easier."

"I don't believe a word you say."

"OK. Go ahead and pump air every twenty minutes. Bail every fifteen. Baby, I can fix it. This time it will work."

"You are a laugh."

"We've got to fix that hole. I pumped every twenty minutes last night."

"And what do you think I was doing? Dancing in a girlie bar in Paris? I bailed every fifteen minutes. I didn't sleep at all. I am dead, worn out, finished, and tired of your tricks."

"I'll push the washer and gasket inside the tube. With the wing nut, I'll tighten the outside gasket and washer against the inside. Guaranteed."

"Guaranteed? Where do I collect the guarantee after you sink the raft and all those beasts eat us up?"

"There's a guy down at the bottom called Davy Jones. He takes care of all payoffs."

"OK, OK. You go down to your buddy Davy with your patch and leave me alone. You tried the same exact method last time, and it didn't work. What's new?"

"Forget it. I won't do it. Let's pump and bail ourselves to death." She's getting on my nerves. But then, suppose it doesn't work?

I fiddle all day with the parts for my new patch. The washer I made for my first try was the core of my problem. It was too big to push through the small hole in the air tube. When I started, there wasn't a real hole. The air leaked from an abrasion. Next time I do it, I must open a hole in the air chamber first to make space for the washer to slip in.

This patch will go on tomorrow, unless Sim attacks me with the knife. Now, it's late and I'm tired. If I screw it up again, Sim will never forgive me. That is, if she survives her heart attack.

"Sim, look. I have the patch all figured out." I show it to her and explain how I plan to stop the leak.

She listens intently and then says reluctantly, "I'm not sure. I'm at the point where I panic when you bring up a new idea. If we have to do it, let's do it. We can't go on like this. This is hell."

"Why don't you read for now? I like the one about the bread and the stone." Sim reads a parable taken from Matthew.

> *What man is there of you, whom if someone asks for bread, will give him a stone? Or if he asks for fish, will give him a serpent?*
>
> *If you then, being evil, know how to give good gifts unto your children, how much shall your Father, which is in heaven, give good things to them that ask him?*
>
> *Therefore, all things whatsoever you would that men should do to you, do you even so to them, for this is the law and the prophets.*

Tonight I ask Sim to read the psalms twice. While she reads, I bail. We no longer settle down for the night. We have to bail and pump and fight sharks without stop. The beasts buffet the raft all night. I fight, pray, and splash the pole in the water. I don't bother to sit up any longer to work the pole. I tie the pole to my wrist, dangle it in the water, and from a horizontal position, move it up and down.

I fall asleep with the pole in the water. A sharp shark whack awakens me, and I find the pole gone. I grope in the dark in real panic. Minutes pass before I recall it's attached to my wrist and floats alongside.

Morning is ever so slow in arriving this day. It's as if night refuses to let go. We perch on our cushions, naked as the day we were born. The black, striped comforter is a wet, lumpy mass, good only for use as a pillow. Simonne sleeps on her life jacket. Buckles and hard foam press into her bony body as she fidgets to get body and cushion in sync. By then, she has to bail again.

I can't ever get comfortable. Sometimes I try to sleep on the bare cushion, which is smooth but hard. Then I spread the soggy foul-weather gear under me, but the creases tear into my sores. Edges in the foul-weather jacket feel like barbed wire. Our semicomfort is completely gone. Bare-bones survival has taken its place. And we are almost down to bare bones.

Once the sun is up and the day portends to be calm, I gather up my courage and announce to Sim, "The time has come for the patch job." I don't know what else to say. The words sound hollow even to me.

"It's OK, Bill, as long as you're sure of what you're doing."

"I screwed up last time. I lost my nerve. I got scared when I heard the air hissing out and didn't push in the screw all the way. This time I will do it right. Don't worry."

"I'm worried to death."

"Relax, baby. Here, look over the patch. Inspect it. Check it out. It will do the trick. It's better than pumping every twenty minutes."

"Twenty minutes is better than sinking or pumping every ten minutes if you botch it again."

"OK. Let's forget it. Let's keep pumping. I'm through arguing. End of subject."

I turn over and extend my back to Sim. I feign disinterest and sleep. A half hour passes.

"Bill, time to pump air."

"I'm through pumping air. Let it sink. What the hell, it's going to sink sooner or later. Or the sharks will get us. Why suffer any longer? Let's get it over with."

Sim grabs the pump and fills the air chamber.

Another half hour passes. The leak gets worse. She pumps again.

Then out of the blue, Sim says, "Bill, are you positive it'll work?"

"I was going to say guaranteed, but . . ."

"OK. Be very careful."

"I'm always careful."

"Baloney. If you're going to do it, get it over with."

"That's the girl. What a raft mate. I'll have it fixed in a jiff."

"Be careful."

Sim pumps air into the chamber until it's tight. I get on my knees and lean over the side. Sim has the screw with the gaskets all assembled and ready to go. I remove the rags and unlace the flaps. I feel for the hole. The slit is so small I can barely feel it. Only the bubbles tell me where it is.

"Sim, hand me your nail file. Then put the pump on and get ready to pump."

"What are you going to do with the nail file?"

"I'm only going to clear some threads away." I keep lying to Sim. If I tell her I plan to shove the file into the air chamber to open the hole, she'll scream or use the knife on one of my vital parts. She hands me the file. I open the hole. Masses of larger bubbles escape. I hand the file back to Sim with a trembling hand.

"Pump up the raft and hand me the patch."

The screw has the two washers and the two gaskets and the wing nut in their proper order. I feel for the hole with my finger, then push the head of the screw inside the air chamber. The washer will not go through. Bubbles increase tenfold when I lean on the screw. The hole is still too narrow. I push harder but can't see what I'm doing for all the bubbles. This is where I was before when I lost my nerve. I push with all my remaining strength. With a pop, the washer slides in and the flexible leather gasket slides in easily after it.

It's then that I notice the wing nut is missing. I look around in desperation. All I see is blue ocean and loads of triggerfish eager to snack on my fingers. The wing nut has fallen off. I've done it again. The frothy burble has never been worse.

I lost the other wing nut yesterday under the cushions but didn't bother to find it since I only needed one. The heavy line of bubbles pours out of the hole. I call out, "Sim, pump!"

Sim screams, "What happened? What are you doing? What's that noise? The raft is getting limp! I can't keep up! Oh God, not again, not again!"

"I'm only adjusting the patch. Be quiet." If Sim finds out I've lost the wing nut, it'll be the big casino. I'll lose my last strands of credibility. I'll probably lose something worse.

I lift the cushion and try to remain and act calm. Inside, I'm frantic. I dig through the accumulation of trash, tiny bits of paper, fish scales, threads, and hair. I'll never find it. Why did I start this project anyway? We could have pumped every twenty minutes. All of a sudden, pumping doesn't seem a major chore. If I can't find the wing nut, I don't dare think of the consequences. The hole I have opened is huge.

I turn the top cushion over, and my heart jumps when I see the wing nut on top of the bottom cushion. I scoop it into my hand and quickly screw it onto the end of the bolt. The squeal of air lessens as I tighten the wing nut. In seconds, I'm finished. The leak is plugged. I lean back slowly. Sim has been pumping wildly and praying aloud. The sudden increase in pressure takes her by surprise. She doesn't know what to expect. "How did it go? Did you fix it?" She appears stunned. She would like to believe it's fixed, but she remains unconvinced.

We pump again, then plug the air valve and wait. A half hour passes. I lean over. Some bubbles still escape, but at a much slower rate. An hour passes.

Sim is overjoyed. "You did it. Baby, you did it!" She embraces and kisses me.

"I didn't think you kissed murderers and terrorists, particularly unshaven, unwashed ones, full of salmonella. Here, look for a spot without fish scales."

She hugs me.

"You are wonderful. What would I do without you?

"Well, let's see. You could marry a guy who likes dry land. Or someone who takes you around the world on the *QE2* with all your finery. Instead, you marry a sailor with a sunken boat and a leaky raft who forgot to bring along your clothes. You are really not all that bright."

Two more ships pass to the east. One heads north, the other south, both less than a mile away. We don't bother to hail or get excited. Sim tunes in new stations from San José and one from Puntarenas, all in Costa Rica. Most come in strongly. There's also a country music station from a town called David, in Panama, advertising a weekend barbecue. Hey, let's go!

We're ready for shore. Two pairs of shorts stored under us in a plastic bag haven't been inspected in a month. Will they fall apart like the two T-shirts we bought in Balboa? Those rotted to the point I couldn't even use them as rags to stuff into the leak.

The first day of our ninth week aboard *Last Chance* dawns clear and bright. A tinge of orange touches all horizons. What sort of an omen is that? My patch job has improved our lifestyle. We now only pump air every hour and a quarter. One less burden. Sim bails every fifteen minutes, day and night.

How can I improve the fix on the hole in the floor of the raft? I should've put a gasket between the edges when we first sewed the hole together. What can I do to slow the leak?

Shark attacks are down from eighty whacks a day to forty. I expected more sharks as we neared the coast, but it's turned out the other way. I've heard that hordes of sharks roam the coasts of Nicaragua and El Salvador. Do we have another great white visiting? Will shark activity get worse as we close with shore?

I fish and make water. Sim bails and looks out. In between, we try our best to find a position that affords a few moments of comfort. Whenever I move, the top cushion slides toward the middle and closes off the space Sim needs to bail. Then I must move again as Sim pushes my cushions back into place.

Sim reads as night engulfs our little world. Though the radio tells us we're moving closer, why haven't we seen a fishing boat? When will the current change? At some point, many miles offshore, the easterly current has to turn either north or south. Or will it turn 180 degrees and flow back out to sea? I fall asleep with a head full of more unknowns than ever before.

Three ships pass between two and three in the morning, all inside us—that is, toward shore. Two are bound for Panama, and the other is headed north. All are too far away to bother signaling. Sim maintains an hourly lookout.

She rarely sleeps. Aware how easily and how deeply I doze, she's afraid that the raft will fill with water or sink from lack of air, or that a freighter will run us down while I have the watch. Several times in the last few days, when I was in charge of bailing, I fell asleep after an hour or so, and the water rose over the cushions and up to Sim's behind. She awakened from her few moments asleep sputtering and furious. What else is new. I'll do my best, but I am dead tired.

Morning arrives on a gray note. A threat of rain is to the north. Simonne looks out the window toward the east and northeast for signs of land. During the past several days, I have often gotten a feeling that she has seen something. Like the island we passed, she will not call "Land ho" until she is 100 percent sure it is land. When she first spied the island, I, the incurable optimist, hoped it was the mainland. As we approached it and until the very last, I hoped to see land attached to it. Despite my earlier convictions to the contrary, that island must have been Isla de Cocos, for no other island is that far from shore.

Sim has been studying the horizon for an entire day. She looks in one direction more than in others. I keep my eye on her lips and eyes for a telltale sign. She maintains her concentration, which, in itself, is heartening.

Curiosity gets the best of me. "Sim, what do you see?"

"I'm not sure. Behind all those clouds, I think I see land. A high line of mountains. When I see it, clouds cover what I'm looking at, and it's there no more. It looks dark blue, darker than the clouds."

How many times in the past weeks have I, and Sim too, stared at a low-lying black line on the horizon? The line would remain fixed for such a long while that we were sure it had to be land. It always turned out to be a cloud.

Simonne rests. I take advantage of the cool of the day to make two liters of water and catch six triggerfish. Afterward I am almost asleep when several sharp slaps announce the arrival of the shark pack. Three pokes later, they leave. Their interest in us is not as intense as weeks ago. Maybe they came by just to say hi to their old buddies.

I remove my T-shirt to dry the sores on my back, then nap. When I awaken, Sim is again scanning the eastern horizon. I pull the binoculars out from under my head, where they have been part of my pillow for at least six weeks. One eyepiece is full of water. The other, although partially blocked, passes some light. I disassemble them using the knife as a screwdriver and wash the eyepieces, the mirrors, and the prisms in fresh water. The sun quickly dries the parts, which I reassemble. With the prisms aligned and the eyepieces replaced, I take a look and still see nothing. Water is trapped inside the eyepiece, which cannot be taken apart. I remove the strap and toss the binoculars over the side.

Sim, ecstatic, cries out, "I can see land! There's no question about it. The same mountain peak is there. Low clouds cover the horizon, but above those clouds, I count three peaks. The mountains are high. It has to be the mainland. We cannot be far."

I lean up and look at gentle valleys that lead up to dark-blue peaks hovering in the sky, three or four thousand feet high. "It could be thirty to fifty miles," I tell her. "We could be closer."

As sunset begins the inevitable retreat of yet another day at sea, Sim reads our daily psalms. The sun sets, and as soon as night takes over from day, we notice lightning in the distance. Soon, we hear thunder.

"Bill, that storm is coming closer. A while ago, I counted to sixty, but the latest thunder came forty seconds after the flash."

"Bath time. Get the soap. I hope it misses us, because it's chilly tonight."

"Thirty."

"Twenty." Both of us count and compare.

"Wow, that was a big bolt. Bill, do you think we could get hit by lightning? What would it do to us?"

"I'd hate to say it couldn't hit us, the way my luck has been running, but it's extremely unlikely. There's nothing to attract it to us except the watermaker. Besides, the swells are still fifteen to twenty feet, and we're under the surface level more than half the time. I wouldn't worry about it."

Sim jumps up. "What's that noise? Listen. It must be a ship!" She looks out and cries, "No! Look! Oh my God, it's rain. It's coming this way."

A flash of lightning lights up the ocean to accentuate a white wall of rain roaring in from the north. I can see it in the darkness, accompanied by a deafening roar. A white wall, the worst type of squall. We zip up and tighten the windows. I pull my blanket out from under my cushion, soaked and cold, and without hesitation, pull it over my seminaked body. Sim covers up with her usual trash bag.

The first gusts of forty knots quickly increase to fifty. Rain hits the raft horizontally. Propelled by gale-force winds, it rushes through the hole between the windows and canopy. I push the canopy up with the fishing rod as water sprays into the raft, the cold wind and rain sending shivers through us. I pull my soggy Andean wool blanket up higher. It's almost warm now. Wool is amazing. Soaking wet, it has kept me warm many a night.

Sheets of rain with hurricane-force winds propel the raft to the southwest, back out to sea. We time a lightning bolt at ten seconds, a mile away. I hold Sim's hand and hang on with the other. Gusts of sixty to seventy knots threaten to blow the canopy off. Our fragile raft hugs the sea. We securely tie the watermaker and pump.

Wind and rain pummel us. Thunder and lightning spend themselves in a powerful show of bravado. Bolts shower down like hail. And just as fast as the squall came, the wind decreases and the rain eases. Soon we hear just a distant rumble. We have survived one more trial. What's next?

Sim bails for the balance of the night at the usual fifteen-minute intervals. I pump air every forty-five. The need to bail every fifteen minutes consumes what little energy we have. When she starts, Sim can quickly remove four or five cans of water. To get the rest, I have to suspend myself by head and feet to get the water to trickle slowly from under my cushion into the well created by the ball of Sim's hand as she pushes down on the floor of the raft.

Weeks ago, she used the sponges supplied with the raft to remove the last dribbles of water. When the sponges thoroughly rotted, she sopped water with pieces of the rotting T-shirts and strips of the cotton blanket. Now we have nothing left to remove these last drops with. Anyway, the tear in the bottom of the raft has left us with a sense of resignation we have been unable to shake. At one time, we busied ourselves drying our covers. Sim has always been the busy housekeeper. Now we languish in our rotting raft, too exhausted to care whether we are wet or dry, filthy or not.

My wool blanket lives in the bilge, thoroughly soaked, under my feet, for there is no other place for it. Sim screams if the rough, salt-water-soaked wool touches her irritated and chafed skin. I try to keep it as far away from her as a raft three feet wide will permit. If I notice that the night is going to be cold and rainy, I wring the blanket out before dark and pull it over me, wet and ice cold. Fifteen minutes later, I am warm as toast. Sim shivers under her plastic garbage bag.

Since Sim mentioned blinis weeks ago, the word has bounced around inside my head louder and louder. It's blini-blini-blini, hundreds of blinis. I've asked Sim never to mention food of any kind again. It's bad enough to put on my wool gloves with "Häagen-Dazs" emblazoned on the back every time I fish. (I "found" these gloves in the ice cream section of a supermarket. When we were checking out, the Häagen-Dazs delivery man came running up and reclaimed his gloves. Then, as we were leaving, he returned and gave me another pair. As *Siboney* was sinking, the gloves were one of the items I threw into the raft. They have proven invaluable when catching triggerfish.) When I get to shore, I'm going to swim in ice cream. "When I get to shore." That'll be the day!

Incredible luck continues to follow us. The three-inch rip in the bottom of the raft could easily have been six inches or ten or the full length of the raft. I shudder at the possibility. Our water-making machine could have dropped through the hole. Water would have flooded the raft instantly. Triggerfish would have nibbled continuously until we bled. There is no way we could have contained the water as we have done with the actual three-inch gash.

We continue to bail, day and night, through calm and storm. Lack of sleep tells on us, particularly on Sim, who needs a long time to fall asleep. I don't make a move to bail while Sim is awake. And she barely sleeps. She hasn't slept for at least two days. I may bail for an hour around dawn, which is the only time Sim naps. While I sleep, she bails and tosses the water out on her own. She overbails. I am unable to convince her there's nothing wrong with a little extra water in the raft. She refuses to listen.

She is as hardheaded as a mule, yet were she not hardheaded, stubborn, ingenious, and resourceful, we would not have made it this far. She's cursed me, humiliated me, screamed and yelled and carried on, but at the same time, she has helped and sustained me. We've prayed and laughed and cried together, and through it all, she's loved me. A warm feeling flows through me with the certainty of my love for her. We could not have survived this long without each other's help. We belong together. We will be saved together, and our life will be even better than before now that we have found God.

ABOARD THE RAFT
LAST CHANCE
0745 SATURDAY • AUGUST 12, 1989 • DAY 59

OLDEN SHAFTS of light overcome the immense, drawn-out dreariness of dawn to put behind us yet another endless night. As if in mock surrender, wind and waves ease. The new day radiates hope and promise. Sim looks to the east and cries out with excitement, "Bill, look! Land! Land! Mainland. Mountains. It's so beautiful. It's so clear, I can see one, two, no, three mountain peaks. And valleys. I can see the entire coast all the way from north to east. It's spectacular! We are getting closer. God, how could I have doubted you so?"

I pull myself up to the window with a last little push by Sim. Pale-blue mountains float high above the morning mist. Below the peaks, valleys cascade into the sea, taking the hills along. We feast our eyes on the ridge of high mountains that extends far to the north. This is true mainland. Mainland Central America. Of that there is no doubt. This is no illusion.

Sim asks the same question that's been on my mind. "How far away do you think it is? It looks so near and at the same time so far away."

"It's hard to tell. The peak, the high one in the middle, could be thirty, forty, even fifty miles away. In Manila, on a clear day, we could see the peak on Bataan, fifty miles away, and it looked about the same. The shoreline is much closer than the peaks that we see, but we won't see it for several days."

We marvel at the vista before us. As the sun rises, its light strikes promontory after promontory, ever changing the panoramic landscape. Between the dark expanses of forests, rectangular fields of cultivation dot the mountains. We cannot believe that our salvation is actually in sight, not a mirage that will fade into the shape of distant clouds.

Is our voyage really almost over? We have traversed more than a thousand miles of open ocean in a six-foot rubber boat. Our fragile vessel has fallen victim to giant seas, violent storms, and assaults by a multitude of vicious monsters of the sea. By a series of miracles, we have survived onslaught after onslaught from above and from below.

Sim's spirits turn as bright as our skyline. She's been a remarkable crew. She has fought to live and has suffered deeply because of it. As I look at her, I see but a shadow of the woman who sailed with me on *Siboney*. She has lived too long in the shadow of death. Many weeks ago, she made peace with the Maker and made ready to accept His will. Now she believes that yes, she will live to tell her story.

Sim's radio picks up signals from San José, the capital of Costa Rica, and from a town called Carthago. Last night she again heard a station out of David, a small town in northern Panama, advertising a dancing, drinking, and eating place with many girls. Wow, we're back in civilization.

The direction of the radio signals tells us our drift is to the south. I wish we had a map to locate all the cities, and how I wish I had paid a little more attention in high school to the geography of this part of the world. The good news is that we are approaching the coast, slowly yet steadily.

We should soon come upon a fishing boat. The calm weather surely will bring out the fishermen, commercial and sport. This is Saturday. The sportfishing crowd will be out either today or tomorrow. Or don't they bother to fish these waters because of all the sharks? Or is it not the marlin season? Tomorrow, Sunday, should bring out a couple of boats.

Land is a blessing, our salvation, an end to the life and death incognito we have lived with for nine long weeks. Yet land comes in a multitude of shapes. Land can be jagged rocks leading to even more jagged and sharp cliffs. A rocky shore would quickly destroy our raft. Will we have the strength to swim? Our raft, structurally weak and leaking water and air, may be safer at sea than at many landfalls. But then, we could wash up on a nice sandy beach. All these thoughts churn continually within me.

Sim reads. Then we pray, full of hope. God wants to save us. He has watched over us through a thousand miles over the high seas. He has tested our faith in one of the world's most perilous oceans. He has shown us His power and His mercy in heavy doses. We have passed His test. So far.

Death knocked thousands of times. Sharks have battered the raft more than eighty times a day, at least four thousand times in the past fifty days. Any of the twelve-foot hammerhead or mako or white-tipped sharks that circled the raft at dusk could easily have done away with the raft, and would have received a hearty meal as a bonus. Or what if the great white shark had been in a feeding mood? Its digestive juices would still be working on our leg and arm bones. But the sharks didn't touch us. Why not? The two ships that missed us by mere feet could have ground us into oblivion. Thank you, dear Lord, for your helping hand.

The hours of night are endless hours of toil. We bail and pump. With every night that passes, we see fewer sharks. In the past days, we have seen just one turtle. We try to nap on our wet, slippery, too-narrow, rock-hard cushions. I don't really care whether I sleep or not. Soon, we'll be safe.

Sim prods me and asks, "Are you awake? There's a massive air search going on." I jump. These are the words I have been awaiting. Sim senses my reaction. "No, they're looking for a congressman lost in Africa. Dozens of planes search for him. Can you imagine? We've been off the scope sixty-five days, and we haven't seen a single search plane."

She's right. We left Balboa eighty-two days ago. More than twenty-five ships have passed close by, and none has seen us. But if there is a search going on now, it will be nearer to Hawaii. Besides, I never ran for Congress.

We are approaching shore, and we will save ourselves. To hell with the Coast Guard and air searches and ships. We got ourselves into this mess, and we will get ourselves out of it. We'll be onshore and safe in a few days. Besides, as we get within a few miles of the coast, a fisherman is bound to come by. A smaller boat can spot us easier than a freighter. If no one sees us, we will drift onto shore.

That is, if the wind blows from the west. Yesterday, after the squall, an offshore breeze pushed us away from land. I fought hard to remain patient, for I was sure the onshore wind would return. We had to wait for the forces of nature to again balance out. And they did. Weak at first, forming mere ripples on the mirrored sea, the westerly breeze increased until once again we were on the move toward land.

Waves will also take us to shore. All debris in the oceans end up onshore sooner or later, propelled by waves and current. Relentless, endless rollers, in tireless succession, head toward shore. They bend around natural barriers, then head in to face their natural end head-on.

The night is dense and black. The moon, which glowed earlier through a heavy layer of clouds, has set. A ship inshore is too far away to bother telling Sim about, though she no longer gets depressed by ship sightings. The first dozen that steamed up and passed without seeing our raft drove her to tears. Now we see a dozen lights around us on any given night, all too far away to risk our last flare.

I try to nap. Sim bails. The cushion arrangement is abominable. yet I cannot think of a better solution. Sim wants to go back to the original, single-layer configuration, but I continue to argue that it will only put us constantly underwater.

When I open my eyes again, our new day, number sixty, is upon us. Sim lies on her cushion face up, mumbling her prayers. Dense clouds cover all.

"Morning, sweetie. Are we onshore yet?"

"There's no land. Low clouds hide everything. I've looked and looked while you snored, but it's hopeless. I'm so depressed. I dreamed last night of trees, big, beautiful green trees, with the wind rustling the leaves and little birds hopping from branch to branch, gleefully chirping. How long have I thought I would never sense the feeling of land again? And now that we are so close, land continues to elude us."

Sim bails. Then she retrieves the watermaking machine, and I prepare to make water. I no longer have the comforter to pad the machine. I put it on my chest to pump. A small rag on my chest and another on my pelvic bone help cut down on abrasions. I pump more slowly now. Two liters will take me an hour. We keep all our containers full. One never knows.

I'm all bone. Actually, a few weeks ago one of my bones gave me a real scare. As I ran my hand over my chest, I felt a new bump. As days passed, the growth became larger. A bone was growing right in the middle of my chest. I continued to check. Desperate, I had Sim feel it. She burst out laughing.

"You dummy," she said. "Bone doesn't grow. You've lost all your fat. That's some damage you did when you were young. That bump is usually hidden by fat."

I hope she's right, but the thing is huge and I never noticed it before. I pump the handle on the watermaker slowly. I do one ridge of the Evian bottle at a time. I rearrange the rags and do another ridge. When finished, I fish, and then clean the catch.

We eat, pump, bail, then nap. As evening approaches, Sim reads, her task each evening made more difficult, as the cards stick together. The sun sets quickly, allowing us but a brief last glimpse of land. Will it vanish like the island? Will our trial never end?

When Monday dawns, land is nowhere in sight. Storms toward shore are dense, dark, and ominous. Menacing masses of gray and black clouds layer the eastern and northern horizons. Bitter disappointment overwhelms Sim.

"I knew it. Every time I get my hopes up, something happens to smash them. I know we have been going backward. The current turned, and we're being taken out to sea. The radio stations from Costa Rica I heard so clearly days ago are no longer there. I hear more Panama and Colombia. Even Radio Sandina from Nicaragua has disappeared. We're no longer going in toward shore. What a cruel joke God is playing on us. He puts hope in our hearts, then takes it away. We're headed out to sea, caught in a circular current, forever adrift, until we slowly die."

"Calm down, baby. Land is still there except that the clouds are hiding it. Visibility is less than five miles. Land is still thirty miles away. As soon as the clouds lift, you'll be in for the surprise of your life."

"I'm going to be in for the surprise of my life if your prediction turns out like all your others. We're probably off Hong Kong for all I know. Butler, you can't prove we drift toward shore. You have no way to tell. Your only reference points are black, ugly clouds. I'm starting to think my seeing land was nothing but a dream."

"Impossible. Your dreams only have monsters or dead men sprawled on the beach or monster sharks munching rafts. Besides, check the wind direction. See, it's from the west. It pushes us east. East is where the land is. Keep your pants on; we'll be there soon enough."

"Speaking of pants, I've got bad news. I have my period again. Is this a curse or what? I'm fifty-one. How long will this go on? Forever?"

"Again? That's three times in less than sixty days. That's another record for Guinness. Like my not pooping for five weeks."

"Stupid. What do I have to do to get a little sympathy on this dumb raft?"

Sim sits up and looks out. She turns around, excited. A ship approaches. I take a look. She's right, and it's heading to pass close by. Sim turns on her knees, and I pass her the fishing pole with her T-shirt tied onto the end. She lifts the pole high and waves it back and forth. I wave the red bag.

As I watch Sim, I have to chuckle. Naked, she waves the pole with a battered shirt at the end exactly the way castaways do it in the movies and in the Sunday comic strips. The ship passes four hundred feet away as it steams toward the Panama Canal. We hear the thump of the engine as it spins the propeller. Each turn pushes it farther away. Sim blows the whistle but gets no more than a low squeak. She lets the ship go without a fuss, now convinced that merchant ships do not post lookouts.

Before we sailed, I asked a friend, a merchant seaman, about bridge routines on long sea hauls. He confirmed my fears. Most ships sail shorthanded. Men on watch keep busy with navigation, instrument readings, radar, and keeping the many logs. They may glance out a window only a few seconds every hour. The small windows on the bridge provide a poor view of the surrounding waters. It's hardly worthwhile for anyone to look. Besides, the radar will sound an alarm if another ship approaches. Our best hope is at night. We have to make good use of our last flare.

As we rest, I notice Sim cock her head. A look of concentration is on her face. She cries out, "Bill, I hear an airplane! Listen. It sounds as if it's taking off."

I now hear the faint sound. It's a propeller plane and it strains to climb. Clouds are higher and look less menacing than they were yesterday. The sound quickly fades away, leaving behind a promising omen.

The afternoon soon turns into evening. Simonne gathers up her prayer cards that she has been drying on the air chamber, and reads. The pictures of her family have faded away completely.

At last light, she cleans my back, a nightly routine, by pouring a little fresh water on the open sores that now run from my neck to my buttocks. How we have gone this long without infection I will never know. Sim says the sores on my back are just abrasions. They are open and ugly, but not infected.

Our night is uneventful. Three or four sharks keep us from falling into a deep sleep. The two A.M. monster does not show.

Tuesday, August 15, dawns on two forlorn castaways. Today is the feast day for Sim's mother's saint. Sim is so sure her mother has followed us daily in her thoughts. Sim wanted so much to be on land today, to call her mother and reassure her, to tell her we are safe, alive.

Clouds cover most of the coastline, yet Sim assumes her usual position by the window, peering toward where she hopes land awaits. I see her smile as she looks over to me.

"I see land. Just a little piece of it. Thank goodness, it's still close. I was so afraid it wouldn't be there. Thank you, God. Forgive me for doubting you. Oh, Bill, I'm so depressed and so very tired. I'm exhausted, but the nearness of the coast keeps me going."

I believe it is just days before we make it to a beach on our own or someone finds us. But even the welcome land, to my distorted eyes, appears hostile and unwilling to receive us. I feel we are being tempted with false hopes only to be bitterly disappointed once again. How will this story end? Is the sea ready to release us? Enraged that we have survived its cruelty and are about to escape, what new hazards and trials will it throw at us?

I catch Sim staring off into the distance again. She mutters thoughtfully, "It looks like we're heading for Panama. If we land in the north, the people shouldn't be as worked up as those in Panama City. I heard Noriega closed the airport in Panama City and has tossed out all the tourists. We may have to go to Costa Rica to make our way home."

I agree. Sim bails while I pump. We remain silent, too excited by the proximity of land. As evening creeps up on us, Simonne reads. Today's sunset evolves into a mass of gray and pale, sickly yellows. Darkness quickly hides our world.

Rain begins after midnight. Large drops seep through the canopy. We await the new day with real fear. Memories of how close we came to the island play before us. What new surprises will we face? Is the sea prepared to relinquish its hold? Are we to drift toward land one day and back out the next, like the tides? We may not reach shore for weeks. Time stands still as day sixty-two on the raft begins.

Land is barely visible below the low-hanging clouds and through the drizzle. It looks closer, but we must wait for clear weather to really tell. I have visions of a sandy beach. Once ashore, will we be able to walk? We have been off our legs since *Siboney* sank, nine weeks ago. What will happen when we try to get out? We tore the raft getting in. So many questions crowd my mind.

Sim is as happy as I have seen her since we left the Panama Canal. "Morning, my sweet," she says. "I have the local news. My foreign press service couldn't get through. Most of the stations are Panamanian. I'm afraid we're headed to Noriegaville. I heard there was an incident with American troops and Noriega's police. There's talk about an international commission taking care of the canal. That situation can't last long."

I nod. "We didn't meet a person when we were passing through Panama who wasn't ready to grab a gun and go hunting for Noriega. Even that quiet taxi driver with the three children wanted to put four big round holes into 'Pineapple Face,' as they call him. When the tables turn down there, Noriega's behind isn't worth a cent. I hope the excitement holds until we get out of here."

Rain falls most of the day, and we face another cold, wet night. Our excellent health is a constant source of amazement. Cold, wet, naked, dirty, and undernourished, we've had not a sniffle. Even Sim's headaches are part of the past.

Sim's third period is almost behind us, which is great, since our supply of old T-shirts is down to the one on my back. Three periods in sixty days! New to me. Her chafed, naked behind rests on salty bedding, but she takes it like a trouper. I can tell she is now convinced we will be saved, that it's only a matter of time.

I still can't get over the lack of sharks. I was sure attacks would increase as we neared shore, but I ended up plumb wrong. They're probably all fished out. Today, so far, we've only had one shark bump the raft. We approach nightfall more relaxed. If the sharks will allow us peace, our dilapidated raft will make it. We'll make it last another week or two until we're onshore.

As the last four weeks have passed, we have found it more and more incredible that no one has been out looking for us. To hell with everyone. We'll save ourselves. Soon we'll be onshore and will need no help from anyone. That is, if we can walk. Every time Sim tunes the radio, I pray she comes up with the news of an air search for two missing sailors. Or did we miss that broadcast?

Rain falls well into Wednesday morning. The dampness has made my warts grow even more black and spongy. Two are as big as dimes. I scratch one and pieces fall off. The sores on my back itch less after last night's rain. I would like to sit up and look out, but don't have the ambition. Sim will surely wake up soon.

Sim dozes. Bedraggled, emaciated, her hair matted, she looks like a Martian what with her face littered with blue flakes shed by the canopy. She rests with an air of peace, her mind momentarily at rest from her daily death-on-the-doorstep trauma. I turn onto my left side, take the bailing cup, and with my left hand push the floor of the raft down. Water rushes up to my wrist. I push the cup down, let it fill partially, then pour the water over the side, careful not to nudge my sleeping beauty.

I quietly repeat the process. Sim so needs her rest. She hasn't had a good sleep for a week. She stirs, opens her eyes, senses I am awake and bailing, and lapses again into one of her special sleeps.

When I empty the bilge, I lean back, rest my body, and close my eyes, heavy with sleep. Yes, shore must be in sight. The wind has been out of the west all night. The current also pushes us east. We should be making almost eight miles a day. Land is twenty to thirty miles off. In three or four days, we will be on a beach.

I close my eyes and see a wide beach with a long, shallow approach. It's ideal. The raft drifts in slowly, edged on by a gentle breeze. The day is bright. We're in a foot of water. I look down. The bottom is sandy. I jump over and pull the raft onto the beach. I help Sim out. We topple into the warm, rich, cleansing water, naked. We roll over and over as we work the grime from our deepest pores. We pull the raft onto the beach, dress, then embrace. We're safe; we're on land. Nothing can hurt us now.

Where are we? We rest on the beach for a day or two, but soon we must walk to the road. There must be a road. At the far end of the beach is a young couple in street clothes, walking along the shore. We walk up to meet them, tell our story, and ask for help. They have a car parked near the beach, on the road. They are happy to help us. We go back to the raft to pick up the life jacket with our passports and money. When we return, the couple has left. We're forlorn. But we've come this far on our own; we can make it the rest of the way. We walk toward the road.

The path away from the beach is even and without the usual thorns. Barefoot, we make good time. We help each other. The path takes us into a forest. It winds around in darkness until it delivers us to a highway. We hear a radio at a small neighborhood store. They have bananas and mangoes. They accept our dollars. I ask them where we are, but they are unable to tell me. We tell them we need help. A young man assures us he will call the local police. We wait and wait until I feel someone shake me. I open my eyes. It's Sim.

"Bill, land is very close. I can see details onshore. The peaks I saw two days ago are farther away and to the north. I see new land to the east. We have been blown to the south. I heard many Panamanian stations last night. That big party with the music and girls is still on in David this weekend."

"Let's go, baby, break out the oars. Can you still do the cha-cha? Any other news?"

"No. Soccer is the main news event in this part of the world. They report soccer scores, and every night there are several soccer games. I like the way the announcer calls out a score as 'Goaaaaalllll!' The people go wild."

I smile and we hold hands.

"Can you distinguish any objects on land, like a tree or a house?"

"No, not yet. What a shame we will miss a landfall in Costa Rica. I so much wanted to visit the shrine of Nuestra Señora de Los Angeles in Carthago. She is the patron saint of Costa Rica. I heard on the radio they have an annual pilgrimage on August 2. They still talk about it. If we make it, we will go to Carthago, a pilgrimage on our own to say thanks." I nod and smile. Yes, of course, we'll go.

By now, it's well after one and time for lunch. I rely on my now standard technique. I have nine triggerfish on board and cleaned in less than an hour. I stuff myself as usual, while Simonne barely eats three fillets. We nap through the remainder of the afternoon. Sim reads. As the sun sets without fanfare, we prepare for the night. The flashlight and our last flare are in their nighttime place next to my head.

Sim scans the horizon for signs of lights onshore but sees none. She bails the raft dry, and I give it an extra-heavy pumping. We return our cushions to their places, and we talk. Or I should say, I nod off while Sim continues to talk. She is too excited to sleep.

Suddenly, she jerks up to a sitting position.

"A ship. I hear engine noise. Listen."

The faint hum of a diesel engine becomes louder. Both of us look out at once. We see nothing. I pull out the oar and row the raft around. The hum turns into the heavy thumping of a large diesel engine. I row the raft in a full circle. We see no lights.

The noise from the engine grows louder. We look at each other in silent amazement and again scan the waters around us. The ship approaches completely blacked out. It's invisible.

"Should we signal with the light? He's still coming closer. Bill, I'm afraid."

"Let's wait. Honest seamen don't travel at night in a darkened ship. I don't like the looks of it. We may be safer where we are than to get mixed up with some bad guys." The heavy pounding of the diesel is upon us. The horizon is as black as the night, so there's no hope of seeing any sort of a silhouette. Will they run us down?

Then Sim spots it.

"There it is, and it's not too far away. It's a small freighter or a big fishing boat. Pass me the compass. They are going almost east, toward shore. What a shame. We could have signaled, but I agree with you, there's something fishy about this fisherman."

The throbbing engines grow fainter, then die out. We are alone again. Our hearts pump furiously. This latest alert has frazzled our nerves. We are beginning our tenth week on the raft. Ten weeks. I can remember back when we considered one week impossible. How did this raft ever last this long?

My thoughts over the past two nights have kept returning to *Siboney* as she lies on her side on the bottom. There is no current to move her sails. New dwellers penetrate her protective crannies to set up residence. Her hull remains in one piece, of that I am sure, for the pressure of the deep equalized as she slowly settled during her two-mile descent.

Her water and fuel tanks are certainly crushed, unless the vents kept the pressure balanced. The three batteries surely exploded when salt water arced across their terminals. Did the propane tanks burst? When I get home, I'll have to work all that out.

The mainsail surely remains set, as do the two jibs. They should last many years. The rigging should keep the mast standing for fifty years or more. The engine is no doubt a mass of rust. My old engine, which we call "Bertha," lies in a Miami warehouse; it is all I have left from my beloved *Siboney*.

There is a host of hardware on board *Siboney* that will last for centuries. I had struggled with rusty chain through fifty years of anchor hauling. For this trip, I bought fifty feet of three-eighths-inch stainless chain. That chain and the three anchors will be intact hundreds of years from now. I can't believe that I didn't throw the Bruce anchor over the side when I plucked it out of the lazarette. Water covered the deck. Nothing could then have saved *Siboney* from going to the deep, but years of habit made me set it down easily on the deck, as if I would use it again sometime.

At Isla de Aves, near Venezuela, we dove for years on a three-hundred-year-old French man-o'-war shipwrecked on the reef. We found anchor chain, chainplates, and spikes in excellent condition. I brought a two-thousand-pound cannon back, tied under *Siboney*. Could we raise *Siboney*? My crazy heart says yes, but I know it cannot be.

Siboney would float. The wood hull, inside the fiberglass hull, would have expanded and sealed the crack. A miniature sub could place several heavy-duty airbags inside *Siboney*, fill them with compressed air, and *Siboney* would rise on its own. On the surface, we could pump out the remaining water, then sail her home. The trick would be finding her.

Enough dreaming. It's time to fish and make water. I want all the water bottles full and a load of fish aboard when we hit shore. We must prepare for any eventuality. I do my chores, eat, then try to nap.

The weather clears, and Sim returns to her position as lookout. The details we saw this morning onshore have vanished in the dense haze. We are still more than twenty miles off. Every hour brings us closer to salvation, both spiritual and physical. We're so close, Lord, bring us to a safe haven. Please!

ABOARD THE RAFT
LAST CHANCE
2100 THURSDAY • AUGUST 17, 1989 • DAY 64

THERE, BILL, more to the left." I see it. A halo of light, a loom, ever so faint. It must be a small town. On the other hand, small towns normally don't make a loom. It must be a medium-sized city. The direction of the radio signal indicates that it's in southern Costa Rica. Though faint and far away, this is our first visual sign of life onshore. We see no distinct lights, but there are surely people.

Sim again echoes the queries I ponder. "What do you think it is? How far?"

"I can't see the horizon, but I sense it is up high in the hills. It could be thirty or so miles away. It has to be a fair-sized city with mercury street lighting. Otherwise the lights would not create a loom."

"I see the horizon. The city is way above it." Sim's keen eyesight starts her thinking. "Can you imagine, if it is a city, all those people sleeping in their homes, secure and dry and warm, while we are out here fighting for our lives. Oh, Bill, it's time this trip ended. It's time for a shower and a *café con leche* and bread. Yes, bread."

"Soon, baby, soon. We're drifting onto shore. In two or three days, we'll be onshore and safe and sound. I don't feel a single muscle in my legs. When we reach the beach, we may have to crawl when we find our legs refuse to do their job."

"That's great news, but don't try standing again. You almost tore the raft apart last time."

Five or six weeks ago, in a fit of anxiety, my legs cramped and aching, I tried to get up on my feet. The exercise almost turned into a disaster. My right foot slipped off the cushion and onto the floor of the raft. The tape that holds the floor of the raft to the air chamber ripped off, and for a moment I thought I'd done it again. After closer inspection, we found that another tape under the floor had maintained the seal. That was the last time I tried to stand.

A light breeze blows out of the northwest. We should move five or more miles closer to shore tonight. That will put us inside the twenty-mile mark. Local fishermen surely come out that far. We could be found and be onshore tomorrow.

Friday dawns on a day made in heaven. At first light, Simonne searches for land. When I awaken, I find her starry eyed. She helps me up. The sky is cloudless. Land, reflected on a mirrored sea, reaches far to the north and to the south. High mountains to the east cast dark shadows on farmland that rush out to meet us. High, forbidding bluffs lie ahead. Behind them, blue-green forests gently rise toward the high land.

Sim calls out excited. "Bill, look, a cruise ship, coming this way. Wow, just like in the ads. It's so large and so white and clean. It's heading north. Oh Lord, bring him to us. Look! There!"

The magnificent white liner cruises slowly near shore, its passengers surely on deck enjoying the same magnificent view. Will no one look our way? The ship comes closer. It's one of the larger ones, almost as big as the *QE2*, but higher off the water. Sim waves her shirt at the end of the fishing rod. As the ship approaches, Sim sees people walking on deck. She screams, and I blow the whistle.

Majestically it heads north, away from the canal, its hold full of the comfort and safety we so badly need. It's probably one of the trips that starts on the U.S. West Coast, cruises halfway through the Panama Canal, then turns around and returns. Passengers are no longer allowed ashore in Panama because of vandalism.

Sim pulls out the mirror and hands it to me. This is the first time a ship has been in line with the sun, and the sun is out and bright. I line up the mirror as Sim waves her shirt. I chuckle every time I see her wave a white T-shirt on the end of the pole, naked, exactly like the cartoons. The ship nears, now less than half a mile away. The sea is perfectly calm, and the visibility is as clear as it has ever been.

Cruise ships have a better lookout system than merchant vessels, and besides, hundreds of passengers have nothing better to do than look out. Except, on this ship, they are surely all looking the other way, at the bright-green shoreline and the stately mountains. We wave frantically. The sun feels good as we bob on gentle swells. Sim hasn't stopped swinging the pole and yelling the entire time the ship passes. We wait in vain for a telltale change in course or a difference in the sound of the propellers. The ship continues on its course and within minutes is but a dot on the northern horizon.

We fall back to pump and bail, exhausted from the exertion and once again deeply disappointed. More than forty ships have now passed close at hand. I don't count the lights of ships we see far off at night. Last night Sim counted seventeen ships, and so far none has seen us—that is, except for the small white ship that sped by early that rainy morning several weeks ago. We wasted two flares that day. I'm still convinced they saw us but didn't stop, the bastards. We have one last flare, although a shortage of flares hasn't made that much difference so far. We haven't had a ship approach close enough at night that we've seen in time.

I catch nine triggers for lunch, fillet all nine, and serve them up. We postpone watermaking until evening. The sun makes it too hot for any heavy work. Besides, we must conserve our energy for the big test that still lies ahead. Sim eats four of the eighteen fillets. I eat until I can stuff down no more, but I'm still losing weight. Neither of us has had a bowel movement for five weeks. I wonder what happens to the two pounds of fish I eat every day. I do cut the fish in minute pieces and chew them well; our bodies must absorb it all.

The sun has worked its way to the west, which makes the shore easier to see. Sim spots trees and several white objects that look like buildings. High rock bluffs rise vertically at the water's edge, but we're still too far away to see the actual shoreline. As the height of the bluffs is unknown, we cannot judge how far away we are.

Individual landmarks are clear. I guess we must be within twenty miles. We drift seven to ten miles a day. In two days, three at most, we'll be onshore. Will we arrive on a dark night in a squall to be thrust upon jagged reefs waiting to extinguish *Last Chance?* We would have to row off until morning. The thought sends a cold chill through me.

Sooner or later, we will have to face up to a landfall, whatever it may bring. Is the sea really ready to release us? Is the land hostile and unwilling to receive us? Are we tempted by false hopes only to be bitterly disappointed again? Another test definitely still lies ahead.

I fish again at five and catch six triggers. Sim doesn't eat at night, so I eat everything but two fillets. I save more than I need, but better to waste a trigger or two than run short now that we're this close. Besides, they are such ugly, mean fish. If I fell in the water, they'd clean off my bones in ten minutes. Hundreds circle under the raft, waiting.

I make two liters of water, now that it's cooler. A fiery sky lingers as we look first at the setting sun, then east toward land as it slowly vanishes under a veil of obscurity. The psalms have more meaning tonight, and we are drawn together as never before. We have suffered so much side by side that we are now of one body. Our differences, whether small or large, arising from our different characters, disappear. We now know we are meant to be saved.

When the sun sets, we see lights high on the hills and the loom of a large town. Sim jumps and calls out, "Bill, a ship!"

I look to where Sim points and see two white lights in a line. Below them, bright red and green running lights are clearly visible. The ship cannot be more half a mile away.

"He's coming our way, Sim. Let's get the flare ready."

"Wait. Remember our agreement. This is the last flare, and you're not going to waste it like you did the first two."

"This is different. Look, the ship is heading straight for us. The two white lights are right in line. He's going to run us over. Let's get the flare ready."

"No, no, no. Wait. I'm not sure. Let's not waste the last flare."

"OK. OK. You hold onto the flare. I'll signal an SOS with the flashlight."

I flash "S-O-S" repeatedly.

Sim shakes me excitedly. "Bill, look! On the bridge. There's a man. He flashed a light twice."

"Damn it, let's fire off the bloody flare!"

"OK, do it."

"Thanks, admiral." I turn over on my knees, lean outside the raft, and remove the wax wrapper from the end of the flare. I take the wooden endcap in my left hand and rub the abrasive on the cap against the end of the flare. The flare fails to ignite. I rub it again. Nothing happens. It's been aboard the raft during all the near-sinkings and is most probably shot.

I scratch the igniter desperately and get nothing. The ship comes upon us at full speed. I keep scratching the end of the flare. It fires! A bright-purple flame erupts from the tip of the flare. Slag spurts in all directions. Sim holds my waist as I lean out the window to hold the wooden shaft of the flare as far as my arm can take it from the raft. The smallest drop of slag on the air chamber, and it will explode. Our voyage would be over in seconds. As the flame heats up, the light turns a bright reddish purple.

The ship steams toward us at a perfect angle. If they hold course, they'll miss us by no more than a hundred feet. The person on the bridge with the lantern shines it our way. A light appears on a lower deck, and several shapes move about. Sim jumps with excitement. "Bill, they've seen us! They're getting ready to throw a line!"

"No question they've seen us! The lantern is still shining on the bridge. Can you see the man holding it?"

"Yes. Are they stopping?"

"I don't know." The flare burns brightly. It burns my fingers, but I hold on as I thrust it toward the ship. In seconds, as soon as the captain can get the order down to the engine room, the ship should be slowing down to pick us up. I can't believe our incredible luck. Tonight we'll sleep away from predation and death, in a dry, clean bed.

Sim screams, "Bill, they're not stopping! They see us, but they're not stopping. HELP! *AUXILIO!*"

I scream too. The ship is abreast, much less than a hundred feet away. We can see its every detail. It's six or seven thousand tons, a small freighter. A man on the lower deck has a big moustache. We scream for help in Spanish, certain they have given the order to stop. The speed of the engines changes. Are they going into reverse, or are they pulling away? They are surely turning. Or are they? What in the hell is going on?

"Bill, they aren't stopping! What's the matter with those guys? That's impossible! We've wasted our last flare! How can they not stop?

Can't they see we're in distress?" Devastated, we continue to yell and
flash the light, but the ship continues on its course and its stern drops
quickly away. The flare burns my fingers and I drop it into the sea,
where it sizzles and sinks. When I look out again, the ship has vanished in the darkness.

A long period of silence overwhelms both of us. I try to encourage
Sim. "Forget them, baby. We'll be onshore soon. We don't need anyone to help us. Besides, they're headed the wrong way. That ship just
left land. Suppose their destination is Korea or who knows where? We
would be taken out to sea on another ocean journey, after we've
worked our way toward land for so long. Forget him. Let him go."

Sim blasts back at me. "You stupid cretin! We would have been
saved. If they had stopped, I would have jumped on board even if
they were headed for the moon. I want to get off this raft no matter
how I do it. If I thought I could swim, I'd be over the side this
minute."

"Sweetie, relax. It'll soon be over. And get the swimming scene
out of your head. The triggerfish would pick your bones clean before
you got ten feet away." She shrugs my words away.

The anxiety of the near-miss lingers with us well into the night.
What was that all about? They saw us and took off. What did they
think we were? I've never heard of castaways being abandoned on the
high seas. May the miserable bastards fry in hell.

On the other hand, land is truly at hand, and we're moving in the
right direction. We'll be ashore in a day or two. We must shrug off
this latest setback and replace it with a strong sense of anticipation,
for soon we'll be on land.

The wind blows out of the west, exactly what we need. Come on,
current, take us to land. Come on, raft, stay afloat. We're almost
there; don't let us down now. Another day, two or three at the most,
and it will be over. Thoroughly exhausted, we drop into the sleep of
the dead.

ABOARD THE RAFT
LAST CHANCE
0100 SATURDAY • AUGUST 19, 1989 • DAY 66

SIMONNE IS UP and leaning against the arch. She paddles gently as she scours the shoreline for some sign of life. Lights seen on nights past are hidden by the light overcast that threatens to envelop the raft. Safety is so near at hand and yet so far. If we could only paddle this raft or come across a fisherman.

Fishermen. Where in the hell are they? The sea is alive with every conceivable variety of fish. We've traversed twelve hundred miles of ocean and have not seen one fishing boat. Sim thinks she saw one off the island we passed, but I still think it was a rock. We'll never know for sure.

Sim continues her vigil by the window. I thought for a while she was onto something, but now I'm sure it's only her anxiety to reach shore and safety. In any case, I'll watch her out of the corner of my eye for any change in expression. How I hope she'll see something. Even a single lightbulb. A fire. Any sign of life.

Now more than ever before, I am confident our trip will end well. We should drift onto shore in a day and a half, and if the weather remains calm, our landing shouldn't be too bad. If we arrive at night, we'll paddle off until dawn. We can do that without too much trouble. We'll take turns like we did so many days ago when the dolphin tore the hole in the bottom. Or both of us can paddle, if need be.

The light overcast delays the arrival of dawn on our sixty-sixth day cast away. Our day really arrives with the dawn; the pitch black of night somehow belongs to the day past. Neither of us sleeps as the skies grow lighter. I pray for a sandy beach. As soon as we can touch, we'll jump over the side and wash off two months of dirt. I'll rub sand into my crotch until it's raw to work out a ton of blood and the guts of hundreds of triggerfish. The blue waterproofing that penetrates every pore should float away in the refreshing water.

The specter of a rough landing at night, though, is all too real a possibility. I visualize sharp heads of coral that break the waves as the wind and waves push us ever closer. Frantic, we paddle, then push off submerged rocks in a last effort to stay off. A larger wave pushes us up and over the reef. The raft tears and deflates. We stay with *Last Chance*. Shore is still too far. If only we had shoes. We pray for daylight, and swim. Dear Lord, protect us; don't leave us now.

The sky clears as six hundred and sixty minutes of darkness begin to yield to the power of the sun. My engineering training keeps my mind busy calculating trivia: we have lived through forty-three thousand minutes of deadly blackness on this voyage. On a raft, an hour is a meaningless measurement. Minutes last as long as an hour on land. Will these odious nights ever be over? Or does our ultimate test yet lie ahead? I recall how we considered it a grand achievement when we had been adrift five hundred hours. We have now drifted more than fifteen hundred hours. Who would ever have thought it possible?

The sky turns dirty gray. Sim sits up with the compass in her lap and paddles the raft until she faces east. Low clouds heavy with moisture obliterate the coastline. Will it be there, or are we to live through yet another disappointment? Will the wind blow fiercely out of the east and push us back out to sea?

The power of the sun eats away at the cloud cover, and soon land is clearly in sight to the east. Yesterday's cliffs rise black and rugged out of the sea to end abruptly at a cape several miles to the south. Low hills rise in the haze beyond the cape, indicating a bay twenty or more miles long running to the east. If we miss a landfall to the north of the cape, we will face another three or four days adrift. Yet inside the cape we have a better chance of being seen by fishermen.

To the north, the high cliffs turn into a long, even headland. As the day grows lighter, the clouds lift to reveal several peaks far inland. Rolling hills lead up to a large mountain or volcano. High, brownish-green mountains rise to embrace the clouds all the way to true north.

I need two reference marks onshore to plot our drift. If I can align two points, one closer to us than the other, I can tell whether we are drifting east toward the bluffs or if we will miss them by falling too far to the south. So far, I cannot detect a single distinguishing feature on the landscape.

The wind shifts to the northwest after midmorning, an unfavorable twist that will tend to move us south. I have no way to measure the effect of the current and still can see nothing onshore to line up as range markers. If this wind continues, we'll miss the cape to the south for sure. Our only chance is to sail the raft. If I row it around so that the bow heads north, the wind against the side might help us move to the northeast. It's worth a try.

I prop my head up with a life preserver so I can see out the window and row the raft around with the paddle tied to one end of the fishing rod, until the headland lines up with the edge of the canopy. When I stop rowing, the end of the raft that heads north drifts slowly to the south. When the headland is out of sight, I row until the headland again appears in the window. I continue to row for the next two hours. I can't tell if I'm doing any good, but at least it does no harm. If we miss the cape, we'll still get to shore.

Why are there no landmarks onshore? The bluffs to the east have not a single distinguishing feature, and even if they had, I see nothing in the highlands behind that could serve as a range mark. As noon approaches, I have my paddling down to an easy routine. Three strokes put us on course. In four minutes, the raft drifts until I can no longer see the headland. I then pull three times on the oar, which I leave hanging over the side when I'm back in line.

The hot sun forces both of us to strip off our shirts. Hope radiates toward us from shore and from above. We will live, of that we are now sure. Our ordeal is almost over. The hazards of the sea are behind us. Or are they?

We have water and food. We've remained healthy. When I think back over our trials of the past two months, I am filled with wonder at how fortunate we have been. We've traveled twelve hundred miles in a torn plastic raft. Tempests and beasts have fought to subdue and destroy us, but we've managed to escape the jaws of death. Twenty miles remain before we will be safely ashore. The thought of seeing our families again buoys our emaciated, tired bodies.

Sim calls out, "Bill, I can see trees clearly, palm trees. The rocky cliffs are about fifty feet high. I see a house toward the north. How far away do you think we are?"

I look out and guess we're fifteen to twenty miles off. I reply, "We'll be onshore in forty-eight hours, if not sooner. The four hours of rowing have made me hungry. How about lunch? Trigger?"

"Sounds terrific," Sim banters back. "Shall we try a little soy sauce on it today?"

"I think I'd rather have a dab of lime juice. I'm tired of the same old soy sauce every day. If you have nothing better to do, pray for a wind shift. We need the wind to shift from north of west to the south or as close to it as possible."

I join Sim in prayer. "Help us, dear Lord. Just a little shift in wind toward the south. Please. If that's not possible, that's OK, too. Thank you for all your help during the past ten weeks. To be alive today, here and now, is nothing less than a miracle, and you are the number one miracle-maker."

My spiritual conversion has been another miracle. Throughout our first days on the raft, I was convinced that my strength and my knowledge of the sea would suffice to see us through to safety. The sharks, more than the violent tempests, brought me ever so slowly to understand that without the hand of God we would never make it to shore. As I look back, each shark whack inched me closer to the Lord. At first, I struggled with the Lord's Prayer, first to remember the words, then to fully fathom the true meaning of each word. "Our Father." What a powerful beginning. He looked after us faithfully through thousands of frightening hours, leading us ever closer into His fold, never pushing or shoving, always tenderly leading me closer to Him, until my faith in Him now totally dominates my day.

Simonne has prayed nonstop since the first day and has recited two or three full rosaries daily. Her faith led me to find mine, at first by assisting me in prayer, later through dogmatic discussions. In recent days, since Simonne heard of Nuestra Señora de Los Angeles, I have been praying that she help get God's attention to our plight and somehow guide a ship toward us. My prayers to la Virgen de la Caridad del Cobre worked miraculously, warding off attacks by the most violent of our predators. My newfound faith has given me comfort and solace through interminable nights of terror, and will forever change my life. Why, oh why, did I not find it earlier in my life?

The skies have cleared, and the green vegetation so near invites us to run up to it and embrace it. The sun is overhead, which means it's time for lunch, for this is no time to weaken. I sit back up and prepare to fish. I put my gloves on backward on opposite hands, as I've worn out the palm of the right glove, which I use to grip the triggerfish. Even so, I have more than forty trigger stings in that hand.

Yesterday's leftover fish spent the night spread on the paddle, which I have found keeps it fresher than stashing it in a can. I cut the bait into one-inch cubes and run it through my hook. The fabulous panorama distracts me. Days ago it was but empty ocean. Now we are near heaven. I feel like that first man so long ago beholding his enchanted garden.

With the baited hook in my left hand, I lean over the side of the raft to check what's swimming around. Many times I've had to postpone fishing until the sharks have left, but today only triggers surround the raft, at a depth of two to three feet. I dip the bait in the water, and right away a dozen triggers surface with their grunting, sucking sound. In a splash of boiling water, my hook is bare. I bait it again and again. The triggers are now wild, hovering inches below the water, each fighting for position. They look up and watch my every move. I move my hand quickly six inches off the water, and a dozen leap at it. They're ready.

I check my glove and touch my bait to the water. My right hand flies out and around a trigger. I grab it too close to the tail, and it wiggles free. I rebait and try again. The second one is too large, and I can't get my hand around it. I must shoot out and grab them before they activate their trigger, a one-inch spine with a barb at the end.

I hold my first caught trigger tightly against the camcorder case turned filleting board and quickly remove both fillets. Gripping it by its tail, I lower it into the water. The sea boils with triggerfish eager to munch on their brother. I grasp a second trigger as I throw the first one ten feet away from the raft. Dozens of triggers dart to the sinking carcass, tearing it apart until it sinks to a depth of about three feet, where a large shark dispatches the remains. I repeat the process until I have ten triggers cleaned.

We eat lunch and nap. When we stir and look out, the wind has shifted to the south. Once again, our prayers have been answered. If this breeze can only blow all night tonight, we will be very close to shore by tomorrow afternoon. As the day wears on, the southwest wind continues to pick up. We couldn't ask for more. There is no need to row.

At four, I prepare to catch our evening meal. I sit up, the paddle on my lap full of bait, when a loud roar out of nowhere startles me. Sim jumps up and cries out, "Bill, a large white boat is going to run us down!" A huge yacht, exactly like the one in my dreams, slaloms down six-foot seas, one second heading as if to run us down, the next to miss us.

"Bill, he's going to run us down! Is it a fishing boat?"

"It looks like a sportfisherman, as in my dream. He's seen us! He's coming right to us!"

Sim cries with joy. "Baby, we are saved! Oh my God, my God! They have seen us. They're slowing down. Oh, it's real. It's not a dream!" She cries and laughs at the same time. Tears flood down her cheeks.

"Quick, get the pants out!" I cry out as the launch slows and turns.

Sim digs a soggy plastic bag out from under the cushions and pulls out pants that have not left the bag for sixty-six days. Sim puts on the last small, dirty, sleeveless shirt and her life jacket, then slips into a pair of her pants.

The boat is now alongside. Half a dozen men are on the rail, looking down. We cry without shame and wave. We can't stop. I see the red Coast Guard stripe on the side of the boat and think it's the U.S. Coast Guard.

I look up, hand cupped to my mouth, and call to the men on deck in English. "Thank you! Thank you!" I cannot find any other words. My head reels.

One of the men throws a line, which I fasten to the raft. They hold the raft a few feet off the patrol boat, which rises ten feet above us and bobs wildly in the waves. The stern rises and falls six or more feet.

Steps that lead to the deck are three feet off the water, a hopeless leap. The crew looks down at us in amazement. We must be a sight, unwashed for nearly ten weeks and nothing but skin and bones. My beard has grown almost three inches. When I boarded the raft, all I had was a slight moustache.

I turn and drink in the expression of sheer joy on Sim's face. I say to her, "Sim, remember what we have been talking about in a rescue. Getting off the raft is dangerous. We haven't been on our feet for ten weeks. I'm not sure we can stand."

"Oh, Bill. I'm going to see my babies again, and my mother." Tears stream down her dirty face.

"Sim, be careful. Sit tight. Let's get the canopy off so we can stand."

I struggle with the zipper of the canopy. It jams, half open.

"Sim, hand me the knife." With it, I slash the remaining half of the canopy. One man, on the bottom rung, hangs out, hand extended. A crewmember pulls on the painter.

"OK, Sim, you're first. Careful. Go!"

Sim turns on one knee. She cannot stand. I hold her as she tries to kneel. The patrol boat heaves in the heavy seas. Sim waits for the bottom rung to drop and lunges for it. I give her a push as the sailor takes her hand. Seconds pass as she dangles in space. I'm ready to catch her if she falls. He pulls her to safety with a single hand. She weighs nothing. On deck, another crewman takes her in his arms and carries her toward the main deck.

I load the sailbag with items I want to save—the logbook, workbook, knife, compass, our psalms—and hand it up to the waiting crew. It's time for me to go. I look up at the wildly gyrating boat, not sure I can make it up onto my legs. Suppose I can't stand up? The crew beckons. I stand and lunge for the ladder in one motion. I hang on and struggle for a foothold. My feet touch the sea. I can't find the rung. And I didn't put on my life vest. My strength ebbs as my hands slip from the rung. As I begin to fall, two men grab my arms and pull me up. With a jerk, I too am safely on deck.

Sim and I crawl to a hot-air vent amidships and sit on the deck. We embrace. And cry. We are safe. The voyage is over . . . after sixty-six days at sea. We have drifted more than eleven hundred and fifty nautical miles. We each have lost more than fifty pounds, but by the grace of God, we are alive. Thank you, dear Lord, for saving these two undeserving castaways. Thank you. Thank you so much.

ABOARD THE COSTA RICAN COAST GUARD VESSEL *PUNTA BURICA*

1800 SATURDAY • AUGUST 19, 1989

I HUDDLE WITH SIM against the hot-air vent. The ship's crew stares at us in amazement. Simonne pulls her life vest tightly around her for warmth. One of the men slips a cushion under us. We speak to him in Spanish, taking him totally by surprise.

One of the men jumps into the raft. Poor guy. I'm glad we dropped the soggy comforter over the side as they came alongside. Still, the raft cannot smell too sweet. He passes up the watermaker, the radio, the flashlight, the cushions, everything.

The crew of the patrol boat have put two lines around the raft and are preparing to lift it. I thought they would surely abandon it. That's why I passed up the sailbag. The raft is quickly on deck. I look over the side from where it came. Hundreds of triggerfish swim aimlessly around, now homeless. They have lost their habitat and their umbrella of protection. Many have been with us for the entire voyage. Tough luck, gang. So long. Though they kept us alive, I am happy to see them no more.

The patrol boat comes to life with a roar. Two men join us, and we tell them pieces of our story, then ask them who they are. We're aboard a Costa Rican Coast Guard patrol boat called the *Punta Burica*, stationed at the port of Golfito. They were out searching for a shrimp boat that had disappeared several days earlier. They found us instead.

They had sailed a random course all day. The helmsman saw what he thought was a buoy. With the captain's permission, he headed for it. Suddenly, they came upon a raft with two gaunt castaways. Our prayers were truly answered. We cannot stop thanking them. They smile, happy for us, still trying to sort out exactly what they've found.

Captain Nuñez joins us as the patrol boat picks up speed. Engines roar. Spray flies. The air from the vent keeps us warm. Sim, with her shredded shirt, looks like someone straight out of *Tobacco Road*. Her life jacket still tightly tied, she leans against a bulwark, starry eyed, unmoving, ecstasy radiating from her face, still unable to grasp all that has happened in such a short time. The entire rescue operation lasted less than fifteen minutes. From the moment we first heard the engines until we were both aboard took less than ten.

The men ask dozens of questions and are amazed at our answers. They offer us hot milk. The captain gives Sim a new T-shirt. All crewmembers vanish as Sim changes. I sit shirtless. My shirt that had been tied to the top of the raft canopy has disappeared. I didn't see the shirt when the raft came aboard, so it may be back with the triggerfish.

The *Punta Burica*, now at top speed, heads north. The captain tells us we are thirteen miles from the coast according to his radar, and that we are heading for Golfito. He says we will be taken to a hospital. We assure the captain a hotel would be fine, that there's really no need for a hospital. A couple days of rest and we'll be ready to travel home. After all, we have been stuffing ourselves with fish and drinking all the water our bodies called for.

He grins, nods, and turns away. I call him back. Sim unbuttons a pocket in her life jacket and removes our passports. I hand them, with the logbook, to the captain. How many times did I rehearse this scene on the raft? It's the way I've seen them do it in the movies.

We remain on deck and chat with the crew. We meet the helmsman who spotted us. This man's sharp eyes made the difference. It turns out the *Punta Burica* had sailed earlier in the day and had headed west, into the Pacific Ocean. The captain ordered a random search pattern. After a long leg to the west, the boat motored south, then east, then north, back west, later south. They were on their return trip east when they came across our raft.

The joy of life is so exciting we find it hard to talk. We give away nearly all our belongings to the crew. The helmsman gets my watch. Sim gives her radio to another young man. The blanket goes to another. We keep the sailbag nearby with the knife, the compass, and other memorabilia. The raft is the center of attention. They cannot imagine how we lived sixty-six days in that flimsy raft. It now looks like a mountain of trash.

A crewman brings out two glasses of warm milk. He asks if we would like dinner. Yes, I could eat anything. He returns below. As we speed along at nearly twenty knots, low, black squall clouds form in our path. It looks like rain. The captain suggests we go to the pilot-house. We help each other walk the two dozen steps. Each step is a shaky, painful trial. They usher us into the pilothouse and close the door behind us. The first big drops hit the deck.

The pilothouse is freezing. The helmsman offers me one of his shirts to wear. They bring Sim a blanket. We sit on the floor and try to stay out of the way of the crew. The captain is on the radio. Another man scans the radar. A crewmember arrives with a plate of food. Captain Nuñez stops him cold. He has just spoken to a doctor at the hospital. We are to have nothing to eat except milk.

My heart, not to mention my stomach, collapses. I have seen the plate of red beans and rice and smelled its aroma. But the captain is adamant, and the plate returns below. Who cares? We're alive and well. Nothing else really matters.

Heavy sheets of rain block our way. A blinding flash of lightning and a clap of thunder shake the very keel of our vessel. The helmsman slows the engines. Two men study the radar. The captain is on the radio in hurried communication until flashes of lightning force him to shut it down.

Visibility is zero until lightning lights up the ocean around us. Otherwise, we see nothing. With the boat slowed and in calmer waters, I struggle to my feet. I hold onto the handrails tightly and find I can stand. I test my legs and balance. I'm not sure I can walk on my own, but at least I can stand.

The plate of steaming hot red beans and rice beckons. The aroma fills the stuffy cabin. I look down the steep stairs and into the galley and dining area. Everything is compact but neat and clean. On the stove there is a pot of rice and another of beans. I salivate for the first time in months. I've forgotten what real food is like.

The stairs down to the galley are almost vertical. Can I negotiate them? I ask a crewmember if I can go below and sit. He says that would be no problem. I study the stairs and handrails again and decide to go for it. I take one step at a time until I reach the bottom. When I sit at the mess table, the crew gathers around. I tell a couple of sea stories. They offer me crackers. I send some up to Sim.

The smell from the beans drives me wild. I try to get a crewmember to serve me a plate. No, he says, the captain said no. But, I argue, the captain is on deck piloting the boat in the storm. Please, *por favor*. They break down. I eat two plates and know I have gone straight to heaven. This is my first hot meal in sixty-six days.

I work my way back up to Sim with a few more crackers. I don't tell her I ate the beans, nor do I dare offer her a plate, for her stomach isn't as tough as mine. The storm is a nasty one. The ship's radar is old and not easy to read as they try to pick their way into a channel among many rocks. A crewman mentions that another patrol boat ended up on the rocks a couple of weeks earlier. Captain Nuñez holds the boat at dead slow. After an hour, when the rain eases, he increases speed, and soon we pass an entrance marker and approach a pier. An ambulance waits nearby. Several dozen people stand on the dock in the drizzle. The launch eases in, and the crew quickly secures it.

The captain helps Sim ashore. The pier gyrates wildly. It's a floating pier. The waves must be monstrous. We cannot walk from all the bouncing around. We greet the people, joke about not walking too well, and enter the ambulance and sit on two wooden benches in the rear. The ambulance heads away with a cough and a roar.

The hospital is just minutes away. I ask the driver to take us to a hotel, but Sim insists that we will be better off in a hospital for a day or two. I can barely walk from the ambulance to the hospital entrance; the hospital spins as badly as the pier. This entire town must float.

We are taken to the emergency room, where a nurse offers us a brownish, sweet drink. We try it. It's fabulous, another gift from God. It's *agua dulce*, sweet water, made of sugar-cane juice. We drink at least three large glasses each.

One of the nurses leads us to a pay phone, where Sim calls her mother in France. She gets right through. Joy overwhelms her mother. She knew we were lost and near death. I call my daughters— Sally in New York and Susan in Texas. Neither of them imagined the true extent of our odyssey. We try to call the boys in Miami without success.

A hospital staff worker summons me into a little office to complete the usual hospital paperwork. With two fingers he pecks away at a typewriter. He enters my name and address. Then he asks my occupation. Without a second thought, I reply, *"naúfrago,"* "castaway" in Spanish. At the moment I feel like nothing else, and so content to be one, a live one at that.

I mention to the young man that someone should do something with that pier where we landed. He asks why. I explain how it bounced around in the waves. He assures me that the United Fruit Company drove those pilings forty years ago and that the pier is as solid today as it was then.

We learn that the United Fruit Company also built the hospital decades ago. Constructed of wood and two stories high, it has room for dozens of patients, a complete operating area, and a large outpatient building. The facilities, though primitive by modern standards, are clean and staffed with nurses and doctors who take a genuine interest in us. We instantly make friends with all.

A nurse draws blood, which I'm sure smells of triggerfish. Then we proceed to shower. Sim is first, for there is only one shower with no door, open to the public. A nurse turns on the water and Sim cringes at the cold and shies away. Sim waits, then asks when the hot water is going to start. Señora, the nurse replies, there is no hot water. Poor Sim suffers through an icy shower.

While Sim showers, I tell sea stories in the emergency room. I am so happy to be alive that I just radiate talk. When Sim appears from the shower, I jump in. I revel in the cold water and use a bar of soap to wash the juices of four hundred triggerfish from my crotch. I feel new.

By the time we finish bathing, it's past eleven in the evening and time to jump into bed. Sim is given one of three beds in the ladies' ward. Under the covers, she feels better than any queen between silk sheets. I end up in the men's ward, also with three beds. We are the only patients. My bed rests against a window, which stretches up to the ceiling, its glass jalousies long gone. A cool breeze flows over me as I prop myself up on my pillow and look out at the full moon. The garden outside glows soft yellow. Royal palms stand majestically, reminding me of a lighthouse. How great to be alive. We have been delivered directly into paradise.

I cannot sleep and really don't want to. Why sleep at a moment like this? I have been born again. Fleecy clouds slip by between the moon and the palm trees. The gentle breeze carries the sweet scent of life. A truly enchanted evening.

Hours slip by. My IV is almost empty, and my bladder is full. I drag the three-legged stand to the bathroom. On my way back, I peek in at Sim. She is holding court, the staff entranced with her sea stories.

I sleep. When I awaken, daylight floods the room. I hear a cough, turn, and notice that both other beds are full. When I get up and start to walk, the pain in my legs makes me flinch. Forgotten muscles complain. It's a good sign. I'm alive.

I peek in at Sim again. She's asleep at last. She didn't get six hours' sleep total during the last week on the raft. An entirely new staff is in place. In no time, I make new friends. Sim awakens for breakfast. She had nightmares in the night, and a gentle nurse sat in the room with her until she was asleep again.

I looked at the breakfast roster while hobbling around and found that there is one cardiac breakfast, whatever that is, two dietetic breakfasts, and six regulars. The dietetics must be for us. To our surprise, we get regular breakfasts.

I join Sim on her bed, and we both clean our plates of *gallo pinto* (red beans and rice), a good piece of fresh cheese, two pieces of bread, and coffee. As I help Sim finish her plate, we feel better already. We surprise the doctor with our good health. Sim is anemic, and we're told that each of us will receive four bottles of various IV solutions during the next three days. They'll check our blood again then.

The doctor tells us the press has called and will arrive soon. Do we want to meet with them? We are so happy to be alive, we agree to anything. The excitement starts before eleven Sunday morning. Several local reporters and photographers drop in for stories.

On Monday, the entire press corps bursts into the emergency room at the little Golfito hospital. At dawn, Channel 7 from San José sets up their cameras in one of the examining rooms. Crews from the four major U.S. networks arrive with their full equipment. They take over the other examining room and an office. Sim talks over the phone to correspondents in Paris and Melbourne.

The hospital has two telephone lines and a pay phone in the lobby that accepts overseas collect calls. Calls come in nonstop over both lines. Why all the fuss? Is our adventure a hot story? When rescued, our main preoccupation had been getting through to our family and friends to tell them we were alive and well.

I take a call from the *National Enquirer*. The man is insistent. He offers a thousand dollars for an exclusive. Instinct tells me to refuse. I'll talk, but without being tied down. At that moment, my body sends a strong signal that a bowel movement is imminent. I ask him to call back. He says he will hold.

I hobble to the toilet, trailing the tripod with the IV. Cramps bring sweat but no luck. I hobble back to the phone. The man from the *Enquirer* is still there. I reply to other questions about the trip until cramps again interrupt. He will stay on the line. I go back to the bathroom. Nothing again.

I return to the phone, answer two more questions, and then rush back to the bathroom. This goes on for half an hour. I haven't had a movement for five weeks. Sim hasn't either. The man from the *Enquirer* stays on the line. I return and complete the interview.

Agence France-Presse calls from Paris, and Sim tells our story. The four U.S. networks beseige us. We are so happy to be alive, we follow their orders gladly. We're in utopia, we're alive, and we will see our families again.

Lunch and dinner again consist of red beans and rice, accompanied by either a small piece of meat or a vegetable. Famished, we devour everything served, though we know this is not what we should be eating. The press leaves. Calls continue from friends and family until late into the night.

The children will arrive in San José tonight and should be here tomorrow. The U.S. embassy calls saying they will meet the children at the airport and transport them to Golfito. The U.S. Coast Guard has called twice from somewhere near San Francisco. They want the name of our boat, its size, and our destination. The nurses at last disconnect the phone so we can sleep.

We soon learn that emergency rooms are noisy. Monday night turns out to be asthma night. Half a dozen people come in with varying asthmatic ailments. Both wards are full with coughing men and women. Every time I walk to the bathroom, I pass people in the lobby using oxygen. The noise continues, but we sleep.

At midmorning Tuesday, my daughter Sally and granddaughter Cody arrive in San José by air, followed by my eldest son, Bill Jr., and Sim's eldest, Cris. They then take the tortuous, six-hour overland route to Golfito with a representative from the U.S. Embassy. Of the people who knew us before, the children are the first to see us. Our physical condition alarms them. They say we look like two people out of a concentration camp. They insist we move to a better hospital, but we refuse. We are happy in the Golfito hospital, where everyone has been so great. Besides, it's the only hospital within miles.

The embassy representative, Steve Groh, offers the services of the U.S. Embassy. We appreciate the offer, but we have everything we need. Our passports, traveler's checks, cash, and credit cards are intact. He can't believe it. Part of his job is to help U.S. tourists who within mere hours in the country have lost their passports, money, and everything else. Lost at sea for sixty-six days, we haven't lost a thing . . . except for a "little" weight—a total of almost a hundred pounds.

I'm alive, and everything else can wait. My trips to the bathroom turn desperate. Many times, I almost faint. My pleas to the doctor yield two tiny baby suppositories. I plead for something more substantial, like a stick of dynamite, but the doctor says to let nature take its course. Two hours go by with no results. I tell Sim that I feel like I'm in labor. She insists that labor is much worse, but I doubt it. My bathroom visits are now every ten minutes, almost like Sim's bailing routine. Every time I pass the nurse's station, the entire staff laughs with me.

At long last, it's over. I feel like a new man. I bathe in delightful fresh water and return to my clean bed. I give Sim the good news. I'm 100 percent alive again.

Simonne faces a problem with a roommate. Sim awoke last night to find a woman sitting on a little stool by her bed, mumbling. When Sim opened her eyes, the lady gave her a disoriented religious dissertation. She kept Sim awake most of the night.

The bright moon, swaying palms, lush trees, and puffy clouds confirm that we are in paradise. I spend a good part of the night either looking out the window or heading to the bathroom. I now have diarrhea, caused by too much chocolate and the wrong food. I should have brought a few triggers with me. Most of my bathroom trips end with a shower and clean clothes. While I run to the head, Sim sleeps soundly.

Wednesday arrives. Nurses remove our IVs in the morning. It's time to bust out of the hospital. Yesterday we talked to the head doctor concerning our departure today. We received neither a yea nor a nay. Today when he arrives, we will try again.

Sim has made friends with a French couple who live in Golfito. They want us to spend a night at their home before flying to San José. The doctor arrives. He wants us to stay until we are stronger. We insist on leaving. He realizes we are eager to fly home and reluctantly approves our release. We leave the hospital amid tears and farewells from our cherished new family.

We move to the nearby home of the French couple, where hot water and a bubble bath await Sim. A chicken dinner around a family-sized dinner table makes us feel on top of the world.

On Thursday, Cedrik, a friend of my second son Jim, flies us to San José, where we are met by TV cameras and the press. Channel 7 of San José and the newspaper *La Nación* practically adopt us. They cover our every move, and their representatives become close friends. We drive to the Sheraton, which has a family room where all six of us fit comfortably: Sim and I, Cris, Sally, Cody, and Bill Jr.

The phone continues to ring while we try to relax. A prayer group of ladies, devoted to the patron saint of Costa Rica, visit. I'm in bed under the covers, and decide to stay there to rest a bit. My legs ache as any newly used set of muscles normally aches. Next comes a priest who operates a small old people's home in a small town in northern Costa Rica. He gives Sim prayer books and religious medals.

Cedrik, who flew us up from the coast, picks us up after dark to join him in a little get-together with friends at his house. After hellos and a few sea stories, out bursts Cedrik with a large plate of sushi. Everyone joins in laughter and banter. I surprise them all by eating the entire tray. His guests can't believe their eyes. Perhaps I should have left a few pieces for someone else. But I was hungry—and there was soy sauce!

On Saturday, we fly to Miami on Pan Am. Customs has made arrangements for the press to gather at a side door so as not to interrupt the normal flow of passengers. They suggest we slip out the main door. We refuse. We've had a good rapport with the press, so why avoid them now?

We head for the exit. Sim follows in a wheelchair, her legs too weak for the long walk down the airport corridors. The door opens. Ten TV camera crews and our family members reach out to greet us. Kisses, hugs, tears, and interviews follow. The English-speaking press on the right catches our attention first, and I banter with them for several minutes.

A voice in Spanish from my left cries, "Give us a chance, too!" We turn to the Spanish-speaking media and run through their queries. I'm having a great time. We're home. We're alive. Dear Lord, thank you. You are infinitely generous. You gave us lives anew. Thank you, thank you for your love and your helping hand.

EPILOGUE

BACK IN FLORIDA, Sim and I settled into my apartment in Coral Gables, where Simonne's son Cristóbal had been living, while we regained our strength, put on weight, and gathered the energy we needed to plan our next move. By December 1989, we decided to take the furniture out of storage and return to live in Simonne's home in South Dade County.

That we had survived our two-month ordeal kept us in a state of wonder. Both of us remained awed that we were alive and safe and ready to continue a life that we had given up for lost. Our newfound faith provided a platform for understanding the why of our trial and grasping the true meaning of our salvation. Days after returning to Miami we arranged a private mass for our family and friends. Father Wally, our parish priest, blessed us and welcomed us back from the dead. From then on, we never failed to celebrate Sunday mass, and remained at all times closely tied to God and His principles.

So many times, while adrift, we wondered whether anyone was searching for us. At first we were sure that our children would worry and initiate some sort of search. As it turned out, Sally was the only one of our children (my five and Sim's two) who did take action. In retrospect, any search would have been "project impossible," as our raft was—for all intents and purposes—invisible to anyone searching either by sea or by air.

By late January, we had both regained our pre-raft energy levels. I began to write our story, and I urged Simonne to do the same, with the expectation that we would merge the best of each. Sim wrote two short pieces, both quite good, but could go no further. I pounded out copy nonstop, almost two hundred thousand words, more than twice the length of this story, in which I retold almost all my lifetime sailing sagas.

But the human spirit can be as inscrutable, contrary, and destructive as it is indomitable, and it began to seem that the bond forged by almost ten weeks of back-to-back struggles against death would not be enough to hold Simonne and me together. As our health returned, so did old hurts—stubborn cankers that I'd hoped the voyage would wash away. Simonne renewed a years-old accusation of infidelity that I'd long since grown tired of denying; it had never been true, unlike her quite justified complaint that I'd dragged her off to sea in an old boat with a life raft not made for drifting ten weeks offshore. And we renewed our continual battle over how I treated her boys—endless arguments that I always lost. I could never convince her that I treated her sons and mine exactly the same.

When a friend offered me a berth as navigator on the 1990 Newport–Bermuda Race, I leapt at the chance to get away and to find out whether the sea and I could once again bond. I had a great time and decided right off that I would soon be back on the water.

By the beginning of 1991, I was as unhappy as I had ever been. It was then that Sim went to a young Latino priest in downtown Miami for confession. During their conversation, he asked if she was married, and she said yes. "In the church?" he asked. Sim said, "No." When he asked why not, she said, "I have two sons, and what would they think if my marriage to their father was annulled?" The priest went ballistic. "You are not married!" he almost shouted. "You cannot live with Bill. If you do, you are living in grievous mortal sin."

We'd been living together fifteen years, married for nine. I now, at long last, understood what Sim had meant by the "promise" she had spoken about on the raft. Convinced that her traumatic experience on the high seas had driven her to the point where she would only be at peace if she lived as a semi-nun, I moved out of her house and into my apartment in early June. Six months later we concluded a fairly friendly divorce. Though the religious reawakening that we experienced while cast away drew us closer, our marriage, in the end, could not survive the old hurts and disagreements.

Shortly after we separated, a one-two punch knocked me out cold. A terrible flu sent me to bed, alone in my apartment, for the entire month of October. While I lay on my back, feverish, virtually unable to move, my mind kept churning over the failure of our marriage. To have survived sixty-six days adrift with Simonne only to have our marriage end up on the rocks seemed too cruel an irony. Depression kept me bedridden most of November. Nothing made sense. I could not move.

In early December, my old sailing buddy Siro Cugini called from Puerto Rico. He quickly detected my condition and invited me to join him and his wife in Puerto Rico for New Year's. Just as quickly, I accepted. When he picked me up at the airport in San Juan, he and his wife announced that we would stop for a glass of champagne with an old friend, Lirio. My first reaction was "Lirio who?" They reminded me that I had met her in 1973 at their home in Venezuela at a party given in Lirio's honor. I barely remembered the event.

Lirio's reaction was similar. When the Cuginis called to say I was coming into town, her first reaction was "What? I saw him on TV after his shipwreck, and he looks like a total loss!" But the meeting kindled a flame, and after I returned to Miami, Lirio and I began a telephone romance. We met in early 1992 at a tall-ship OPSAIL event in San Juan, and again later in Florida. There was little doubt I was falling in love.

Right after my divorce from Simonne, I had contacted a couple of used-sailboat brokers and told them I was looking for a forty-foot ocean racer. In March 1992, I found what I was looking for, a North American 40. I bought it and renamed it *New Chance*. In April, I asked Lirio, who had never married, to be my bride, and she said yes. When I told my buddies that I had bought a new boat and was going to remarry, they all said, "Some guys just never learn!"

Lirio and I married in San Juan on July 4. On July 27, with my son Joe and buddy Ty Norton, we headed across the Atlantic to the start of the Columbus 500 regatta in Spain, the very objective Sim and I had had in mind when we sailed away in 1989 aboard *Siboney*.

We didn't win the regatta but had a great sail, after which *New Chance* made San Juan its home port. In 1994, I assembled a great crew and we sailed through the Panama Canal and down the western coast of South America to the Strait of Magellan. Within three miles of Cape Horn, our way was blocked by a full gale. After four attempts, it became obvious that my goal of rounding the Horn was not to be. Disappointed, we headed north past Argentina and Brazil, and back to San Juan, arriving home in mid-1995 after circumnavigating South America.

In 1997, I sailed *New Chance* once again across the North Atlantic to Amsterdam, where I dropped the mast and, together with Lirio and another couple, headed up the Rhine to Mainz, across the Main to the canal that connects with the Danube, then downriver across the historic heart of the continent to Istanbul, a spectacular ninety-day voyage.

In the spring of 2000, I headed out of San Juan Harbor bound for Oslo to visit an old college buddy. We had a great sail up the East Coast, past Cape Hatteras, through New York Harbor, up the East River and Long Island Sound to Maine and Nova Scotia. Upon leaving Halifax on a clear day, at eleven in the morning, under power, my helmsman fell asleep and put *New Chance* on the rocks. I struggled during the next ten hours to save my beautiful boat, fully loaded for the long passage to Ireland. I failed, and we had to swim to shore, the boat a total loss, Bill Butler once again a castaway. I closed out the log of *New Chance* at 40,968 nautical miles.

After that, I honestly convinced myself that it was time to stay ashore. Confusing scripture with baseball, I e-mailed my dear friend Rafael, who had provided me with daily weather forecasts from the Canary Islands, that I considered my three shipwrecks a clear signal from the Lord to stay away from the sea. He jumped down my throat. Who in the hell did I think I was, expecting the Lord to grant me three chances? The Lord gives one chance and no more. Take Adam and Noah, he blasted away. They each got one chance and that was it.

Weeks later, still confused and infuriated over the loss of my boat, I presented my quandary to my friend and priest, Father Wally. I told him I had been unable to reconcile two powerful and conflicting feelings. One was the urge to strangle this man who had driven my boat onto the rocks, to squeeze his throat until he gasped no more. But I also felt a need to thank God that He allowed this accident to happen on a calm, clear day with the shore an easy swim away. Had we continued, this same man, at some point during the next three thousand miles—sure to include severe ice, gales, and shipping—likely would have slept on his watch and killed us all. "Father Wally," I asked, "how do I reconcile my emotions?"

Father Wally stroked his chin, thought for a minute, looked me in the eye, and said, "Bill, the Lord will send you a signal."

Darn, a signal, I thought as I walked away. I sure hope it's not a lightning bolt! I spoke to Father Wally on a Monday morning. On Wednesday, I opened an e-mail from my good friend Alfred Schubert in Caracas. His sailboat *Teresa V* had been tied next to *Siboney* for years at a marina in Venezuela. His e-mail read:

> Bill. I had lunch yesterday with Ramoncito who told me all about your shipwreck in Nova Scotia. I am so sorry you lost that beautiful boat. What a shame. I really cannot conceive of you not having a boat. I have retired and have moved to the Canary Islands. I want you to accept my boat as a gift.

I was stunned. This was the signal! I gratefully accepted Alfred's gift, and in early 2001, with members of my transatlantic and Cape Horn crew, we sailed *Teresa V* to Puerto Rico in six days. I've since been cruising nearby islands with a gaggle of grandchildren. In August 2003, I renamed the boat *Pallas*, the name of my first pram in Cuba sixty years earlier.

As for future plans, I'd sure like to sail *Pallas* across the North Atlantic to say hello to my friends in the Canary Islands . . . if Lirio ever looks the other way!

APPENDIX: SURVIVAL

THOUGH SIXTY-SIX DAYS at sea in a small "deflatable" raft would hardly qualify me as an expert on survival, I would like to share what little I can claim to have learned.

Alan Villiers has aptly stated, "All loss of ship at sea is due to error." My error was to sail in a vessel that did not respond to the demands of the sea. Shipping containers, other vessels, and rocks can sink a vessel just as surely as maddened whales. A ship's hull must be sound, seaworthy, and strong enough to withstand gales, grounding, collision . . . even whale attacks. Obviously, *Siboney* did not meet this requirement.

Go to sea in a strong boat made of wood, aluminum, steel, or heavy, solid fiberglass. You want a stout rig, and I for one feel safer with a full keel. Do not venture offshore without a 406 mHz emergency position-indicating radio beacon (EPIRB). Satellite phones are great but work only when charged and dry. The battery on the EPIRB drains *only* in emergencies and is designed with a minimum life of five years. When turned on, an EPIRB will transmit a signal detailing your position, your name, your vessel's name, and your designated contact information for several days.

No matter where else you might skimp, do not skimp on your purchase of an EPIRB. When you register it—and this is as important as buying one—provide several reliable, twenty-four-hour shore contacts, people who know what you are up to. The search-and-rescue (SAR) system in place is fabulous. It can work wonders at getting help to you.

Develop a strong shore team that has at hand your proposed sailing schedule. Keep in touch with them on a regular basis, whether by sat phone or single-sideband (SSB) radio. I left behind a detailed four-year plan for our circumnavigation with my children and friends. I spoke via SSB almost daily with one of them thanks to an assortment of amateur radio operators.

The EPIRB we had aboard our raft used 1989 technology. The satellites in use at the time, unable to store a contact in memory, needed to be within line of sight of a shore station at the moment an emergency signal was received. With no shore in sight, our signal was lost, like the two of us. Today, nearly two dozen satellites store signals until they can be downloaded to a shore station.

We resorted instead to mental messages. In our case, they apparently got through to my daughter Sally. She repeatedly tried to get the Coast Guard to search for us. But the U.S. Coast Guard knew it would be next to impossible to initiate a search no matter how much she insisted. Given the uncertainty as to our location at the time of sinking (and remember, they did not know when or even if *Siboney* had sunk), the area airplanes or ships would have needed to search was equivalent to finding a small rowboat adrift somewhere in the Great Lakes. Lesson: Don't leave home without an EPIRB.

EPIRBs aren't the only signaling devices that work. Another, thousands of years old, worked for us. On July 6, day twenty-two on the raft, convinced beyond a doubt that we would never make it to shore and safety, that we would die and no one would ever know our fate, we resorted to an age-old message-posting device—a message in a bottle. Our bottle eventually washed up on the beach in Costa Rica that we had been approaching when rescued and was picked up by Santiago Rojas Acuña, a member of the Rural Police. A reporter for the local paper obtained our note and made it public.

The find settled my quandary as to whether we would have washed up on Punta Burica or missed it and landed in Panama. If we had not been picked up by the *Punta Burica*, we would have preceded the bottle to land by some ten days, thanks to the push we got from the wind and waves.

After an EPIRB, the next items to consider are a raft, a watermaker, a satellite phone, a VHF (very high frequency) radio, flares, a global positioning system (GPS), and stores in an exit bag. Buy the best of these you can afford and fit aboard, and stow them so they are handy.

You cannot survive long in the water; thus, the most simple of rafts is a minimum requirement. The EPIRB will get help to you in less than twenty-four hours unless you are in the real boonies. Then it may take several days to divert resources. But you *must* get out of the water.

Select a raft (or rafts) that will hold your entire crew and is compatible with the trip you plan to undertake. The Switlik four-person coastal raft I purchased was perfect for cruising the Bahamas and the Florida Keys, but we pushed its designed life of just weeks to way past its limits.

And we were lucky. Had we sunk on the leg from Honolulu to Yokohama in icy waters, we would not have made it. Coast Guard–approved rafts provide additional insulation and ballast as well as being strong and durable.

We are alive today because we had a machine that provided us with all the drinking water our bodies required. An inexpensive manual desalinator could keep you alive in the event you lose or damage your EPIRB and your time adrift is extended.

Know your body and be aware of what it needs to keep functioning. I found that my body required a glass of seawater a day to keep me from getting horizontal vertigo. Everyone's body is slightly different except for one fact: We all need to drink at least one liter of fresh water per day to continue to function.

Lots of people, mostly women, approach me at boat shows and say, "I would have died out there. I would never have made it." I argue back that they are wrong. Our bodies are built with an automatic internal survival system that switches on when we need it. Simonne more than met the test. Though she insisted almost daily that she was going to die and that she wanted to die, there is no question in my mind that she would have expended her last ounce of energy to survive. Most humans will. She stood up well during a sixty-six-day struggle punctuated by moments of extreme terror and intervals of intense despair.

The will to survive is essential. Throughout our odyssey, both Simonne and I yearned to continue to live. No matter how many times Sim screamed that she wanted to die and have it over with, these were but passing fits of fear and frustration that had nothing to do with throwing in the towel. In every crisis, such as when I loosened the patch and we almost sank, or when dolphins tore a hole in the floor of the raft, Sim responded with the vision and energy needed to salvage the situation.

She wanted to continue living, and so did I. Battered incessantly by sharks, with death always hovering, we both knew we would fight ferociously until the very end.

Having been asked about this many times, let me say that in extreme situations the will to live eclipses absolutely the will to procreate. Or at least that was our experience. Before *Siboney* sank, Sim and I had been great lovers. Aboard the raft, we were elbow to elbow, hip bone to hip bone, day and night, during those nine-plus weeks adrift, totally naked. Never, not for one microsecond, did my sex drive kick in, and neither did Simonne's. Though I teased Sim, my brain was 100 percent in survival mode.

Back to selection of a raft: most, if not all, raft manufacturers allow the buyer to select additional equipment to be included inside the raft package when it is packed. How many times did I rue not buying another dozen patches of different sizes, shapes, and types? I should have also included a variety of fishhooks, fishing lines, dried food, and gloves. Before you buy a raft, spend time at various boat shows and shop around. Ask each manufacturer for a list of extras that they provide. A provision to catch rain would be a helpful feature.

We are alive because we were aboard a fully ballasted raft. Ballasting is achieved through the use of cloth bags suspended under the raft that fill with seawater when the raft is launched. At boat shows, you will see a variety of ballast bags, many of them triangular in cross section with the apex of the triangle at the deepest point, thus reducing the ballast volume exactly where maximum ballasting is needed. In contrast, our Switlik raft had a large rectangular bag along each side of the bottom and two more at each end. Chain on the bottom of each bag kept the bags full of water, and that rectangular cross section gave us maximum water ballast down low. Though slammed by hundreds of twenty-five-foot breakers, we never flipped over.

It's a good idea to watch the inspection of your raft to better understand how the raft is packed, what it contains, and where its contents are stowed. At the inspection, the raft will be manually filled since the canister will overpressurize the raft.

But do also schedule at a boat show an observation of a raft inflated with the canister. In inky darkness, with the deck awash and whales alongside, I pulled the inflation cord on our raft with a jerk and received the shock of my life when the raft, with an unexpected boom and hiss, almost blew me away. I had no idea what to expect!

The raft did inflate, was launched, albeit dramatically, and did take us across a good part of the Pacific Ocean through much heavy weather. We displayed it at boat shows and during conferences until Hurricane Andrew swallowed it as the hurricane passed through Simonne's home in August 1992.